Routledge Revivals

Taxation and Economic Development

The tax system is one of the instruments said to be available to translate development policy objectives into practice. The wide-ranging papers collected together in this volume, first published in 1978, explore different aspects of the link between national development objectives and the tax system. Attention is particularly focused on traditional aims such as growth, fair distribution and economic stabilisation and development. Articles written by distinguished experts in the fields of public finance and economic development clarify the concepts of taxable capacity and tax effort, and examine the connections between growth and changes within the tax system.

Taxation and Economic Development

Twelve Critical Studies

J. F. J. Toye

Routledge
Taylor & Francis Group

First published in 1978
by Frank Cass and Company Limited

This edition first published in 2013 by Routledge
2 Park Square, Milton Park, Abingdon, Oxon, OX14 4RN

Simultaneously published in the USA and Canada
by Routledge
711 Third Avenue, New York, NY 10017

Routledge is an imprint of the Taylor & Francis Group, an informa business

Publisher's Note
The publisher has gone to great lengths to ensure the quality of this reprint but points out that some imperfections in the original copies may be apparent.

Disclaimer
The publisher has made every effort to trace copyright holders and welcomes correspondence from those they have been unable to contact.

A Library of Congress record exists under LC control number: 79302871

ISBN 13: 978-0-415-83108-6 (hbk)
ISBN 13: 978-0-203-49923-8 (ebk)

TAXATION AND ECONOMIC DEVELOPMENT

Edited by

J. F. J. TOYE

Assistant Director of Development Studies, University of Cambridge.

FRANK CASS

First published 1978 in Great Britain by
FRANK CASS AND COMPANY LIMITED
Gainsborough House, Gainsborough Road,
London, E11 1RS, England

and in the United States of America by
FRANK CASS AND COMPANY LIMITED
c/o Biblio Distribution Center
81 Adams Drive, P.O. Box 327, Totowa, N.J. 07511

British Library Cataloguing in Publication Data

Taxation and economic development.
1. Underdeveloped areas—Taxation—Addresses, essays, lectures 2. Underdeveloped areas—Economic conditions—Addresses, essays, lectures
I. Toye, J F
336.2'0091724 HJ2351
ISBN 978-0-7146-4028-0

Contents

Preface vii

Introduction: Taxation and Economic Development: Answers and Questions from Recent Research.
J. F. J. Toye 1

Part One: TAX CAPACITY AND TAX EFFORT

1. The Taxable Capacity of a Country.
A. R. Prest 13
2. Assessing Tax Performance in Developing Countries: a Critical Review of the Literature.
R. M. Bird 33
3. Tax Effort in Developing Countries: What do Regression Measures Really Measure?
B. R. Bolnick 62

Part Two: TAX REVENUE AND ECONOMIC GROWTH

4. Estimates of Revenue Elasticity and Buoyancy in Central America, 1955–1974.
D. Sykes Wilford & W. T. Wilford 83
5. Exports, Taxes and Economic Growth: the Case of El Salvador.
L. R. Caceres 102
6. The Fiscal Crisis of the Latin American State.
E. V. K. FitzGerald 125

Part Three: EQUITY ASPECTS OF TAXATION

7. Income Tax Evasion and Income Distribution.
N. C. Kakwani 161
8. Progressive Public Utility Rates as an Income Redistribution Device in Developing Countries: the Case of Municipal Water.
M. T. Katzman 174
9. Transfer of Resources from Agriculture to Non-agricultural activities: the Case of India.
M. Lipton 193
10. Equity *versus* Ease in Indian Land Tax Policy.
J. F. J. Toye 222

Part Four: ECONOMIC EFFECTS OF TAXATION

11. Domestic Price Stabilisation of a Staple Export Crop: an Evaluation of the Rice Premium Tax in Thailand.
N. V. Lam 249
12. Fiscal Incentives for Firms in some Developing Countries: Survey and Critique.
S. M. S. Shah & J. F. J. Toye 269

Index 297

Preface

From the amount of bad academic economics that is published, I had until recently concluded that no good piece of work would have difficulty in reaching the public. So I was somewhat alarmed to discover myself, as one of the managing editors of the *Journal of Development Studies*, with many more good contributions awaiting publication than could be published given the present size and frequency of the *Journal*. This was particularly unfortunate because five of them were in my own field of special interest, namely tax policy in underdeveloped mixed economies. My first debt of gratitude is to the Journal's publisher, Frank Cass, for his ready response to my suggestion that these papers should form the core of a volume of collected essays on the subject of taxation and economic development.

My second debt is to those contributors who, when told of this project, kindly offered me papers which would allow the production of a volume that was reasonably balanced in its range of topics, its geographical coverage and its diversity of intellectual styles.

My third debt is to the University of Cambridge's Overseas Studies Committee, under whose auspices my own researches into equity aspects of Indian taxation have been conducted. The Committee has materially assisted my own research and the preparation of this volume, which is intended to be an addition to available teaching material for courses on public finance for overseas administrators.

Most of the essays in this volume have not appeared in print before. But acknowledgement is due to the publishers of *Finanzarchiv* and *Modern Asian Studies*, and to their editors Professor Norbert Andel and Dr Gordon Johnson, for permission to republish Chapters 2 and 10.

Various kinds of secretarial and administrative assistance have been provided by Corinne Benicka and Catherine Thomas, and I wish to thank them both very much.

January, 1978 J. F. J. TOYE

Introduction

Taxation and Economic Development: Answers and Questions from Recent Research

J. F. J. TOYE

The governments of most poor countries profess a desire to stimulate and guide the economic and social development of their nations. This aspiration can be found enshrined in the many hundreds of development plans which have gushed forth from the government printing offices of the underdeveloped world in the last thirty years. Seemingly undeterred either by the enormity of their ambition or by the frequency of undeniable failure, many governments of poor countries continue to reach out for the goal of government promoted and directed development.

The tax system is often identified as one of the most powerful levers available to these governments to move their economies from their present, by definition sorry, states to the distinctly happier positions which invariably characterise the final year of a development plan. Thus the link between taxation and economic development implied by the title of this volume of essays is the link between a universally desired end and a form of government action which is widely believed to be a means to that end.

The belief in the possibility of such a link is of quite recent origin. Fifty years ago, taxation was generally seen as the regrettable necessity that followed hard on the heels of government spending, a kind of public hangover. That taxation might after all be 'functional' in some sense or other was the argument of the American disciples of Keynes in the 1940s. The specific function that they envisaged for taxation was the regulation of the overall level of economic activity by altering the amount and composition of taxation in relation to public expenditure. That function, as is now well appreciated, is irrelevant to the development of poor countries, because:

(a) its time-horizon is 'the short term', twelve to eighteen months ahead, during which the capital stock can be reasonably taken as fixed;
(b) it requires the assumption that some part of the capital stock lies idle because of generalised lack of demand, whereas typically in a poor country unutilised capacity results from some particular supply bottlenecks which persist despite powerful internal demand for those products;
(c) it assumes that the origin of macroeconomic fluctuations lies in sagging investment demand following 'loss of confidence' by domestic private investors, whereas typically in a poor country macroeconomic fluctuations arise from exogenous influences transmitted by foreign trade from the international economy.

To argue in this fashion that post-Keynesian stabilisation policies have no place in the policy-making context of poor countries is not, of course, to argue that taxation there can have no function. For example, if we believe that fluctuations are transmitted to a poor country from outside via foreign trade, taxation can perform a stabilising function under certain conditions. If a poor country derives the bulk of its export revenues from a small number of primary commodities, taxes on the export of these commodities can be varied so that high tax rates choke off demand from the booms in advanced capitalist countries, and high subsidy rates help to sustain demand even when these countries are in the trough of their cycle.

Export taxes on primary commodities designed for economic stabilisation will have a number of undesirable side effects, even if they succeed in achieving the stabilisation objective. Inevitably they will encourage smuggling and under-invoicing. They will stimulate the diversification of the primary producing sector and the growth of untaxed types of output. The government revenue derived from them will, *ex hypothesi*, fluctuate considerably, and it may be gathered at the expense of the saving of the private sector rather than its consumption.

What usually happens is that export taxes originally introduced for stabilisation purposes are allowed to become a continuing source of revenue. Instead of high tax rates alternating with high subsidy rates, the alternation is imperceptibly transformed until it is between high tax rates and low tax rates. Then this form of taxation becomes a way of redistributing real income away from the rural sector and towards the urban sector, which most observers would be inclined to regard as the most favoured of the two in the first place.

Leaving aside these undesirable features of export taxation, export taxation is like any other stabilisation instrument in that its successful use requires vigilant monitoring of the economic conjuncture, speedy decision-making and policy action and a minimal time lapse between the government's taking action and the effects of such action being felt by the economy. These requirements have rather rarely been satisfied in underdeveloped countries. In Chapter 11 of this volume, Dr N. V. Lam examines the Rice Premium Tax in Thailand and concludes that its potentialities as a stabilisation instrument were never fully realised. Following a distinguished tradition of fiscal analysts, he recommends that the variation of premium rates should be made automatic, on the basis of a sliding scale relating rates to world rice prices, since the government seems to have shown, with one exception, very poor economic judgment in the exercise of its discretion. Dr Lam's study very usefully documents some of the practical pitfalls awaiting governments which try to use export taxation as an economic stabilisation device.

But the catchphrase of 'taxation for development' normally envisages quite different functions for taxation in a developing economy than stabilisation. These specifically developmental functions are the promotion of economic growth and the improvement of the distribution of income. The basic thinking behind these two functions of taxation during economic development is set out very clearly by Kalecki in his essay on problems of financing economic development in a mixed economy. The Kaleckian analysis starts from a distinctly old-fashioned and mechanical conception of the engine of economic growth. The economy grows because population growth is accompanied by positive net capital formation and the relationship between the latter and the growth of output is given by an assumed constant incremental capital/output ratio. The tasks of taxation are then first, to restrain consumption so that the amount of investment needed for non-inflationary growth can be undertaken, and second, to do so in such a way that the consumption of higher income groups is restrained more, proportionately, than the consumption of the lower income groups. If these tasks are successfully performed, economic growth will take place and the distribution of income should be improved, or at the least not worsened, in the process of growth.

Formulating the growth and distribution function of taxation in this way helps to clarify a number of issues. The collection of additional tax revenue ceases to be, as it usually seems to Finance Ministers and their top officials, an end in itself. The need for additional revenue is limited by the balanced growth rate which the economy can achieve given the sluggishness of growth in the agricultural sector; and by the expected value of the incremental capital/output ratio. The kind of tax which stimulates development is shown to be not any kind of tax, but only taxes which inhibit private consumption. Taxes that reduce private saving should be avoided, except when the channels which direct private saving into desirable investment are blocked or non-existent. The groups whose extra consumption should be most tightly constrained are those whose absolute levels of consumption are already relatively high, and not those whose basic needs are not yet adequately met. In principle, the kinds of taxes required to meet the growth and distribution function of taxation are, among direct taxes, a progressive expenditure tax supported by wealth and gift taxes; and, among indirect taxes, excises and sales or value-added taxation differentiated to bear very heavily on a class of luxury items.

The question of how to assess the tax performance of a poor

country's government, in relation to the growth and distribution functions, is thus clearly a complex one. Ideally, it should be done in the context of a full-dress macroeconomic plan, or a post-mortem on a past plan. The essays in this collection which touch on this question are concerned mainly with pointing out the fallacies involved in using a certain type of intellectual short-cut in assessing tax performance. An approach frequently encountered is to measure tax performance by the size of the actual revenue yield in comparison with the taxable capacity of the country. But the concept of taxable capacity, like many others in writing on public finance, has been given different meanings at different times and in different contexts. Professor Prest in Chapter 1 disentangles these different meanings, and with masterly skill succeeds in resolving a good deal of conceptual confusion. What he has to say on the use of inter-country comparisons to define taxable capacity is by implication critical of the methods used by international organisations, and particularly the IMF, to measure tax performance. Such methods are addressed directly by Professor Bird (Chapter 2) who, after a sparkling review of the literature on this topic, finds himself forced to conclude that economists will make more progress in understanding the links between the fiscal system and development if they restrain an 'apparent tendency to become the high priests of a new version of the old mystique of numerology'. If any reader is tempted to dismiss this stricture as a piece of intellectual Luddism, he should turn to Chapter 3. In this paper, Dr Bolnick develops a simple aggregative model of resource allocation between public and private sectors, and then uses it to clarify the analytical basis of the measures of tax effort applied by international organisations to poor countries' tax performance. He concludes from his rigorous analysis that the usual measures are actually hybrids which confuse differences in performance relative to desires with differences in desires themselves between countries.

If most of Part One is devoted to criticism of some simple-minded (though apparently very sophisticated) methods of assessing tax performance, Parts Two and Three attempt to be more constructive. Since global comparisons require, almost by definition, a theoretically naive approach, more constructive research seems to call for a severe narrowing of focus to individual countries, or, at most, to a few countries which share a basic institutional and cultural heritage.

In an interesting macroeconomic study of El Salvador in the 1960s, Dr Caceres (Chapter 5) explores, with a ten-equation model, the consequences for the public sector of a strategy of import-substituting industrialisation within a regional common market. He shows that the loss of import duties on intra-regional trade, the loss of revenue arising from generous tax concessions granted to foreign investors and the falling off of revenue from coffee export taxes led to an actual contraction of government investment. El Salvador's fast *laisser-faire* growth increased the country's dependence on imports, without apparently raising the welfare levels of the population. The picture of a sluggish growth of revenue relative to national income growth is corroborated in the broader fiscal study of the Central American Common Market undertaken by Professor D. Sykes Wilford and W. T. Wilford for the period 1955–74. All five C.A.C.M. countries are shown, in this careful and scholarly study, to have a revenue structure which is highly stable, as evidenced by tax revenue buoyancy and elasticity of close to unity throughout the period.

In Chapter 6, Dr FitzGerald examines the proposition that dependent industrialisation in countries on the periphery of the world economy generates contradictions which are manifested, in part, as a 'fiscal crisis'. Using fiscal statistics for six countries (Argentina, Brazil, Chile, Colombia, Mexico and Peru), he argues that state activities have expanded substantially since 1945, but the growth of tax revenues has lagged markedly behind. Thus a growing budget deficit has been financed by domestic borrowing through state banks and from social security funds, by foreign borrowing (with enhanced foreign control) or by direct resort to the printing press. In addition, to the extent that tax revenues have been increased, the source has been the earnings of labour rather than the profits of capital. The failure of taxation both in its growth and its distribution function is here argued to be a structural phenomenon.

The question of the impact of additional taxes raised to finance development on the distribution of income is, perhaps, the most important question of all for students of public finance in poor countries. But it is also an extremely difficult question to tackle, and its difficulty has all to often been used as an excuse for pushing it into the background. All that this volume claims to do is set out some recent contributions to selected aspects of the problem. Dr FitzGerald's hypothesis of tax pressure increasing more on labour than on capital has been mentioned. The implication of the Wilfords' finding of low revenue buoyancy and elasticity is that the tax system as a whole in the countries they studied was proportional in its effects rather than progressive. In Chapter 7, Professor Kakwani analyses the effect of income tax evasion on income distribution. One notable result is his conclusion that, if the tax system is proportional, the after-tax distribution of income will be more unequal than the before-tax distribution in the presence of income tax evasion, provided (as is usually true of poor countries where corruption has gained a good grip) that the probability of detection is a decreasing function of income. Even with a progressive tax system and a constant probability of detection, tax evasion increases the inequality of the income distribution.

The remaining chapters in Part Three are all, in one way or another, concerned with tax policy and income distribution. Professor Katzman considers the desirability of making public utility prices a positive function of quantity purchased. Using data for water consumption in Penang, Malaysia, he demonstrates that a 'progressive' tariff could not be relied on to improve the distribution of income because the income of households is not positively correlated with the quantity of water they consume. Professor Lipton, in Chapter 9, forcefully challenges the doctrine which was very widely held in the 1960s, and still persists today, that the agricultural sector in India is, in some sense, 'undertaxed' compared with the non-agricultural sector. *Per contra*, he argues that the taxation of Indian agriculture has exceeded the 'fair' amount (relative to ability to pay) by between 1½ per cent and 2½ per cent of agriculturists' incomes. Chapter 10 does not consider whether or not the existing tax levies are fair, or the vexed question of what would constitute equity between economic sectors (as distinct from equity between individuals or households). Its purpose is to examine whether one set of proposals to reform the taxation of agriculture in India, those made by the Raj Committee in 1972, fully satisfies its own criterion that 'equity should be the major consideration'.

The last chapter of the volume picks up a problem which was touched on by all the papers in Part Two. Very many tax systems in poor countries feature extensive concessions to private enterprise firms which are supposed to act as 'investment incentives'. These concessions are one of the causes of the sluggish growth of tax revenues even when economic growth, as measured by the national accounts, is proceeding quite rapidly. Yet both Wilford and Wilford and FitzGerald comment that the concessions appear to be ineffective in stimulating additional investment. Chapter 12 is an attempt to investigate, on the basis of a survey of tax legislation in 28 developing countries, the phenomenon of tax concessions which are both widespread and apparently ineffective in achieving their stated purpose.

It will be clear to readers of this collection that the contributors belong to no single school of opinion on fiscal matters, or indeed on wider social and political issues. The editor has done his work on the assumption that readers would prefer the clashes and contrasts produced by a variety of approaches, rather than a single song sung in well-rehearsed unison. He has always received the greatest intellectual stimulus from listening to the disagreements of intelligent but tolerant people.

The topics on which contributors take opposite sides are interesting ones. Four perhaps should be pointed out. First, one notes a difference of view about whether the notion of an economic surplus has any place in the theory of tax policy. Is the notion of surplus so hopelessly vague and relativistic that it can never be quantified and thus be made operational? Or is it the case that, although it is imprecise to an extent, the magnitudes involved can be approximated by simple calculations like that in FitzGerald's note 14? Attempts have been made to operationalise the concept of surplus in both developed and poor country contexts. These efforts by, for example, Stanfield and Phongpaichit, could serve as the basis for further critical enquiry and research effort.

Secondly, can indirect taxes, which are contributing an ever-increasing share in the tax revenues of poor countries, be a progressive set of taxes, as they are required to be in the Kaleckian analysis of development finance? The Wilfords adduce evidence of indirect taxes in Central America that are 'far more progressive than is typically the case in developed countries'. On the other hand, it is normally assumed that heavy reliance on indirect taxes prevents the tax system as a whole from being very progressive. This particular dispute would be illuminated by a detailed and theoretically sound case study of a tax system in which indirect taxes succeeded in both generating substantial revenue and imparting to the entire tax system a marked degree of progressivity. Perhaps such a case study exists, but has so far eluded the gaze of this editor. If not, it should be a high priority in the fiscal research agenda.

In third place, the concept of 'tax blindness', which is often, incidentally, given as the explanation of poor countries' heavy reliance on indirect taxation, can evoke two quite opposed responses. Dr FitzGerald dismisses the argument from political invisibility when considering why Latin American governments decide to use other methods of financing their expenditure than taxation. Other contributors argue that political visibility can affect both the level and composition of tax revenues, and the choice between an investment incentive given as a tax relief and as a direct government cash grant. It would be a useful task to clarify the exact nature of the disagreement here, and to explore whether these differences are reconcilable or not.

Fourth and finally, what difference is made to fiscal processes by the presence of democratic institutions? Professor Prest suggests that the potential disincentive effects of a high tax ratio financing free provision of consumer goods prevent actual tax ratios from being set too high, even in countries without democratic institutions. He thereby endorses a modified version of Clark's view that tax ratios are limited by purely economic influences. It follows that the autocrat's ability to repress political opposition does him no good (at least in the long run) in the area of tax policy. On the other side of the question are those who argue that it is precisely political influences which hold down tax ratios in poor countries, because their governments are leant on by leaders of dominant classes to connive at tax avoidance and evasion by those who, in a just society, would contribute most to the exchequer. The establishment of democratic institutions, in this view, is the first (but certainly not the last) step towards the rational use of taxation as a tool of planned development. Democracy is a necessary but not sufficient condition for the achievement of a socially progressive path of development, it would be argued.

This fourth difference of opinion is manifestly more fundamental than the previous three, to each of which, however, it is linked by logical implication. Of course, one hopes that fresh research will vindicate one side or the other, or provide a reformulation of the question that is less contentious. In the meanwhile, since specialists in public finance, as in most fields of the social sciences, tend to gravitate towards either the claim that (putting it crudely) economics is king, or that class politics rules, the reader should keep the existence of this dispute clearly in mind. He is also advised to read with a severe critical scrutiny those passages which seem to him to have a bearing on this central issue. For, in the words of Ignacy Sachs, 'when it cannot destroy illusions, reason finally delivers itself into their service; and the more persuasive it is technically, the more devastating the possible effects of its enslavement'.

REFERENCES

Kalecki, M., 1972, *Selected Essays on the Economic Growth of the Socialist and the Mixed Economy*, Cambridge, Cambridge University Press.

Phongpaichit, P., 1978, *The Economic and Social Transformation of Thailand, 1958–73*, Ph.D. Dissertation, Cambridge, Cambridge University Library.

Sachs, I., 1976, *The Discovery of the Third World*, Cambridge, Mass., M.I.T. Press.

Stanfield, R. J., 1974, *The Economic Surplus and Neo-Marxism*, Lexington, Mass, D. C. Heath and Company.

PART ONE

TAX CAPACITY AND TAX EFFORT

An earlier version of Chapter 1 was published in the Greek periodical *Spoudai*.

Chapter 2 is based on a seminar originally delivered at the University of Puerto Rico in October 1974. Although helpful comments on an earlier draft were received from Fuat Andic, Roy Bahl, Luc De Wulf, Daryl Dixon, Ved Gandhi, Richard Goode, Gerald Helleiner, Carl Shoup, Roger Smith and Vito Tanzi, it is important to emphasise that none of these necessarily agree with the author's analysis or conclusions. This essay was first published in *Finanzarchiv*, Band 34, Heft 2, March 1976, pp. 244–65 and is reprinted here with permission.

Chapter 1

The Taxable Capacity of a Country

A. R. PREST*

The topic of taxable capacity is an ancient one in public finance literature.[1] After being dormant for a number of years, it has recently come to the fore again in a variety of different contexts.[2] In this paper the different strands of thought embedded in the idea are set out to show how they relate to one another.

Section I will be concerned with the estimation of actual tax yields as proportions of national aggregates. Although no one would claim that such data in their unvarnished form tell one anything about taxable capacity, it is nevertheless necessary to know, before proceeding further, something about the snags in such calculations. Section II examines one historical strand in the literature about taxable capacity: the notion that it is connected with justice or fairness in tax assessment. Section III turns to what seems at first sight to be another theme, and one which has received a lot of attention in recent years, i.e., the notion of reasonableness as judged by the standards of tax-raising in other countries with similar characteristics. In Section IV we come to the proposition that taxable capacity relates to an upper limit beyond which tax ratios cannot be raised. Finally, we shall draw a few conclusions.

*Professor of Economics, London School of Economics and Political Science.

It can quickly be seen from this very brief description of the content of this paper that it is much more concerned with pulling together a number of threads from the literature and examining their implications than in developing brand new ideas. It is only right that this point should be made explicit at the beginning.

I THE RATIO OF TAX YIELD TO A NATIONAL AGGREGATE

Obviously, no calculations or estimates of ratios of tax yield to a national aggregate are going to tell us anything directly about the notion of taxable capacity. The latter conveys some idea of potential yield, as distinct from actual yield, and therefore the former is not likely to enlighten us more than minimally. As we shall see, the concept of taxable capacity is extremely elusive. But our concern at the moment is simply to clear the ground by sorting out what is commonly measured by these calculations so as to produce a foundation for later discussion.

I propose to refer to two sets of recent calculations. The earlier one[3] covers a large number of countries, but inevitably relates to data which are now older than one would like. The later one[4] refers to a smaller number of countries, but has a more recent coverage.

The conventional conclusion is that the ratios of tax yield to GNP in developing countries are quite substantially lower than in the developed countries. If one takes the Chelliah data one finds that for 47 developing countries the ratio of taxation to GNP in 1966–68 was 13·6 per cent; and in 1969–71 the average was 15·1 per cent. On the other hand, the corresponding figure for sixteen developed countries in Europe and North America in 1969–71 was 26·2 per cent. If one wishes to amplify the data for developed countries one can see from the paper by Messère that the ratio for fifteen OECD countries in the year 1974 was 36 per cent (including social security taxes).

Two obvious conclusions follow. One is that there is a wide gap between developed and developing countries. Indeed this is greater still if social security revenues are included, because these tend to be proportionately greater in developed countries. A second conclusion is that the Chelliah figures show that the ratio in developing countries is tending to increase over time.

The conclusions drawn from these data differ sharply between developing and developed countries. The usual inferences drawn for the former are that the ratio of taxation to GNP is some sort of national virility symbol, and that they should try to emulate the ratios of developed countries, or, at any rate, that those developing countries occupying low positions in their own league table should try to mend their ways and increase their ratios, so that they are closer to those of the leaders. On the other hand, in developed countries in recent years it has become much more a matter for national despondency or complaint if the tax/GNP ratio is seen to be higher than in comparable countries. The fact that such opposing conclusions are drawn should put one on one's guard against the tendentious use of this ratio.

In interpreting data of this sort there are three major points to make. As I have dealt with the subject elsewhere at some length,[5] I propose not to go into extensive discussion, but simply to list the major problem areas. The first is what one is *not* concerned with in measures of this sort. The second is the consideration of the right principles for these sorts of measures. The third is the way in which the conventional calculations depart from these principles. Let us now look at each of these subjects in turn.

If we are trying to establish what we are *not* concerned with in this area it is easy enough to compile a very long list. Putting it into a nutshell, one is clearly not going to establish from measurements of the ratio of tax to GNP either the proportion of real resources which is absorbed by the public sector, or the proportion of value added in the economy as a whole which comes from the public sector. Still less shall we obtain any indication of the degree of government intervention, or any such complicated concept.

In principle, one could start by saying that one is trying to measure the cost of the payments which the communtiy has decided to make on a collective or non-market basis. In other words we are concerned with what Shoup[6] has called the proportion of expenditure about which individuals and corporations are not allowed to please themselves. At least this is an approach to the correct principle. But it is clearly not sufficient, in that it is essentially concerned with the proportion of public *expenditure* to the national aggregate, rather than public *revenue*. If, as here, we want to concentrate on public revenue, the appropriate concept is the flow of income which is compulsorily diverted from individuals, corporations and the like, and so is not at their direct disposal.

We now come to the ways in which the standard calculations depart from this concept. Let us look first of all at the measurement of tax revenue and then, secondly, the national aggregate.

As far as tax revenue goes there are a number of major issues. One is how the profits of public corporations should be treated; another is social security contributions; another is capital taxes; and another is the inflation tax, a concept which has been made familiar in recent years by the writings of Professor Friedman[7] and others.

One can hope to set up an appropriate measure only if one can establish a set of general principles. Those which seem to be relevant are, first of all, to know whether any particular payment to the government is compulsory or not; and, secondly, to have some method of deciding whether the profits of state corporations should be treated as part of total revenue. For reasons which I have set out in detail elsewhere,[8] it seems to me that the appropriate measure in the second case is a concept relating to the excess profits of public corporations, i.e., those profits in excess of a 'normal' return, however defined. Obviously, there are plenty of difficulties in defining a normal return. But if we do not follow such a rule, we are likely to find that comparisons between countries of ratios of tax to the national aggregate are completely distorted because one country happens to have profits from, say, a nationalised steel industry, whereas another does not. This argument also ties up with the notion of that part of spending power which is *compulsorily* diverted to collective provision. People are not normally compelled to buy specific amounts of those goods or services which are sold by State organisations.

If we follow these concepts through, we find that the standard data are affected in various ways. I do not propose to refer to these in detail but obvious examples are the treatment of social security contributions, capital taxes and, in an age of inflation, the inflation tax. All these various contributions to the State fit in with the principles set out above just as much as income tax and there are really no reasons for excluding them. To the extent that international calculations do exclude them, they are including only a portion of the total tax revenue in each country.

If we turn to the concept of the appropriate national aggregate there are plenty of issues to be considered here too. We can divide them into two groups:

1. The first arises if one wants to take a conventional national accounts aggregate such as GNP or GDP. This raises all the usual problems about whether one wants a national or domestic concept, a market price or factor cost concept and so on. I do not propose to say any more about this here.
2. The other major issue is whether one wishes to have a concept which differs from the usual national aggregate, and if so, whether one wants something larger or smaller. There are numerous choices here, but my own preference would be to say that the most appropriate notion would be something like personal income (including personal capital gains) plus undistributed profits of companies (together with corporation taxes paid) and, in addition, the trading surpluses or net property income of public corporations. This would correspond much more closely to the stream of income from which tax payments are made than, say, a national aggregate concept which excludes transfer payments. No doubt, there are plenty of statistical problems in producing comparable data for this sort of concept in different countries. But that is really no excuse for churning out, year after year, tax ratios based on measures of national aggregates which are quite obviously inappropriate.

To summarise this section, we can say that the standard international calculations lead to well-known conclusions about differences between developing and developed countries, conclusions about positions in the international league table and so on. But these conclusions are really based on concepts which are more than a little suspect, quite apart from any deficiencies in the national accounts data themselves. Nor is it sufficient to argue that one gets the same results whichever set of data one takes. This is simply not true as one can quickly see from comparisons of different tax/national aggregate ratios for individual countries over periods of time or in respect of comparisons between countries. For example, in the U.K. we can conclude that the ratio for 1974 was 44 or 54 percent, depending solely on whether one takes a factor cost or market price concept of GNP and on how one treats public corporations.

II TAXABLE CAPACITY AND TAX JUSTICE

The interpretation of taxable capacity as being connected with the amount of tax which could be justly or fairly imposed on an individual is an ancient one among economic theorists. The sacrifice principle as enunciated by Edgeworth and Pigou essentially led to the conclusion that a rich man's capacity to pay tax was disproportionately greater than that of a poor man. The Haig/Simons principle in effect maintained that relative capacity to pay was best measured by a concept of income embracing all net accretions of assets as well as consumption. The modern school of optimal taxation theorists is concerned, at least on the income tax side, with the optimal degree of progressivity.[9]

The same idea has long been applied to relative tax burdens on the different sections of a country or on different countries joining together for some co-operative purpose. In case anyone thinks that the division of tax contributions agreed between, say, member countries of the E.E.C. or NATO allies has raised brand new concepts of taxable capacity he would do well to study the 1896 Report of the Royal Commission on Financial Relations between Great Britain and Ireland.[10] Thus the first two headings in the terms of reference read as follows:

> (1) Upon what principles of comparison and by the application of what specific standards the relative capacity of Great Britain and Ireland to bear taxation may be most equitably determined.
>
> (2) What, so far as can be ascertained, is the true proportion under the principles and specific standards so determined between the taxable capacity of Great Britain and Ireland.

Going even further back one might quote from the speech of the Younger Pitt in the House of Commons during the debates in 1795 on the commercial treaty between Great Britain and Ireland:[11]

> The smallest burthen on a poor country was to be considered, when compared with those of a rich one, by no means in proportion with their several abilities; for, if one country exceeded another in wealth, population and established commerce in a proportion of two to one, he was nearly convinced that that country would be able to bear near ten times the burthen that the other would be equal to.

So there can be no question about the distinguished ancestry of the proposition that the notion of taxable capacity is inherently bound up with the idea of a just and fair distribution of a given tax burden among a group of individuals or countries.

Nevertheless, one is bound to feel less than satisfied with this interpretation. The first reason is that a large number of disparate strands of thought are covered by this umbrella; and some of them suffer from well-known limitations—the cardinal utility concept behind the sacrifice principle and the very severely limiting assumptions of the new optimal taxation school, for instance. The second reason is that the notion of what is fair or just as between individuals or countries (whichever of the many possible interpretations one places on fairness or justice) is not going to tell us everything about the maximum feasible amount of taxation which can be imposed in any given country at any given time. Elusive as this idea itself may be, until it has been examined in some detail we cannot claim to have drained the concept of taxable capacity of intellectual content.

III TAXABLE CAPACITY JUDGED BY INTER-COUNTRY COMPARISONS

Since the pioneering work of A. Lewis and A. Martin some twenty years ago[12] there have been a very large number of econometric studies in this field, many of them appearing in *IMF Staff Papers*.[13]

Basically, these econometric studies are defining taxable capacity on the basis of what one might expect a country with given characteristics to do in the taxation field. In other words, if country A has similar characteristics to country B (leaving aside for the moment what we mean by characteristics) but raises a much smaller fraction than Country B or, for that matter, other countries like A and B, then one can at the very least say that A is out of line with its peers.

Some ten years ago the procedure, as developed by Lotz and Morss, was to regress the tax/GNP ratio on income per head and a measure of overseas trade or openness of the economy. This set up a norm or standard for what one could expect the tax ratio to be for any given country; and then one could in turn measure the intensity of tax effort in that country on the basis of the relationship between the predicted and the actual ratio.

Latterly this approach was refined, essentially by Bahl, in the following way: Bahl's regressions consisted in relating the tax ratio to two variables. First, the share of minerals and oil in GNP and, secondly, the share of agriculture in GNP. The former is really a proxy for the openness of the economy (with the implication that one would expect the coefficient to be positive); the latter is a proxy for income per head, or at least a negative proxy for income per head, with the implication of a negative coefficient. The regression equation as originally formulated by Bahl and subsequently utilised by Chelliah[14] is as follows:

$$\frac{T}{Y} = \underset{(11{\cdot}07)}{15{\cdot}66} + \underset{(4{\cdot}44)}{0{\cdot}35}\ Ny - \underset{(2{\cdot}37)}{0{\cdot}08}\ Ay \qquad \bar{R}^2 = 0{\cdot}442$$

where $\frac{T}{Y}$ = tax ratio, Ny = share of mining in GNP & Ay = share of agriculture in GNP.

As an alternative which, it was argued, would make for clearer distinctions, the following equation was also used:

$$\frac{T}{Y} = \underset{(7{\cdot}84)}{11{\cdot}47} + \underset{(0{\cdot}38)}{0{\cdot}001}\ (Yp - Xp) + \underset{(5{\cdot}45)}{0{\cdot}44}\ Ny + \underset{(1{\cdot}17)}{0{\cdot}05}\ X^1_y$$

$$\bar{R}^2 = 0{\cdot}376$$

where (Yp − Xp) = per capita non-export income in $ US and X^1_y = export ratio excluding mineral exports.

These two alternatives explored by Chelliah *et al.* gave similar results (at least in terms of country ranking for tax effort) and so we shall not spend time here analysing the differences between them.

On the basis of either of these regression equations a distinction can be drawn between taxable capacity and tax effort. Taxable capacity is measured by the ratio of tax to GNP as predicted by the regression equation, i.e., this would represent normal use of the taxable capacity of a country if that amount of revenue was raised. Tax effort, on the other hand, is an index obtained by dividing the actual ratio of taxation to GNP by the predicted ratio.

As a result one therefore has the two concepts of capacity and effort and hence four possible categories in which countries may be placed. As examples we can quote the following:

High capacity and high effort	—	Brazil
Low capacity and high effort	—	Sudan
High capacity and low effort	—	Trinidad
Low capacity and low effort	—	Pakistan

Although on the Chelliah (1975) version there is a small tendency for high taxable capacity to be associated with high tax effort this was not very marked.

Before considering the contribution of these mainstream econometric studies, it is worth noting that an alternative approach to measures of taxable capacity and tax effort was made by Bahl[15] on the basis of work done on yields of representative tax systems. There have been a number of examples of this sort of work in the past.[16] Essentially, the idea is to take a standard tax system, to look at the yield one can predict in a given country on the basis of certain characteristics (such as income per head) and then to compare predicted with actual yield. Bahl showed that one could by this means develop a measure of tax effort (defined as actual tax yield divided by yield of representative tax system) and a measure of taxable capacity (defined by yield of representative tax system divided by GNP). The yield of the representative tax system was in turn given by the average of effective tax rates for the sample as a whole multiplied by the relevant base for an individual country. For example, one would take the average of income tax rates for the sample and multiply by the income total for any given country. I do not wish to go further into this approach, but it is worth noting that the ordering of countries in terms of taxable capacity and tax effort came out much the same as with the earlier approach.

What contribution do studies of this sort make to illuminating the concept of taxable capacity? Obviously there is a host of statistical problems ranging from the (in)accuracy of the data to the acceptability of the econometric techniques, but I leave these entirely on one side.

The logic of the approach is that the explanatory variables chosen reflect in some sense or other a capacity to pay tax rather than a demand for public expenditure.[17] The proposition that the estimated tax ratio for any given country is a measure of the tax capacity it might reasonably be expected to have, in the light of what happens to other countries, is clearly dependent on this assumption. Equally clearly, the justification for this assumption is not self-evident: as Bird[18] points out the income variable is likely to incorporate demand-for-government as well as supply-to-government ingredients.

Secondly, one must ask whether this notion of taxable capacity differs fundamentally from that outlined in the preceding section. A little reflection will show that it does not do so. Suppose, for instance, one were to include as an explanatory variable a measure of income incorporating an element of progressivity (Y^2, for instance).[19] We then have something which is on all fours with the notions of sacrifice or justice which we were discussing in the preceding section. But the omission of any such progressivity elements does not mean that the equations as usually formulated belong to a different *genre;* they simply embody a proportionality rather than a progressivity norm.

Finally, if this particular approach is fundamentally the same as that in the preceding section the same comments hold as before; we are only being given a glimpse of what tax yield might be 'fair' or 'reasonable' (or whatever other anodyne word one can think of). In no sense are we grappling with the notion of a maximum exaction.

IV TAXABLE CAPACITY AS THE UPPER LIMIT TO TAXATION

The concept of an upper limit to the tax burden which can be imposed on a country has a long history. Basically, it is a Marxist-style notion of a surplus which can be drained off for governmental purposes. As Kaldor once put it:[20] 'The taxation potential of a country depends on the excess of its actual consumption over the minimum essential consumption of the population.' The idea of creaming off the surplus above subsistence level and equating this with the notion of taxable capacity has its origins in, or at least finds support from, the notion of what happens in a major war. Thus it can be argued that in the U.K. in the Second World War the needs of the population at large were cut down to a minimum level, by various types of rationing devices, queues, shortages, taxation, monetary measures and so on. Hence it is often argued that developing countries, for instance, should emulate this kind of example; if they were to do so, we should then have a measure of the maximum feasible tax ratio they could hope to reach. Alternative applications of the concept can be found in discussions in 1918 or 1945 about post-war reparations,[21] or the history of Soviet Russia in the days of industrialisation under Stalin.

The first point to emphasise about any such notion is that it is impossible to pin down with any finality.[22] The concept of a subsistence level is highly elusive and is dependent not just on known physiological needs, but also on people's willingness to have their consumption standards squeezed. This in turn depends on the acceptability of the cause for which their standards are being squeezed.

Nevertheless, even though there is this very considerable element of vagueness about what might constitute an upper limit to the tax ratio, it is worth exploring in some detail why tax ratios in practice will tend to be below any such levels. We shall spend a very short time on the more political reasons; and a much longer time on the more economic reasons.

The sorts of situations in which something approaching a maximum limit is reached—wartime, post-war reparations, dictatorship—all have common elements. Political opposition to such taxation levels is likely to be less the more autocratic the dictatorship or the more popular the cause for which taxes are being raised (e.g., a truly national war; or taxes earmarked for particular purposes of which people may approve, such as the relief of the neediest elements of the population). But even the most absolute of dictators has to face the long run threat of revolution; and even the most popularly acclaimed war is likely to pall after a time, carrying with it the threat that a government may lose office at the next election. If we can designate these arguments as political—and obviously, there is a shadowy borderline here—we can say that there are very clear political constraints on the freedom of governments to approach or maintain tax ratios which are anywhere within sight of the maximum conceivable levels.

With that, I propose to leave the political arguments to those better qualified to discuss them. But I do want to spend some time on the more purely economic reasons why very high tax ratios cannot be made to stick, at least for long periods. There are three topics over which I should like to range: the relationship between economic incentives, taxation and the composition of expenditure; inflationary consequences of raising tax rates; and problems arising from the composition of any given revenue total. We shall find that all three topics point to reasons why taxable capacity in a country may be constrained well below the level that would be required fully to drain off the surplus.

On the first topic, I shall draw heavily on an unpublished paper by Shoup.[23] Essentially, one asks how far the effects of a particular increase in tax revenue on incentives to work or to take risks depend on the particular purpose for which that increment to tax revenue is used. Shoup distinguishes four cases which I shall now discuss briefly.

Case A

The first case is where the government spends its extra tax revenue on the acquisition, and subsequent free provision, of goods and services to the population at large. Suppose that this additional largesse is financed by income tax. Then we can say that the income tax would have income and substitution effects in the usual way, but that the additional expenditure would only have an income effect. Hence (concentrating on work incentives only from now on) there would almost certainly be a disincentive to work, and the overall result may well be to act as a break on government expenditure of this kind. In Shoup's terminology, when work effort and reward for work effort become disassociated we must expect a reduction in work effort and this would have inevitable consequences in imposing limits on government spending. There is one qualification to this argument: when the free distribution by government is complementary to private purchases. For instance, if better roads can only be enjoyed if a man buys a car then the disassociation effect will be that much less strong. In effect, we can think of government expenditure as being an indirect way of subsidising the purchase of automobiles or, alternatively, of the demand for automobiles as being complementary with the demand for roads. We have here an effect on all fours with the well-known complementary effect analysed some years ago by Corlett and Hague.[24]

Case B

Supposing that the income tax is now used to pay people transfers which are in no way connected with their work effort. Once again, the tax creates two sets of income effects and a substitution effect with the probability of adverse reactions on work effort. Once again, there is a qualification. If the transfers are paid to an inactive section (e.g., the retired element of the population) and income tax falls on an active section, then the two sets of income effects do not impinge on the same people. But even here we must acknowledge that today's worker knows that he will be tomorrow's pensioner. We cannot, therefore, separate the income effects in a straightforward fashion.[25] So *net* income effects will be small; and we are still left with the substitution effect of the tax.[26]

Case C

As a third alternative assume that the government uses the income tax to finance individuals' purchases of goods and services in the market by large-scale non-selective subsidies. The effects can be seen clearly enough if we take the extreme case with, say, a 95 per cent average rate income tax and assume the whole of the sum raised in this way to be distributed in subsidies. The net result in this case is less adverse to work effort, in so far as the reduction in the price at which goods and services can be bought (or, on alternative monetary assumptions, the increase in factor incomes which can be obtained from producing those subsidised goods and services) will be such as to offset the substitution effects of the income tax. In other words, we now have the tax being responsible for both income and substitution effects and the subsidy being similarly responsible for both income and substitution effects. Therefore there is no reason why one should now have strong disassociation between effort and reward. The story is much the same if one has selective rather than non-selective subsidies.

Case D

If the government spends its revenue on defence or something similar from which the recipient does not consider he derives an income, we no longer have income effects on both the revenue and expenditure sides. In the limiting case where there is judged to be no accession to income from government spending, we are left with the income and substitution effects of the taxation side alone. Disincentives to work will now clearly be less than in cases A and B, at least on the assumption that the income elasticity of demand for leisure is positive. Hence the 'tax capacity' limits to expenditure of this sort are not as low as when expenditure is useful. Nevertheless, one cannot push the argument too far; people cannot live on the guns which are possible if they sacrifice their butter.

Obviously, there are many qualifications which can be made to this kind of argument. One is that the choice is usually not as simple as that between working and not working. In so far as there are opportunities for untaxed work the disincentive argument is a much more complicated one than text books are liable to allow, as indeed is shown by the inability of the large number of investigations which have been made in this field to come to any firm conclusions.[27] Another qualification relates to the fact that governments may finance expenditure by borrowing rather than by raising taxes. In so far as additional borrowing enables more capital expenditure to be made, this would be likely to have an effect similar to that of defence spending (Case D); but in so far as borrowing enables the government to expand its consumption expenditure we must then revert to Case A. The other complication in the borrowing case is whether people take any account of the fact that taxation may have to increase in later years in order to finance the interest on and repayment of the debt.[28]

In addition to considering non-tax forms of revenue one should also consider other expenditures. For instance, interest payments, if they are paid abroad, are likely to have incentive effects similar to defence expenditure. But if they are paid at home they are likely to resemble transfers. Despite these qualifications and further complexities, the analysis of incentive effects of expenditure composition must clearly be a major ingredient in one's thinking about the economic limitations on the tax ratio in a country.

Another line of thought about the economic limitations on tax ratios goes back to a well-known article by Colin Clark.[29] The author attempted to show that there was a maximum feasible tax/GNP ratio of around 25 per cent under peace-time conditions. We need not spend any time on the statistical part of the argument. But we do need to note that the conclusion was arrived at by an entirely different process of reasoning from the incentive argument developed by Shoup. Essentially, Clark's proposition was that in an economy at any given time some forces favoured price rises and some forces inhibited them. If taxes rose beyond a critical level, anti-inflation forces would be weakened at all levels—whether in government, among employers or employees. Prices would tend to rise, and so the attempt to raise the tax ratio would be frustrated.

This article has often been criticised,[30] not without some justification. Nevertheless, it contains a proposition the general nature of which has found favour in a number of different quarters in recent years, i.e., that attempts to raise taxes generate unacceptable inflationary developments or reductions in consumption standards (leading to strikes) or reductions in business profitability (leading to low investment).[31] Without discussing the detailed merits of these propositions, one may note that we do have here a different class of reasoning about why, beyond a certain point, tax rises may have unacceptable effects on the economy.

One further point is worth making. On the Clark argument,

the limitation on tax ratios was deemed to be automatic in that the initial increase was hypothesised as leading to price rises and an increase in nominal GNP, thus tending to restore the original ratio. This argument was never convincing in that it neglected the additional tax yield generated by the increase in nominal incomes. But if rising tax ratios caused strikes or unemployment, real output would fall, so that tax ratios would not fall to their original level automatically. The constraint on tax ratios in such contexts arises from purposive steps to reduce tax rates once the consequences of rising tax ratios become unacceptable.

To turn to the composition of revenue, we now have to ask whether disincentive effects of some taxes are much greater than those of others. I do not propose to discuss the voluminous literature on the incentive effects of, say, regressive *versus* progressive income taxes. I would rather take up the concept of 'tax blindness', i.e., the question of the extent to which the authorities can minimise the disincentive cost of raising a unit of revenue by adopting one form of tax rather than another. Witholding of income tax rather than taxpayer payments is an obvious instance. If witholding can be extremely accurate and obviate the need for an annual return by a taxpayer (as is often the case in the U.K.), tax blindness may be greater still compared with, say, a system of approximate witholding and self-assessment, as in the U.S.A. Similarly, it may be easier to raise revenue if goods and services are shown inclusive of sales tax rather than the latter being an additional, separate element. In so far as people think that VAT is a tax to be passed on rather than to be paid by them, this tax scores high marks from this standpoint. Similarly, in so far as government can obtain more revenue surreptitiously through the inflation process, this again may be an easier form of tax-raising. We are primarily concerned here with people's psychological processes—what tax burdens are perceived or thought to be perceived by taxpayers and so on. But there is some empirical evidence in the U.K. to show that this subject is an important one.[32] In short, there is a lot of scope for the crafty art of disguising the true import of taxes by such means as the above.

We can now that there is a whole variety of economic effects which may prevent a government, however strongly entrenched politically, from pressing up to the limit of taxable capacity. Professor Shoup has analysed the circumstances under which disincentives to work (or to take risks or to save) are most likely to arise for any given tax structure: essentially, the answer is that expenditure on freely provided goods and services or transfer payments is more disincentive than expenditure on subsidies or 'non-obvious' goods and services. Another line of thought is that rising tax rates may, given appropriate monetary conditions, trigger off inflationary or other unwelcome developments. Still another is that the composition of revenue—the degree of 'tax blindness' or 'tax opaqueness'—will be another constraint on the power to raise tax ratios.

V CONCLUDING REMARKS

If we are content with a notion of taxable capacity which has a connotation of reasonableness in the light of what similar countries do, the econometric type of analysis outlined in Section III is a sensible and helpful approach. But once we try to complicate matters by incorporating elements of progressivity explicitly into the analysis, subjectivity may take over.[33]

If one thinks the concept of taxable capacity ought to contain some notion of maximum possible tax levels, it is very hard to envisage any satisfactory empirical tests of whether countries are operating up to capacity or not. Comparisons of actual tax ratios will tell us very little, if anything, by themselves.[34] One thing we can do is to look for indirect guidance on the lines suggested by Professor Shoup.[35] The socialist economies of Eastern Europe are careful not to distribute large amounts of consumer goods free; defence expenditure is substantial; turnover taxes score high marks for opaqueness. Such observed patterns of behaviour strongly suggest that the potential disincentive effects of high tax ratios to finance free provision of consumer goods are strong enough to keep these ratios within bounds, even under regimes not subject to the political constraints found in democratic countries.

We have not produced definitive conclusions about the

notion of taxable capacity. It would be foolish to expect to do so. The most one can hope to do with such an essentially elusive and intangible subject is to try to approach it from a number of different angles and point out which considerations are possibly relevant, and which claims are patently false.

NOTES AND REFERENCES

1. See, for instance, J. C. Stamp, *Wealth and Taxable Capacity,* (P. S. King, London, 1922); and especially, Royal Commission on Financial Relations between Great Britain and Ireland, *Final Report,* C 8262, HMSO, London, 1896.
2. There have in recent years been a large number of studies of tax effort and tax performance, many of them emanating from the IMF Fiscal Affairs Division. See R. M. Bird, 'Assessing Tax Performance in Developing Countries' *Finanzarchiv,* Vol. 34, No. 2, 1976, and reprinted as Chapter 2 of this volume, for a recent assessment. See also Carl S. Shoup, *The Limits on the Taxation Capacity of a Country* (International Tax Conference, Nairobi, 1976) for another approach on which we shall draw extensively.
3. R. J. Chelliah, H. J. Baas and M. R. Kelly, 'Tax Ratios and Tax Effort in Developing Countries 1969–71', *IMF Staff Papers,* March 1975.
4. K. Messère, 'Tax Levels, Structures and Systems. Some Intertemporal and International Comparisons' (to be published).
5. 'Government revenue, the National income and all that' in R. M. Bird and J. Head (eds.), *Modern Fiscal Systems,* (University of Toronto Press, Toronto, 1972). See also 'Public Activities in Perspective, a Critical Survey', to be published.
6. C. S. Shoup, *Public Finance,* (Aldine, Chicago, 1969), p. 499.
7. See e.g. M. Friedman, *Monetary Correction,* (Occasional Paper 41, Institute of Economic Affairs, London, 1974).
8. 'Government revenue, the national income and all that', *op. cit.*
9. For a recent summary see D. F. Bradford & H. S. Rosen, 'The Optimal Taxation of Commodities & Income', *American Economic Review,* May 1976.
10. *Op. cit.* in note 1 above.
11. *Ibid.*
12. A. M. Martin and W. A. Lewis, 'Patterns of Public Revenue and Expenditure', *The Manchester School,* September, 1956.
13. E.g. J. R. Lotz and E. R. Morss, 'Measuring "Tax Effort" in Developing Countries', November 1967; R. W. Bahl, 'A Regression Approach to Tax Effort and Tax Ratio Analysis', November 1971; R. W. Bahl, 'A Representative Tax System Approach to Measuring Tax Effort in Developing Countries', March 1972; R. J. Chelliah *et al., op. cit.*
14. *Op. cit.* in note 3 above.

15. 1972, *op. cit.* in note 13 above.
16. E.g., Advisory Commission on Intergovernmental Relations, *Measuring the Fiscal Capacity and Effort of State and Local Areas* (Washington, D.C., 1971); V. Tanzi, 'Comparing International Tax Burdens: a suggested Method', *Journal of Political Economy*, October 1968.
17. *Cf.* R. M. Bird: 'The successful measurement of taxable capacity used in these studies depends critically on the *a priori* justification of the explanatory variables as affecting only taxable capacity and not at all either demands for higher public expenditure or willingness to tax.' *Op. cit.*, p. 253, and this volume, p. 43.
18. *Ibid.*
19. *Ibid.*, p. 262; see also Lotz and Morss, *op. cit.*, p. 494.
20. N. Kaldor, 'The choice of Taxes in Developing Countries', in E. F. Jackson (editor), *Economic Development in Africa*, (Blackwell, Oxford, 1965), p. 156.
21. *Cf.* the often quoted speech of Sir Eric Geddes at Cambridge Drill Hall in the course of the December 1918 election campaign. 'We will get everything out of her (Germany) that you can squeeze out of a lemon and a bit more . . . I will squeeze her until you can hear the pips squeak.'
22. *Cf.* Kaldor, *op. cit.*
23. Shoup, *op. cit.*, in note 2 above.
24. W. J. Corlett and D. C. Hague, 'Complementarity and the Excess Burden of Taxation', *Review of Economic Studies*, 1953–4 (I). See also R. A. and P. B. Musgrave, *Fiscal Policy in Theory and Practice*, (McGraw-Hill 1973), p. 470.
25. This is, in fact, a more general point, e.g., an income tax on the 'rich' may be used to make a transfer to the 'poor'; but the 'rich' of to-day may become the 'poor' of tomorrow.
26. If the transfer payment itself declines with earnings the substitution effects become even more adverse to work effort. *Cf.* R. A. Musgrave, *The Theory of Public Finance* (McGraw-Hill, 1959), pp. 251–4.
27. See M. J. Boskin, 'On some Recent Econometric Research in Public Finance', *American Economic Review*, May 1976, p. 105: 'No clear consensus on elasticities of labour supply has emerged.'
28. For an analysis of such problems *Cf.* A. R. Prest, 'Compulsory Lending Schemes', *IMF Staff Papers*, March 1969.
29. Colin Clark, 'Public Finance and Changes in the Value of Money', *Economic Journal*, December 1945.
30. *Cf.* J. Pechman and T. Mayer, 'Colin Clark on the Limits of Taxation', *Review of Economics & Statistics*, August 1952.
31. *Cf.* D. Jackson, H. A. Turner and F. Wilkinson, *Do Trade Unions Cause Inflation?*, (Cambridge University Press, Cambridge, 1972); and R. Bacon and W. Eltis, *Britain's Economic Problem* (Macmillan, London, 1976).
32. *Cf.* C. V. Brown, 'Misconceptions about Income Tax Incentives', *Scottish Journal of Political Economy*, February 1968; also, C. V. Brown and E. Levin, 'The Effects of Income Taxation on Overtime: The Results of a National Survey', *Economic Journal*, December 1974.

33. To quote R. M. Bird again: 'The only feasible approach in fact is probably to try various standards and see which one results in a ranking which looks "about right", that is, accords with one's judgement as to the right weight to be given to divergences in income levels', *op. cit.*, p. 263 and this volume p. 55. This seems to be a classic example of the tail wagging the dog.
34. However, it may be possible to make some progress by comparing countries which are broadly similar in general characteristics such as income per head, but which differ radically in public expenditure composition. Thus if the tax ratio is the same in a country where defence expenditure is a large proportion of public spending as in one where free public provision of consumer goods is the main component, there is a presumption that the latter is operating nearer to taxable capacity than the former.
35. *Op. cit.*

Chapter 2

Assessing Tax Performance in Developing Countries: A Critical Review of the Literature

RICHARD M. BIRD*

From the point of view of an international agency, the problem of assessing the performance of a developing country is analogous to the problem of 'success indicators' in centrally-planned economies. Like the central planner, the international aid official cannot simply be content with such qualitative appraisals as 'country X is doing all right' or 'country Y seems to be slacking'. He wants some quantifiable and comparable indicator of performance, preferably a simple one, so that he can tell which of his 'clients' are doing well and which are not—or, in somewhat stronger terms, which among the many poor countries with which he is concerned are the 'deserving poor', in that they are trying hard, and which are the 'undeserving poor', who are not really doing as much for themselves as they can or should. He may therefore turn to the economist for such an indicator—and also, perhaps, for a clearer formulation of the standard of performance which should be expected of various countries. The performance of a country, its 'effort', may then, of course, be defined in terms of how closely the indicator approaches the standard.

Such a standard with regard to tax performance may be established in at least two ways. One approach is by postulating some ideal (or, some might say, minimum) tax level

*Professor of Economics, University of Toronto.

and structure which any developing country which is 'serious' about development ought to achieve. Perhaps the clearest example of this is found in the work of Sir Arthur Lewis.[1] Presumably such an ideal is based on both pre-determined norms and the observation that at least some countries have in fact attained the specified level, which is taken to mean that it is feasible for others to do so.

An alternative approach to the establishment of a norm, which is now far more common, is to take the average performance of countries defined to be similar in certain respects: in effect to say, as the head of the Philippine planning office recently did, that 'judging from the tax efforts of more progressively developing countries, the low tax effort in our country can only suggest that there is . . . room for further taxation'.[2] In this formulation, the average performance of neighbouring countries is taken not only to show what a particular country could do if it wanted to, but also what it should do.[3] It is this interpretation of the recent 'tax effort' work, which I have found to be common among both national planners and international bureaucrats, if seldom put quite so explicitly, which I am most concerned to refute in this paper.

The paper is organised as follows: Section I outlines a number of reasons that have been put forward in support of the international comparison approach to assessing national tax performance. Section II then reviews the major varieties of such studies which have been carried out to date, with special attention to the recent group of 'tax effort' studies. The paper concludes with some briefer comments on certain other fiscal performance measures and with some modest suggestions as to what might be done to make future empirical work in this field both sounder and more useful for policy purposes.

I. WHY THE CONCERN WITH THIS PROBLEM?

An examination of the literature suggests that there are at least seven reasons which have been put forward at various times in support of the need for, or usefulness of, international tax comparisons. Both for their own interest and because one would logically expect that the intended purpose of a measure should affect both its design and its interpretation, these reasons are reviewed briefly here.

(a) *The Simple Arithmetic of Growth*

The first reason that so much attention has been paid to this question is simply because most economic formulations of the development problem suggest, in essence, that the adequate mobilisation of domestic resources is the key to self-sustained growth. In the oft-quoted words of Arthur Lewis: 'The central problem in the theory of economic growth is to understand the process by which a community is converted from being a 5 per cent to a 12 per cent saver.'[4] The arithmetic underlying the usual development plan, for example, may be crudely summarised as follows: a certain rate of growth is required (or desired, or considered feasible); to attain this amount of growth, a certain amount of new capital formation is needed; but this level of investment can be achieved without unwanted inflationary pressure only if it is equalled by *ex ante* savings; and since private and foreign savings can be expected to amount to only x per cent of G.N.P., x being less than the required amount, there is a need to increase public savings through taxation to make up the difference. More succinctly, 'the simple arithmetic of growth involves mainly an increase in tax revenues'.[5]

One rationale which has been put forward in support of international tax comparisons is therefore to determine '...whether a given country could not, if it wanted to, raise more taxes without seriously "burdening" the economy. In this connection, a comparison may be made with the performance of other developing countries....'[6] A first rationale for comparative studies is thus to see if a country can, 'if it wanted to', achieve the level of taxation required to attain plan targets. In the extreme, as noted earlier, the levels achieved in other countries considered to have an 'accepted' level of performance can even be taken to set some sort of absolute standard, as when Lewis argues that 'most underdeveloped countries need to raise at least 17 per cent of gross domestic product in taxes and other government revenues, taking central and local authorities together'.[7]

Views such as these assume, of course, that an increase in taxes does not cut saving to any significant extent. This proposition was questioned some years ago by Please, who suggested that increased taxes in fact often resulted in increased current government expenditure and hence made no net contribution to total saving.[8] Indeed, if one assumes that increased taxes also reduce private saving, more tax 'effort' might even mean worse savings 'performance'! This hypothesis led to a lot of statistical work but no very conclusive results, although several recent studies have found some support for the Please hypothesis and thus reopened the question.[9] The point of mentioning this here is simply to remind readers of the obvious fact that taxes are not all that matters in resource mobilisation and to point out yet another area in which both theory and fact are in a rather confused state, and where there would appear to be scope for solid and useful empirical work, including perhaps some on a limited comparative basis.[10] This issue, like the debatable assumption that increased government expenditures will result in a higher level of welfare, is not further discussed in the present paper.

(b) *Domestic Appraisal of Domestic Policy*

A second rationale which has been put forward in support of systematic international comparisons is that, whether or not they have a plan to fulfil, officials and politicians are in fact in the habit of comparing themselves with others, so that such comparisons are sometimes an important part of the domestic appraisal of domestic policy. In short, '... government decision makers often resort to the use of comparisons with other countries to gauge the performance of their own fisc'.[11] That this proposition is true is obvious to anyone who has worked in a Finance Ministry in any country, whether developing or developed. Those with such experience can also testify, usually with feeling, that the comparisons which are made are all too often oversimple, misleading and irrelevant. A classic example occurred in Colombia a few years ago when a study which compared the taxes which several hypothetical taxpayers with the same absolute income in U.S. dollars would pay in the United States and Colombia was widely used as 'proof' of the excessive progressivity said to characterise the Colombian fiscal system.[12] The fact that policy-makers are thus drawn to, and impressed by, 'bad' international comparisons appears to most economists to be a good enough reason for trying to make such comparisons better. (This rationale is therefore closely related to one commonly put forward in support of the studies of fiscal redistribution which were reviewed recently in another paper.[13])

(c) *The Macroeconomic Effects of Aid*

If we now change the perspective back from the internal formulation of policy in developing countries to the external interests of the international organisations with which the paper began, several other rationales for international comparisons spring to mind. The issue which has received most attention in this regard in the last few years is undoubtedly the contention that, in contrast to the additive model postulated in the simple capital formation view mentioned above, foreign capital, particularly aid, has tended to replace, or substitute for, domestic saving in recipient countries. Have foreign capital inflows resulted in increased consumption, that is, lower domestic savings, as some have charged, or not?[14] While strictly speaking, the concern in this discussion is with total domestic savings, in fact the mechanism usually assumed to result in lower domestic savings is that the receipt of foreign aid leads to taxes being lower than they otherwise would be. Any possible offsetting increases in private savings as a result of lower taxes are considered to be negligible.

In essence, then, the problem here is exactly the same as that concerning the effect of intergovernmental transfers on local tax effort—a subject on which a very lengthy list of quantitative studies has been carried out in the United States over the last decade.[15] Just as in that literature, most of the studies which have so far been carried out with respect to the effects of foreign capital on domestic savings have suffered from inadequate and partial specification on the questions to which the cross-sectional analysis is directed.[16] Nevertheless, whatever the defects of such work, the obvious policy importance attached to this question by the aid donors has given a new impetus to studies of saving (and tax) effort and performance.

(d) *The 'Leverage Effects' of Aid*

The question of the extent to which foreign saving is substituted for domestic saving is really a variant of a much older question in the aid field related to the problem of 'project aid' *vs.* 'programme aid'. A major criticism which was made of project aid in the 1960s, for example, was that it could not really be tied to specific projects, and that aid givers would therefore be better advised to focus their attention on the entire development programme rather than on the particular part of it they wrongly thought they were financing.[17] That this proposition is generally mistaken (provided there is any price-elasticity of demand for the aided project[18]) is beside the point here: what is ironic is that we now see programme aid being similarly criticised for financing things—namely, tax reduction—other than those the donors thought they were financing.

In any event, the growth of so-called 'programme aid' over the last few years brings up another important reason for the considerable attention which has been paid recently to measures of fiscal performance. To put the argument shortly, programme aid in its 'pure' form is conditional on the attainment by the recipient country of satisfactory standards from the point of view of the donor with respect to certain performance criteria. Given the centrality of saving in the usual development model and the relatively ready availability of fiscal data in most countries, it should not be surprising that measures of fiscal performance—usually either tax effort or the central government's surplus on current account (taken as a measure of government saving)—appear to be dear to the hearts of those concerned with using the 'leverage' of aid in this fashion to affect key domestic policies.[19]

(e) *Allocation of Aid*

A more explicit use of international comparisons in relation to aid might be as a basis for allocating aid, both among the recipients and the donors. While not in fact used for either purpose to any significant extent yet, this possibility has been canvassed in a number of studies.[20] The cruder versions of this approach generally suggest some sort of simple per capita income basis for allocating aid. In fact, however, it would seem very likely that any such scheme to be acceptable would have to take into account additional circumstances of the countries concerned which were considered to be relevant. In particular, experience with intergovernmental aid in federations suggests strongly that it would not be long before some sort of measure of 'fiscal effort', probably based on some comparatively-derived standard, would come back into the discussion.[21] These measures are not only more (politically) necessary in federal states, however, but also usually much better based, both conceptually and statistically, than any existing international comparisons of developing countries. Nevertheless, measures of fiscal effort might also become relevant and significant in areas which are becoming economically more integrated and hence sharing more joint expenditures and revenues. Should the world become more unified in this sense, this use of international comparisons of tax performance, while at the moment more hypothetical than actual, may in the long run turn out to be the most important of all.

(f) *Aid Creditworthiness*

Another use of international comparisons which is sometimes made in respect to aid is as one component of the assessment of creditworthiness, that is, of the ability of the recipient to pay back a loan without undue internal or external financial strain. Tax capacity and the willingness to make use of it are clearly as relevant to this question as the resources and character of a prospective borrower are to a bank manager—and, as we shall see, both of these factors are very often judged by some internationally-determined average standard.

(g) *Intellectual Curiosity and Academic Bonus Points*

The final reason for examining tax performance in quantitative terms is simply that it is a very interesting question. Even if one does not accept the simple capital formation model of development put forward above, it seems clear that no poor country can get very far without in some sense 'mobilising' more resources at least to some degree through taxation. The extent to which it is judged to be able to do so is therefore an important intellectual concern for those interested in the improvement of mankind's lot. Furthermore, the availability of a large body of superficially comparable financial data appears to lend itself to many of the techniques of quantitative manipulation with which most students of economics are imbued these days. Experience suggests that in these circumstances the data will indeed be so manipulated, almost regardless of the point of doing so.

Whatever the motivation—and there are no doubt others not mentioned here, good and bad—there thus seems every reason to expect still more quantitative international comparisons of fiscal performance in the future. It is therefore of particular importance at this time to examine the current state of the art critically and systematically. This is the task of the next section.

II. THE ASSESSMENT OF TAX PERFORMANCE

(a) *The Determinants of the Tax Ratio*

Many studies on tax structure have been carried out without any reference to their rationale, to why we are interested in them. As Professor Shoup noted in a review of some of this literature: 'Too often the information is hardly more useful, directly, than data on the proportion of taxation imposed on inhabitants over six feet in height.'[22] This characterisation applies most appropriately to the earlier studies of the determinants of national tax ratios (the share of government revenues in the national income). Many of these studies can properly be characterised as 'completely empirical, with no real theoretical basis underlying the choice of variables or techniques'.[23]

Despite their severe theoretical limitations, however, the earlier studies did provide some interesting information on the statistical association between various measurable characteristics of a country and the size of its tax ratio. Perhaps the most interesting of these results was the apparently significant influence exerted on this ratio by the size of the foreign trade sector. Some authors (notably Hinrichs and Musgrave) also used their essentially cross-sectional analysis as support for a theory of the evolution of tax structure over time, generally focusing on the declining role of foreign trade taxes and the rise of various income-related taxes.[24]

The most recent and thorough studies of the determinants of national tax ratios have been those conducted at the International Monetary Fund (IMF). Although these studies have been closely integrated with the extensive work on tax effort analysis done at the Fund in recent years, I want here to comment separately on the explanatory or 'positive' part of these studies, as opposed to the normative interpretation which has been made of them.

The 'average tax ratio' in a group of 47 developing countries is shown in the most recent study to have increased, for example, from 13·6 per cent in 1966–68 to 15·1 per cent in 1969–71, with the ratio increasing in almost four-fifths of the countries covered and not falling significantly in any.[25] (These figures exclude social security taxes.) The composition of taxes did not change much over this period, however, with 'income' taxes (which include mineral royalties) accounting for 27 per cent, property taxes 5 per cent, foreign trade taxes 32 per cent, and internal transactions taxes also 32 per cent of the total in 1969–71. That is, so-called 'direct taxes' yielded only about one-third of total revenues in this group of developing countries, although there had been some minor shift towards direct taxes in a little over half the countries covered. Finally, there were marked regional variations in both the level and pattern of taxation, with, for example, the Central American and Caribbean region having the second lowest regional tax ratio (out of five regions) although it was one of the higher income regions. As was noted in an earlier Fund study, 'the "tradition" ... in Central America and the Caribbean seems to be in the direction of low tax ratios'.[26]

(b) *The Measurement of Taxable Capacity*

The presentation of figures such as this, which presumably have some general informative value, is only the first step in these studies, however. The next step is to attempt to 'explain' statistically the observed difference in tax ratios. The 'explanation' which fitted best statistically in the most recent IMF study was:

$$T/Y = \underset{(11{\cdot}07)}{15{\cdot}66} + \underset{(4{\cdot}44)}{0{\cdot}35}\, N_y - \underset{(2{\cdot}37)}{0{\cdot}08}\, A_y \qquad R^2 = 0{\cdot}442$$

where the figures in parentheses are t-ratios. T/Y is of course the share (in per cent) of taxes in national income, A_y = share of agriculture in Gross Domestic Product (GDP), and N_y = share of mining in GDP. In other words, the tax ratio can statistically be best 'explained' in terms of the sectoral composition of the GDP, with mining making a positive and agriculture a negative contribution.

Although one might at first be surprised at the absence of such factors as the average level of income and the degree of openness from this specification, a moment's reflection may reduce the surprise considerably, given the generally close correlation of these factors to the composition variables which are included in this specification. What the statistical analysis tells us, then, is that a good deal—but by no means most!—of the variations in national tax ratios are statistically associated with the shares of agriculture and mining in national output. This is perhaps interesting, but it can hardly be considered to be very exciting or to have much policy significance in terms of evaluating fiscal performance.

Largely for this reason, this equation 'with the greatest statistical merit'[27] was rejected in the IMF study in favour of the following specification:

$$T/Y = \underset{(7{\cdot}84)}{11{\cdot}47} + \underset{(0{\cdot}38)}{0{\cdot}001}\,(Y_p - X_p) + \underset{(5{\cdot}45)}{0{\cdot}44}\, N_y + \underset{(1{\cdot}17)}{0{\cdot}05}\, X_y$$

$Y_p - X_p$ is per capita non-export GNP (in U.S. dollars), X_y is the export ratio excluding mineral exports, and N_y and T/Y are defined as before. This equation has a lower $R^2 = 0{\cdot}376$ and an insignificant coefficient at the 5 per cent level on the first variable. Why is this statistically inferior equation the equation of choice? The reasons appear to be as follows: (1) 'per capita income has considerable normative significance in considering taxable capacity and in assessing tax effort'; it should therefore be included.[28] (2) On the other hand, 'there are grounds for believing that the share of the agricultural sector affects not only taxable capacity but also, perhaps more importantly, the willingness to tax'; it should therefore be excluded.[29] (3) As for mining, however, 'because of the heavy fixed investment associated with extractive industries, operations tend to be confined to a few large firms and as long as world demand conditions ensure high profitability, there exists a combination of taxable "surplus" and administrative ease'; the mining share ought therefore to be included.[30] (4) Finally, the non-mining export ratio is needed to 'make allowance directly for the export factor in countries where mining is not so important'. In short, this equation is used because the purpose of the exercise is not to 'explain' variations in the ratio among different countries but rather to measure 'taxable capacity'.

The successful measurement of taxable capacity used in these studies depends critically on the *a priori* justification of the explanatory variables as affecting only taxable capacity and not at all either demands for higher public expenditures or willingness to tax.[32] The problems with this approach are therefore obvious: the inherently debatable nature of the variables chosen, for instance, is surely clear from the quotations in the preceding paragraph. Per capita income, for example, is presumably included because it is a proxy for a potentially higher tax base, or a larger 'taxable surplus'. But in fact income is surely as much a 'demand' as it is a 'supply' factor: the identification problem seems insuperable in this respect.

Similarly, to argue that the agricultural share should not be included because '... many developing countries have found it difficult to tax agriculture adequately, for historical and political reasons'[33]—an incontestably true statement!—and that this means that the size of the agricultural sector reflects not just capacity to tax but also willingness to tax, is hard to understand in light of the inclusion of the mining share. One might just as well say—equally true—that many developing countries have, for historical and political reasons, found it easy to tax the mining sector (which is controlled by foreigners in many countries and employs relatively few people).[34] That is, if one share can be said to affect 'willingness' as well as 'capacity', then so can the other, on equally firm (or infirm) grounds. The point of this discussion is simply to demonstrate that the distinction between 'capacity' and 'willingness' is a terribly fuzzy one: indeed, one might say that 'capacity' without 'willingness' is not really 'capacity'—or 'effective capacity', if I may coin a term—at all.

In short, it is inherently extremely difficult to specify correctly any model of (usable) taxable capacity—to quantify what Musgrave has called the 'tax handles' available to a country. Any particular specification may be criticised, as has been done above. More important, it seems conceptually impossible at this stage of development of what might be called the positive theory of the public sector—by which I mean that body of analysis, economic and noneconomic, which attempts to understand and explain the observed level and pattern of government activity over time—that any specification of taxable capacity can be developed, let alone measured, that will be fully satisfactory.[35] An academic purist will, therefore, never find this sort of analysis very satisfactory.

The world was not made for purists, however, so many more such attempts will no doubt be forthcoming. Anyway, the practical man will doubtless continue to say 'What's all that to me? I want a number'—and the economist will doubtless continue to give it to him, even if he should not.

(c) *'Tax Effort' Indices*

Let us then return to the numbers game, accepting for the moment the fiction that something called 'taxable capacity' is adequately represented by the equation cited earlier. The next step then follows immediately: the calculation of tax effort, defined as the ratio of the actual tax ratio in a particular country to that which would be predicted on the basis of the taxable capacity equation. Since, by assumption, all capacity factors are allowed for in the equation, the observed difference—the residual—presumably measures the 'effort' which a country makes to exploit this capacity. In the usual form of this analysis, regression equations like those specified above are used to calculate the predicted tax ratio directly, which is equivalent to saying that 'taxable capacity' is that tax ratio which would result if a country utilised its tax bases to the average extent they are used by the sample.[36] Thus a tax effort ratio of less than 1·0 means that the country exploits its estimated tax potential less than the average, in other words, that it has a 'preference' for a level of taxation below the average, or a low tax effort.

Bearing this definition in mind, we can now look briefly at the most recent IMF calculations of 'tax effort' in this sense.[37] These calculations show, for example, that in 1969–71 Brazil had by far the highest tax effort (1·806—that is, it collected 80·6 per cent more taxes than predicted), followed by Tunisia, Egypt, the Ivory Coast, and the Sudan. In all, 22 countries had an effort index greater than 1, with Ecuador, at 1·002, just squeaking over the line—and 25 an index of less than 1, ranging from Jamaica at 0·993 all the way down to Nepal at 0·374.

What is the point of this calculation? In the first place, the ranking thus derived is substantially different from that obtained by ranking countries simply in terms of their tax ratios: only three of the first ten countries ranked by the tax ratio to make it into the first ten in the tax effort league. It might therefore be argued, with some substance, that if for some reason one insists on ranking countries by some simple tax index, the picture suggested by this 'effort' index is less misleading than that suggested by the simple tax ratio. Much the same result, however, can be obtained simply by dropping those countries with a significant mining sector—Zambia, Zaire, Guyana, Iran, Venezuela, etc.—from the sample.[38] Basically, all that the new ranking tells us, therefore, is that countries which can tax substantial natural resources tend often to levy less than average taxes on the rest of the economy; it does not tell us whether this result ensues because they do not want to do so, or because they do not have to do so, or because they are in fact unable to do so for some reason.

The more usual interpretation of these tax effort figures, however, is not in terms of ranking but rather that if a country has a low index, one can conclude that '...the main impediment to a higher tax ratio is the unwillingness of the Government to raise taxes'.[39] In other words, an increase in taxes is judged to be quite feasible, given the country's measured taxable capacity (in the sense used above). While those who carry out these exercises are usually scrupulous in stressing that one should not pay much attention to the rank of a particular country,[40] they have no hesitation in putting forward the calculated index as a guide to the feasibility—not the desirability, although as noted earlier, this inference is in practice often drawn from these calculations—of raising additional revenues. The lower the index, the easier it should be to do so: lucky Nepal! The use of this calculation as one guide in judging the scope for additional taxation in individual countries is thus stressed and the 'international league table' aspect of the exercise is played down.

My own emphasis would be precisely the opposite. There appears to be some marginal merit to adjusting the tax ratios in this way in order to produce a less misleading comparison than would the unadjusted tax ratio, if one must make such comparisons: indeed, my own early contribution to this literature (which took rather different lines) was, for example, undertaken for exactly this reason.[41] So long as pressure from 'practical' men compels the compilation of such international comparative exercises, the use of adjusted ratios is more likely to give rise to useful questions—not answers—than unadjusted ratios. At its best, then, the tax effort approach may give rise to a pertinent question or two.

The most important point to be made, however, is that there is no merit at all in the contention that the difference between predicted and actual values in this kind of exercise measures in any meaningful way the scope for change in any particular country, or the gap that can (or should) be closed through additional 'effort'. The residual three-fifths of reality which is not 'explained' by those chosen independent variables is far too complex and particularistic to be captured by this kind of mechanistic approach. There is no way that 'success' in levying taxes, or the lack of it, in any country can be measured by such crude methods, as anyone with experience in any particular country can testify. In short, the tax effort approach is simply not a very useful way of analysing evidence pertinent to the assessment of fiscal performance in any country, since in the interests of simplistic comparisons most of the relevant information (for example, in political and administrative realities) is left completely out of account.

(d) *A Critique of Tax Effort Studies*

As a critic of my earlier paper on international tax comparisons truthfully said, 'the economist can contribute nothing of use toward the resolution of any policy question ... unless he grapples directly with data on the operation of each tax system'.[42] My reply then was that such shorthand efforts may nevertheless be useful at early stages of policy formulation.[43] On the basis of another decade's experience and several substantial studies in the field, I would now take even this back and say, as I did in my most recent book, '... that to be effective as part of development policy the tax system of each country must be tailored carefully to the peculiar circumstances and objectives of that country'.[44] Just as general theorising as usually carried out is an inadequate guide to the appropriate tax policy in any country at any time, so comparative quantitative studies are even more inadequate—especially since, to date, they have seldom even been related to good theorising.

While those who carry out these studies recognise these points—'due caution must be exercised', says the most recent IMF paper, 'in interpreting the tax effort indices'[45]—they do not seem to appreciate the power which numbers, particularly 'scientifically' derived numbers such as these, have on people's attitudes. In fact, it has become common practice in the international agencies to use such 'tax effort' calculations to assess tax effort in particular countries. As Vito Tanzi noted with regard to tax structure in a recent paper:

> 'If we believe, as we all seem to do, that the tax structures of most developing countries are far from what they should be and that they should be changed, why should we use as our reference point the average of all these distortions? A statistical average of 30 or 50 distorted tax structures cannot give us the norm against which a country should evaluate its own tax structure. And if those statistical relations don't do that, what do they do then?'[46]

It's a good question: I, for one, have to answer 'Not much', both with respect to tax structures and tax levels.

The basic criticisms I would make of the recent tax effort studies can now be summed up in five propositions (not all of which have been mentioned earlier) before turning more briefly to some other types of international comparative studies which have been (or could be) carried out, as well as a few other considerations which need to be mentioned to round out this survey and critique.

(1) There is inadequate *a priori* justification for the use of the selected variables as measures of taxable capacity. Furthermore, it is far from clear that this concept can be measured in any meaningful sense. The complex problem of the relation between government revenues and expenditures—are there differences in the demand for public services, for example?—is only one of the many problems which are obscured in this exercise.

(2) The data are very bad. Everyone who works in the comparative game recognises this; presumably they have all read Oskar Morgenstern's classic critique of the data even in the most advanced countries[47] but they proceed to ignore his strictures and their own intuition. One cannot really take per capita income figures seriously in most developing countries, for example, and even the fiscal data in many countries are questionable. These data problems are very serious, and no one can truthfully claim to be aware of all the biases they impart to the result. In short, any policy use of these studies is suspect for this reason also.[48]

(3) Virtually all of the work which has been done on quantitative international comparisons is cross-sectional in nature: yet the policy inferences which are drawn from (or, in a weaker version, supported by) this work are invariably concerned with changes in particular areas. As Kuznets has eloquently demonstrated with respect to Chenery's early work on comparing patterns of growth, there are few exercises more questionable than drawing inferences about changes from data on differences.[49] The choice of the sample, its comparability, the possibility of technological innovation in the tax field (the value-added tax), and the problem of 'tastes' and international demonstration effects—all these suggest what a treacherous exercise this use of cross-section data is. Cross-section data may provide—they often do—the only game

in town. But to say this does not imply what it is too often taken to do, that we should therefore play this game, or at it.

(4) Yet another problem concerns the nature of the norms which are applied in the tax effort analysis. One difficulty here concerns the distortions to which Tanzi draws attention, as noted above. Another way to put a similar point is that 'one must design a tax system for the economic, political, and administrative conditions which one finds in a particular country, and not for some average abstract hybrid of all countries'.[50] There is thus no meaningful sense in which the average can be considered a standard, nor is it conceptually useful—though it may sometimes act as an additional persuasive argument in political or quasi-political debate—to take the average as showing what is feasible in any particular country. The implicit norm in the usual use of the tax effort index may also be criticised as being proportional, a point to which I shall return later.

(5) Finally, it cannot be said too often that, despite the cautions so copiously sprinkled through the relevant literature on the limitations of the exercise and its limited usefulness for policy purposes, in most cases, the same literature negates its own cautions.[51] More important, these exercises are in practice commonly used to imply (a) that country X should reach some computed ratio or (b) that country X can readily reach this ratio, if it wants to do so. It should by now be plain that I consider both of these inferences to be improper and that my experience convinces me that, as presently constituted, the exercises are more likely to be misused in this way than not. A fifth critique of the now conventional tax effort exercise is therefore that it lends itself too readily to misuse to be worth further attention at this stage of our knowledge. As matters stand, undue attention to such international comparisons is more likely to detract from than illuminate the needed analysis of problems and policies in individual developing countries. The effort which has gone into effort studies would contribute more to both knowledge and policy formation if it were redirected to perhaps less

glamorous but almost surely more rewarding studies of particular problems in particular countries.

III. SOME OTHER DIMENSIONS OF THE PROBLEM

This section reviews more briefly some of the other areas in which quantitative international comparisons bearing on the fiscal system have been made and makes some suggestions of directions for future empirical work which might possibly prove more fruitful.

(a) *Taxable Capacity and Economic Surplus*

It was noted earlier in the discussion of taxable capacity that, in effect, the mining section had a large 'surplus' which could be readily tapped, while whether the agricultural sector had a 'surplus' or not, it was very difficult to tax. The question of the 'agricultural surplus' and the need to tax it has of course long been a concern of development economists, so it is rather surprising so few attempts appear to have been made to measure it.[52] Since it is hard to become educated these days, particularly in a developing country, without being exposed to a fair amount of Marxist thought, it is even more surprising that no one appears to have tried to measure 'economic surplus' and hence 'taxable capacity' in the broad sense.[53] 'The starting point for any realistic theory of public finance for underdeveloped countries must,' it has been said, 'be the concept of the economic surplus generated in the economy.'[54]

Indeed, the first attempt to consider this question in an international context which I have seen was carried out only last year in an UNCTAD study which took an extremely crude notion of 'surplus'—basically, non-wage income—and used the ratio of domestic savings to this 'surplus' as an indicator of savings effort.[55] While the indicator turned out to be highly correlated with the ratio of domestic savings to GDP, the notion of measuring 'surplus' directly is surely an attractive one, worthy of more development. If there are any quantitatively-oriented Marxists (and such, though rare, are not unknown), they may find fun and enlightenment in this pursuit and so, perchance, may the rest of us; however, any such efforts would of course inevitably be very crude and at least as suspect as the measures criticised in this paper.

(b) *Measures of Tax Performance*
More immediately relevant is the fact that the notion of effort evoked in the attempt cited in the previous paragraph is totally different from that common in the tax effort literature. No longer does one examine residuals (or entrails!); instead, one in effect tries to infer something about effort from a direct examination of behaviour. The framework of the UNCTAD study is interesting in this respect. The average savings ratio (S/Y) is interpreted as a measure of savings performance, while the marginal propensity to save (out of expected income) is interpreted as a measure of savings behaviour, and there is really no measure of effort except the abortive 'surplus' one mentioned above. It is clear that 'effort' in this context must mean something very different from what it does in the tax context. In effect, this study interprets the effort it takes to behave in a certain way in terms of what Musgrave calls the 'ability to give up', while the recent IMF studies[56] really interpret effort in terms of the 'ability to collect'.[57]

In fact, it may be suggested that there are four concepts which need to be distinguished: (1) tax performance (as measured by the adjusted tax ratio, for example); (2) tax elasticity (as measured, for example, by the 'automatic' marginal tax rate or the income-elasticity of the tax system); (3) tax effort (as measured, for example, by the buoyancy of the system or some other measure of the total change in the tax ratio), and (4) tax sacrifice or burden (as measured under some sort of progressivity norm). While the terminology in this field is already so confused as to render this attempt at redefinition no doubt hopeless, it might nevertheless be of interest to elaborate slightly on the last three of these concepts.

The cutting edge of policy in the capital formation approach mentioned earlier is, for example, clearly the marginal rate of taxation. 'The most important way to ensure an automatic increase in the ratio of government revenues to gross domestic product is to have a tax structure such that the marginal ratio exceeds the average ratio', or in other words an income-elasticity greater than unity.[58] The primary interest of those concerned with domestic resource mobilisation must therefore be in the behaviour of the tax system over time. This behaviour has two components, however, the automatic component and the discretionary component. For some purposes, it seems suggestive to think of the former (tax elasticity) as tax 'behaviour', in the sense that it is a characteristic of the existing tax structure at any point in time, while the latter, which incorporates both changes in the tax structure and changes in administrative effort, might perhaps be interpreted as an indicator of tax 'effort'. More precisely, one measure of tax effort might be the 'buoyancy' of the tax system (its historical or *ex post* elasticity) less the automatic component due to changes in the tax base. 'Effort' thus defined would then measure the political and administrative efforts to increase effective tax rates or the coverage (base) of the tax system made during the period under examination.[59]

The importánce of paying attention to these dynamic aspects of tax performance has of course often been recognised, for example, by Chelliah.[60] Owing to data problems, however, it has not generally been possible to separate the 'automatic' and 'discretionary' components in the revenue services for most countries. Recently, however, useful standard methods have been developed—again largely at the IMF—for this purpose and applied to such countries as Paraguay.[61] While there are many problems with this statistical exercise also, the point of mentioning it here is simply to suggest (1) that it is concerned with more policy-relevant variables than the static studies of so-called 'tax effort', (2) that it is focused properly on the development over time of a particular system—though no doubt, as more such data is assembled, someone will begin to make international comparisons![62]—and (3) most relevant in the present context, that the results may perhaps be interpreted as suggested above. The process of separating the 'elasticity' from the 'buoyancy' is of course analogous to that of separating 'capacity' from the residual and consequently subject to some of the same objections; but it is at least more meaningful and useful for policy purposes in that it focuses in the right place, on the margin, where policy changes in fact occur. In addition, the presentation of, in effect, three indices of tax performance (the adjusted tax ratio, tax elasticity, and discretionary changes) would be a substantial improvement over the present over-emphasis on the first index—which is probably the least meaningful—alone.

(c) *Tax Sacrifice*

All the measures discussed to this point are really concerned with the 'ability to collect'. As suggested earlier, however, there is also the relevant question of measuring the 'ability to give up', for which the term 'tax sacrifice' was suggested above. Any such notion as this is fraught with all the difficulties of utilitarian comparison: yet, 'regrettable as it may seem to most welfare economists, virtually all economic policies must rest on such interpersonal utility comparisons'.[63] One might follow Musgrave in simply bypassing the crucial question of the nature of the relationship between the tax ratio and the level of per capita income at which equal 'sacrifice' is assumed.[64] The trouble with this procedure is that there appears to be a 'felt need' to say something more explicit about this relationship, and that, more immediately relevant, the 'tax effort' studies reviewed in this paper embody an implicit relationship between the tax ratio and income which is unlikely to be acceptable if it were explicit.

Basically, the tax effort studies employ an implicit norm of proportionality with respect to the 'ability to give up'. The use of the usual tax effort formula to set the underlying standard for normative purposes presupposes that the tax ratio (T/Y) should increase by the same amount for equal absolute changes in per capita income (Y_p) at all levels of Y_p. Because this norm is in contravention of all usual equity standards—however questionable the latter might be—it can be argued that progressivity should be explicitly introduced into the formula. The only authors who have done this in the literature surveyed appear to be Lotz and Morss.[65] They calculated 'tax effort' using a constant progressivity standard[66] and found (a) that the calculated equation fits better and (b) that middle-income countries showed up better and high and low income countries showed up worse. While there is no more reason to use this progressivity standard for all countries than there is to use the proportionality standard of zero (as in the usual comparisons), it is surprising this early exercise has not since been further developed.

An interesting formulation of this problem has been suggested by Luc De Wulf, on the basis of earlier work by Gandhi and, especially, Sahota.[67] Let $t = y^a$, where t = per capita taxes, y = per capita income, and x = income elasticity. Then $x = dt/dy \, / \, t/y$ and $dt/dy = x(t/y)$, that is, the marginal tax rate is equal to the average tax rate times the elasticity. The degree of progressivity of the system may then be measured by the rate of change of the marginal tax rate (the second derivative). If $x > 1$, the system is progressive, that is, as income rises, taxes rise more quickly. If $x < 1$, the system is regressive, and if $x = 1$, it is proportional. The rate of change of progressivity is then shown by the third derivative, which works out so that if $x = 2$, progressivity is constant and if $x < 2$, progressivity decreases (as it does in most actual tax rate schedules).

My 1964 formulation (and the Lotz and Morss exercise) in effect assumed constant progressivity. This rather drastic assumption means that complete income equalisation is the normative standard assumed, as can be seen if one realises that $x = 1 + r$, where r is the Gini coefficient. If the Gini coefficient is zero, then incomes are completely equally distributed, while if the coefficient is one, all income is in the hands of one person. The proportionality ($x = 1$) in most studies therefore in effect assumes that no equalisation of incomes is needed or desired, while the constant progressivity norm ($x = 2$) means complete equalisation is desired. What Gandhi and Sahota did was to assume that $x = 1{\cdot}5$, thus taking a less extreme standard, in fact, the 'middle of the road' solution, and getting results which they felt to be intuitively more reasonable. At this point, however, something very interesting occurs, because it so happens that an elasticity of 1·5 corresponds to the 'magic number' thrown up (at least for poor countries) by Pareto's Law of income distribution.[68] Indeed, for essentially this reason, the same figure of 1·5 has recently been put forward as the 'correct' elasticity of marginal utility with respect to income, albeit with considerably more certainty than the proposition seems to merit.[69] Another 'magic number' thus appears to be entering the literature under various guises.

Clearly, the question of how to introduce some 'progressivity standard' is a highly controversial one, and no particular formulation seems particularly persuasive, even to those who find this sort of question meaningful. (The others presumably stopped reading some time ago.) The only feasible approach in fact is probably to try various standards and see which one results in a ranking which looks 'about right', that is, accords with one's judgment as to the right weight to be given to divergences in income levels.[70] The problem here is therefore exactly the same as that in choosing a progressive income tax rate schedule in any particular country, and as in that case there is no easy answer. The point of raising all this here is simply to note that the recent 'effort' measures have completely ignored this question of 'sacrifice' and, in doing so, have in fact adopted a 'sacrifice' standard (proportionality) which would almost certainly be unacceptable to most readers if they knew what was going on.

IV. CONCLUDING REMARKS

To conclude this review of the state of the art in international fiscal comparisons, I would like to make five points which, if taken to heart, might make future work in this field more useful than I judge the work to date has been.[71]

(1) The data problem is fundamental. Much more work is needed with raw numbers before we can in all conscience proceed with many of the internationally comparative games we play. Anyone who has worked with these problems is aware of the difficulties, and we all mention them *pro forma*—but then usually forget about them in drawing our conclusions. Economists have shown themselves too willing to believe that available numbers, whatever they might be, not only mean something but can be used as proxies to represent theoretically meaningful concepts; they have therefore grossly overloaded a weak data base with technique. Fortunately, the on-going programme of the international agencies to improve the quality and comparability of fiscal data should within a few years greatly improve matters in this respect.[72]

(2) The impending improvement of the data base makes it even more important that we specify logical, complete and explicit models which can be tested. Some recent work shows that this can be done in an illuminating and suggestive fashion, particularly for individual countries or small groups of similar countries.

(3) In general, empirical work will be more useful to policy-makers the more it focuses on changes and on details, for the actual reality and basic issues of policy lie there. Careful detailed quantitative study of particular issues in particular countries is the kind of empirical research which is really needed in development finance. There is little glamour here, but much useful work to be done.
(4) Even if these prescriptions are religiously observed, the connection of many of these exercises with the policy process will continue to be very tenuous. Economists should not be too ambitious in this respect because we do not really have all that much to offer. (Parenthetically, it is perhaps worth noting that the 'misuse' of the tax effort studies referred to earlier should not be taken to mean that countries have done much in response to the urgings of those who may think these indexes mean more than they do. They have not: the polity, like the economy, is a much more stable aspect of the social structure than some of us seem in our more 'social engineering' incarnations to believe.)
(5) Finally, economists should be humble in all their policy pronouncements, whether based on 'scientific' work or not. The reason is simply that, as suggested throughout this paper, we have a lot to be humble about, although it is admittedly tempting to forget the deficiencies of economics when the even more flagrant deficiencies of everyone else are so often made obvious in their pronouncements on policy. Too often when one listens to a sociologist or political scientist, one feels, to paraphrase Sir Winston Churchill, that economics may be the worst of all the social sciences—except for all the others. Economists have made progress in understanding the complex aspects of social reality which are tied up in the fiscal system and development. We will, I am sure, make more progress—but we are likely to do so, I have attempted to argue, if we advance with some caution and restrain our apparent tendency to become the high priests of a new version of the old mystique of numerology.

NOTES AND REFERENCES

1. See especially his *Development Planning*, 1956 (London: George Allen and Unwin, 1956), pp. 115–16, 128.
2. Gerardo P. Sicat, *Taxation and Progress* (Manila: National Economic Council, 1972), p. 3.
3. For another Philippine example, see National Economic and Development Authority, *Four-Year Development Plan FY 1974–77* (Manila, 1973), Chap. 5. A more sophisticated version of the same position may be found in R. A. Musgrave, *Fiscal Systems* (New Haven, Conn: Yale University Press, 1969), p. 166, where this is called 'the only feasible approach'.
4. W. A. Lewis, *The Theory of Economic Growth* (Homewood, Illinois: Richard D. Irwin, Inc., 1955), pp. 225–26.
5. Gerardo P. Sicat, *op. cit.*
6. Raja J. Chelliah, 'Trends in Taxation in Developing Countries', *IMF Staff Papers*, Vol. 18, July 1971, p. 259.
7. W. A. Lewis, *Development Planning*, p. 129.
8. Stanley Please, 'Saving Through Taxation—Reality or Mirage?', *Finance and Development*, Vol. 4, March 1967, pp. 24–32.
9. See the review in Stanley Please, 'The "Please Effect" Revisited', International Bank for Reconstruction and Development, Economics Department Working Paper No. 82, July 1970; also R. Mikesell and J. E. Zinser, 'The Nature of the Savings Function in Developing Countries: A Survey of the Theoretical and Empirical Literature', *Journal of Economic Literature*, Vol. 11, March 1973, pp. 15–17.
10. An excellent example is the fine paper by Peter Heller, 'An Econometric Analysis of the Fiscal Behaviour of the Public Sector in Developing Countries', (University of Michigan, Center for Research on Economic Development, Discussion Paper 30, October 1973), which the author thinks supports the Please hypothesis, although, as Please himself has noted, it is in fact hard to see how *any* type of statistical association can be a test of the political mechanism which he envisaged at work.
11. Roy W. Bahl, 'A Regression Approach to Tax Effort and Tax Ratio Analysis', *IMF Staff Papers*, Col. 18, November 1971, p. 573.
12. See the reference to this study in the statement by a member of the Colombian Commission of Tax Reform in R. A. Musgrave and Malcolm Gillis, *Fiscal Reform for Colombia* (Cambridge, Mass.: Harvard Law School International Tax Program, 1971), p. 196, and the rebuttal by Musgrave, *ibid.*, pp. 219–20.
13. See R. M. Bird and L. H. De Wulf, 'Taxation and Income Distribution in Latin America: A Critical Review of Empirical Studies', *IMF Staff Papers*, Vol. 20, November 1973, pp. 639–82.
14. A number of recent studies bearing on this point are reviewed in Mikesell and Zinser, *op. cit.*, pp. 12–15.
15. See the review of this literature in Edward M. Gramlich, 'The Effect of Federal Grants on State-Local Expenditure: A Review of the Econometric Literature', *Proceedings of 62nd Annual Conference on Taxation* (Columbus, Ohio: National Tax Association, 1970), pp. 569–92.

16. The principal exception is the excellent paper by Heller cited above.
17. See Hans W. Singer, 'External Aid: for Plans or Projects?', *Economic Journal*, Vol. 75, September 1965, pp. 539–45.
18. If this condition is satisfied, project aid will always in fact stimulate the aided project relative to other non-aided projects, although *local* expenditure on the project may or may not fall (see R. M. Bird, 'A Note on the Influence of Foreign Aid on Local Expenditures', *Social and Economic Studies*, Vol. 16, June 1967, pp. 206–10).
19. For a strong critique of this approach to aid, see A. O. Hirschman and R. M. Bird, *Foreign Aid: A Critique and a Proposal*, Princeton Essays in International Finance, No. 69, July 1968.
20. See, for example, A. M. Strout and P. G. Clark, *Aid Performance, Self-Help, and Need*, Office of Program and Policy Co-ordination, Agency for International Development, Department of State, A.I.D. Discussion Paper No. 20, July 1969 (in which the growth of tax revenues is one of the indicators of growth performance); P. N. Rosenstein-Rodan, 'International Aid for Underdeveloped Countries', *Review of Economics and Statistics*, Vol. 43, May 1961, pp. 107–38; and Douglas Dosser, 'Allocating the Burden of International Aid for Underdeveloped Countries', *ibid.*, Vol. 45, May 1963.
21. See Advisory Commission on Intergovernmental Relations, *Measuring the Fiscal Capacity and Effort of State and Local Areas* (Washington, 1971). Incidentally, the 'representative tax systems' approach pioneered by this Commission is not discussed in this paper, although it has been applied to international comparisons by Roy W. Bahl, 'A Representative Tax System Approach to Measuring Tax Effort in Developing Countries', *IMF Staff Papers*, Vol. 19, March 1972, pp. 87–122.
22. Carl S. Shoup, 'Quantitative Research in Taxation and Government Expenditure', in *Public Expenditures and Taxation*, Fiftieth Anniversary Colloquium (New York: National Bureau of Economic Research, 1972), p. 40.
23. Frederic L. Pryor, 'Elements of a Positive Theory of Public Expenditures', *Finanzarchiv*, Vol. 26, December 1967, p. 425. For a related critique of a recent German study (by A. Wagner) along these lines, see Suphan Andic, 'Tax Problems of Developing Countries', *Finanzarchiv*, Vol. 32, 1973, pp. 155–59.
24. See H. H. Hinrichs, *A General Theory of Tax Structure Change during Economic Development* (Cambridge, Mass.: Harvard Law School International Tax Program, 1966), and Musgrave, Chaps. 5–6.
25. R. J. Chelliah, H. J. Baas, and M. R. Kelly, 'Tax Ratios and Tax Effort in Developing Countries, 1969–71', *IMF Staff Papers*, Vol. 22, March 1975, pp. 187–205. A shortened version of this paper was published in *IMF Survey*, 3 June 1974, pp. 162–64.
26. R. J. Chelliah, *op. cit.*, p. 286.
27. R. J. Chelliah, H. J. Baas, and M. R. Kelly, *op. cit.*, p. 191.
28. *Idem.*
30. R. J. Chelliah, *op. cit.*, p. 295.

31. *Ibid.*, p. 297.
32. See R. W. Bahl, *op. cit.*, pp. 571–73, for by far the clearest explanation of the significance and limitations of this approach.
33. R. J. Chelliah, *op. cit.*, p. 297.
34. This is clearly recognised by R. W. Bahl, *op. cit.*, p. 590.
35. For an argument to this effect, see R. M. Bird, *The Growth of Government Spending in Canada* (Toronto: Canadian Tax Foundation, 1970), pp. 103–07.
36. R. W. Bahl, *op. cit.*, p. 572.
37. *IMF Survey*, 3 June 1974, p. 162, also R. J. Chelliah, H. J. Baas and M. R. Kelly, *op. cit.*, pp. 192–93. In addition to the other Fund studies cited earlier, see also the pioneer effort by J. Lotz and E. Morss, 'Measuring "Tax Effort" in Developing Countries', *IMF Staff Papers*, Vol. 14, November 1967, pp. 478–97.
38. If a 'significant' mining sector is defined as one in which at least 5 per cent of total domestic production or 20 per cent of total exports is accounted for by mineral extraction, 35 developing countries qualify (data from United Nations *Yearbook of National Accounts Statistics 1970* and *Yearbook of International Trade Statistics 1969)*. Eleven of these countries appear in the top 20 countries when ranked by taxes as a per cent of GNP (*IMF Survey*, 3 June 1974, p. 162). If these eleven countries are simply omitted and the new 'top 20' listed in order of simple tax ratio, the ranking thus obtained is significantly correlated (at the 1 per cent level) with the 'tax effort' ranking derived from the regression approach (Spearman's coefficient of rank correlation is 0·89).
39. R. W. Bahl, *op. cit.*, p. 572.
40. See, for example, R. J. Chelliah, *op. cit.*, p. 300.
41. R. M. Bird, 'A Note on "Tax Sacrifice" Comparisons', *National Tax Journal*, Vol. 17, September 1964, pp. 303–08. This use of the 'effort' data is recognised, but played down, by R. J. Chelliah, *op. cit.*, p. 299.
42. H. Aaron, 'Some Criticisms of Tax Burden Indices', *National Tax Journal*, Vol. 18, September 1965, p. 316.
43. R. M. Bird, 'Comment', *ibid.*, p. 317.
44. R. M. Bird, *Taxing Agricultural Land in Developing Countries* (Cambridge, Mass.: Harvard University Press, 1974), p. x.
45. *IMF Survey*, 3 June 1974, p. 164.
46. Vito Tanzi, 'The Theory of Tax Structure Change During Economic Development: A Critical Survey', *Rivista de Diritto Finanziario e Scienza delle Finanze*, Vol. 32 No. 2, 1973, pp. 207–08.
47. O. Morgenstern, *On the Accuracy of Economic Observations* (2nd ed.; Princeton, N. J.; Princeton University Press, 1963).
48. For a recent general critique of international comparisons stressing the data problems, see David K. Whynes, 'The Measurement of Comparative Development—A Survey and Critique', *Journal of Modern African Studies*, Vol. 12, No. 1, 1974, pp. 89–107. Whynes' conclusion is equally applicable in the present context '. . . The sooner L.D.C.s choose to disregard institutionalised methods of measurement and concentrate on their own internal problems, then the more hopeful will be their chances of development' (p. 107).

49. Simon Kuznets, *Modern Economic Growth* (New Haven: Yale University Press, 1966), pp. 433–37. Vito Tanzi has made this same point about the studies which are the concern of the present paper in his survey cited above (pp. 203–07).
50. R. M. Bird, 'Optimal Tax Policy for a Developing Country: The Case of Colombia', *Finanzarchiv*, Vol. 29, February 1970, p. 31.
51. To give only two instances, compare R. J. Chelliah, *op. cit.*, p. 300 *vs.* pp. 256 and 299, and R. A. Musgrave, *op. cit.*, p. 166 *vs.* p. 159.
52. R. M. Bird, *Taxing Agricultural Land*, esp. Chaps. 1, 2 and 10, refers to the few studies of which I am aware; see also two excellent review papers by Stephen Lewis, Jr., both reprinted in part in R. M. Bird and O. Oldman, eds., *Readings on Taxation in Developing Countries* (3rd ed.; Baltimore: Johns Hopkins Press, 1975).
53. The only quantitative attempt at measuring 'surplus' in this sense which I have seen is for the United States in P. A. Baran and P. M. Sweezy, *Monopoly Capital* (Penguin Books, 1968), pp. 355–77.
54. R. J. Chelliah, *Fiscal Policy in Underdeveloped Countries with Special Reference to India* (London: George Allen & Unwin, 1960), p. 65. Dr Chelliah cites Baran as his principal authority in this regard; he could, in a sense, have equally well cited Ricardo (see Carl S. Shoup, *Ricardo on Taxation* (Columbia University Press, 1960), Chap. 13).
55. The reference is to a draft paper by Paul Robertson, 'The Mobilisation of Domestic Resources: Measurement and Analysis of Saving Performance and Behaviour' (UNCTAD, New York, 1974).
56. Except in part for J. Lotz and E. Morss, *op. cit.*, pp. 480, 494.
57. R. A. Musgrave, *op. cit.*, pp. 159, 161.
58. W. A. Lewis, *Development Planning*, *op. cit.*, p. 116.
59. Clearly the distinction drawn in the text is artificial in that this period's 'effort' becomes next period's 'behaviour'. Nevertheless, the trouble here is more semantic than real, and if one insists on thinking about these concepts in simple quantitative terms, doing so in the suggested fashion seems more meaningful than the way this question is now conventionally approached.
60. R. J. Chelliah, *op. cit.*, pp. 261–67, and especially pp. 301–05. In fact, Chelliah clearly preferred a combined dynamic and static index for the evaluation of tax performance, Nevertheless, it is the latter which has received by far the most attention, even though, as argued at length in the text, it is both conceptually and statistically highly questionable.
61. The only published example of this work is C.Y. Mansfield, 'Elasticity and Buoyancy of a Tax System: A Method applied to Paraguay', *IMF Staff Papers*, Vol. 19, July 1972, pp. 425–43. There are also important unpublished methodological papers by Roy Bahl and by R. J. Chelliah and S. Chand.
62. See R. J. Chelliah, *op. cit.*, p. 302.
63. R. M. Bird, 'Comment', *op. cit.*, p. 318.
64. R. A. Musgrave, *op. cit.*, p. 160.
65. J. Lotz and E. Morss, *op. cit.*, pp. 494–95. This approach has also been further developed by Gandhi and Sahota: see Ved Gandhi, *The Tax*

Burden on Indian Agriculture (Cambridge, Mass.: Harvard University International Tax Program, 1966), Chap. 2, and G. S. Sabota, 'The Distribution of Tax Burden in Brazil' (Mimeographed; Sao Paulo, 1968).

66. This is the standard used (implicitly) by Bird, 'A Note on "Tax Sacrifice" Comparisons'; the explicit formulation ($T/Y = BY_p^{\beta}$, where B is the index and β is the progressivity parameter) is attributable to Aaron. Both straight tax ratio comparisons and 'tax effort' comparisons in effect take β as 0.
67. In an as yet unpublished paper. See also the references in note 2 above.
68. That is, a Gini coefficient of 0·5. For a sceptical view of Pareto's 'Law', see Jan Pen, *Income Distribution* (Penguin Books, 1974), pp. 234–44.
69. Shimo Maital, 'Public Goods and Income Distribution: Some Further Results', *Econometrica,* Vol. 41, May 1973.
70. There are of course many other problems with such exercises, including the treatment of different income distribution patterns in countries with the same per capita income level.
71. The similarity of some of these points to those made in a recent review of another large body of quantitative work is not coincidental: see Bird and De Wulf, 'Taxation and Income Distribution in Latin America'. Many others (including such eminent figures as Kuznets and Leontief) have of course made similar criticisms of the tendency of many economists to use quantitative data rather too lightly.
72. See especially the important recent Draft Manual released by the International Monetary Fund, *A Manual on Government Finance Statistics* (June 1974) and *Government Finance Statistics Yearbook,* volume 1, (September, 1977).

Chapter 3

Tax Effort in Developing Countries: What do Regression Measures Really Measure?

BRUCE R. BOLNICK*

I. INTRODUCTION

During the past decade a number of studies[1] have attempted to measure the 'tax effort' of less developed countries (LDCs) from cross-section regression analysis. Typically, factors thought to be important determinants of tax capacity are chosen as independent variables partially explaining behaviour of the tax ratio (i.e., tax revenues as a percentage of aggregate income). The residuals are then taken as crude measure of tax effort in the sense that a higher residual would suggest a greater tax yield relative to tax capacity. In short the 'fitted' values of the tax ratio are used as proxies for tax capacity.

Although its limitations have been widely acknowledged,[2] the regression approach to measurement of tax effort has been defended as an improvement over use of raw tax ratios for purpose of international comparisons. If indeed such comparisons have influenced policy decisions in LDCs, or the allocation of international payments,[3] then the analytical foundations of the measures being used should be clearly defined. In this paper a stylised model of government decision-making is used to clarify the conceptual and quantitative meaning of 'tax effort'. Section II discusses in broad terms the interaction between supply and demand influences on the tax ratio. In section III we present a simple aggregative model for

*Assistant Professor of Economics, Duke University.

analysing this interaction. Section IV applies this model to an evaluation of the regression approach to tax effort comparisons. Section V briefly examines an additional measurement problem arising from the choice of functional form. Section VI then concludes the paper.

II. THE BASIC PROBLEM: SIMULTANEITY

In virtually all of the LDC cross-section studies of government taxation or expenditures the interaction between 'getting and spending' is addressed, yet not employed in the derivation of the econometric models. As Gupta has noted, 'empirical studies concerning the size of the public sector have too often estimated mongrel functions . . . lack(ing) a priori analysis of the factors affecting the demand and supply sides separately' [*Gupta, 1969: 62–3*]. As a result the tax ratio regressions yield inappropriate measures of tax capacity.

The basic issue is closely akin to Samuelson's fundamental general equilibrium conception of public sector activities [*Samuelson, 1954*]. As Musgrave explained, 'it is hardly possible to measure tax effort without regard for the expenditure side of the budget. Rather than thinking of the ability to give up the private use of resource use, one should inquire into the appropriate division of resource use between public and private goods.'[4] However this normative criterion is consistently tempered by more practical considerations: 'Allowance must also be made for a county's ability to collect taxes and hence to meet its desired revenue target.' [*Musgrave, 1969: 191*].

We thereby arrive at the tax handle or supply constraint theory of public finance in low income countries. During the early stages of development we find 'demands for government services that cannot yet satisfactorily be met by government' [*Hinrichs, 1966: 48*] because 'taxable capacity influences dominate expenditure demand influences' [*Bahl, 1971: 571–2*]. As development proceeds, 'economic growth increases the relative taxable capacity of a country and permits the government to obtain a larger share of national product' [*Thorn, 1967: 23*].

Embodied in this scenario are serious problems affecting the measurement of tax effort. How are supply and demand influences to be segregated and estimated? What precisely is meant by 'tax constraints' or 'tax capacity'?[5] What meaning can be attached to the notion of 'desired revenue target' as distinct from the availability of tax handles? We can only achieve a useful clarification of these issues by referring to an analytical model of government budget determination.

III. AN AGGREGATIVE MODEL OF GOVERNMENT BUDGET DETERMINATION

Our analysis proceeds from a simple normative model of resource allocation, modified to emphasise the interaction between desired levels of government output and the costs of levying taxes. Assume that there is a single homogeneous private good and a single homogeneous government service, the respective output quantities being Q_p and Q_g. All resource control initially lies with the private sector and must be transferred to the government sector for producing Q_g; increasing marginal opportunity cost (in terms of the numeraire private good) characterises this transference activity.[6] As a further simplifying assumption, the government must fully finance its expenditures through taxes.[7] We also assume a set of preferences, $U(Q_g, Q_p)$, embodying continuously diminishing marginal rates of substitution between the two goods.[8]

In Figure 1, let the product transformation curve ptc° limit the set of attainable output bundles when there are zero transference costs. Given the society's preference mapping, E° is the preferred output choice, with the corresponding private/public goods mix being $(Q_p/Q_g)_o$.[9] Since the transfer of resources to government *itself* requires the direct use of resources plus reduced efficiency or incentives in the private sector, the actual product transformation curve, ptc^a lies below ptc° by the vertical distance $c(Q_g)$, which defines the transference cost incurred for any level of Q_g. Thus:

(1) $\text{ptc}^o\colon Q_p = f_o(Q_g),\ f_o' < 0,\ f_o'' < 0.$

(2) $\text{ptc}^a\colon Q_p = f_o(Q_g) - c(Q_g),\ c' > 0,\ c'' > 0,\ c(0) = 0.$

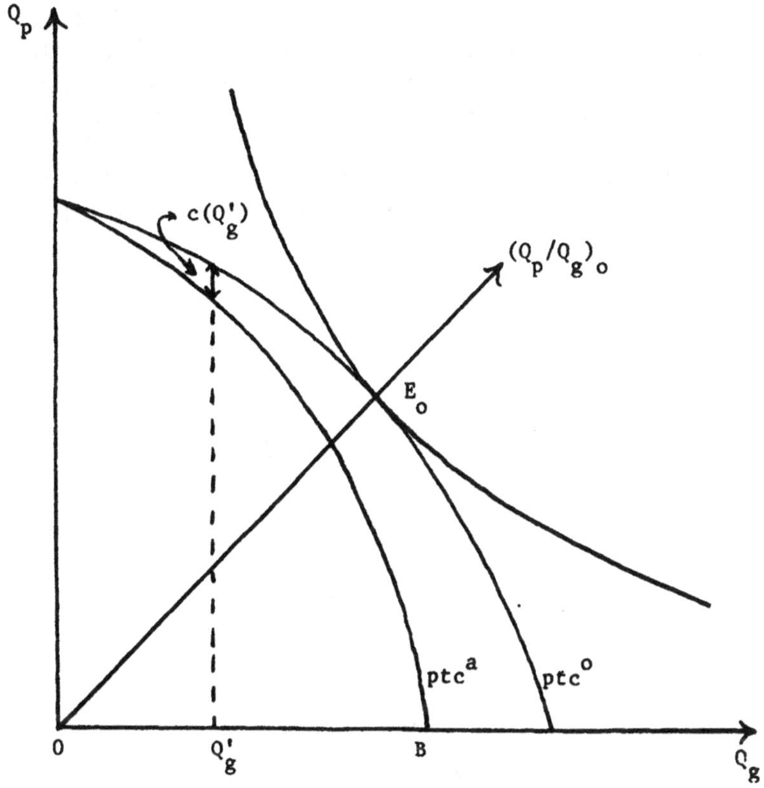

Figure 1

To discern the 'optimal' division of resources we need three sets of information: (i) ptc^o, (ii) $c(Q_g)$, and (iii) $U(Q_g, Q_p)$. We can combine (i) and (ii) to define ptc^a and then seek the most preferred point on ptc^a. Our approach however will be to combine (i) and (iii) instead, to form a 'demand' relationship which can then be compared with a 'supply' function derived from (ii). While less conventional, this approach has the advantage that the tax cost is isolated. This appears to be the most appropriate procedure for analysing the behaviour of the tax ratio during economic development.

The marginal social opportunity cost of transferring resources to the public sector is $c'(Q_g)$, defined over the domain

$Q_g \in [0, B]$.[10] Defining government's share of national income in accounting terms as $G \in [0, 1]$ let us assume that G is a strictly monotonic function of Q_g/Q_p (and thus of Q_g). We can now reformulate the transference cost as a function of G; i.e., we now have C(G), such that $C'(G) > 0$, $C(0) = 0$. Let S_s represent a set of factors determining the precise position and shape of the C curve. Our 'supply' function will then be:

$$(3) \quad C' \equiv F^s(G;S_s),\ \partial F^s/\partial G > 0.$$

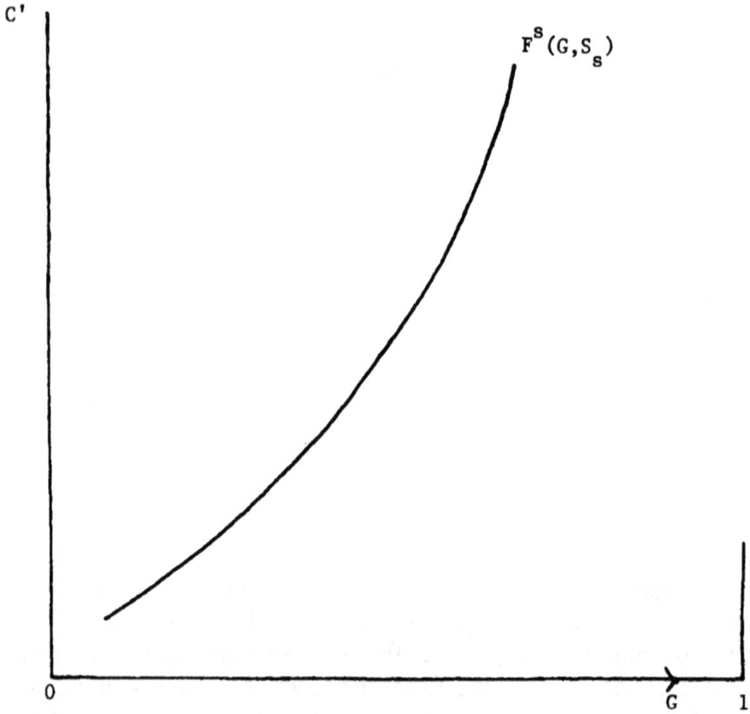

Figure 2

This function, shown in Figure 2, defines the marginal tax cost of achieving each allocation of resources, given the set of relevant economic and structural characteristics of each country.

Given our definition of supply the appropriate 'demand' concept is the *desired* G for any given marginal transference cost. Beginning with ptc^o in Figure 3 we have a family of product transformation curves, $ptc^{c'}$ defined by:

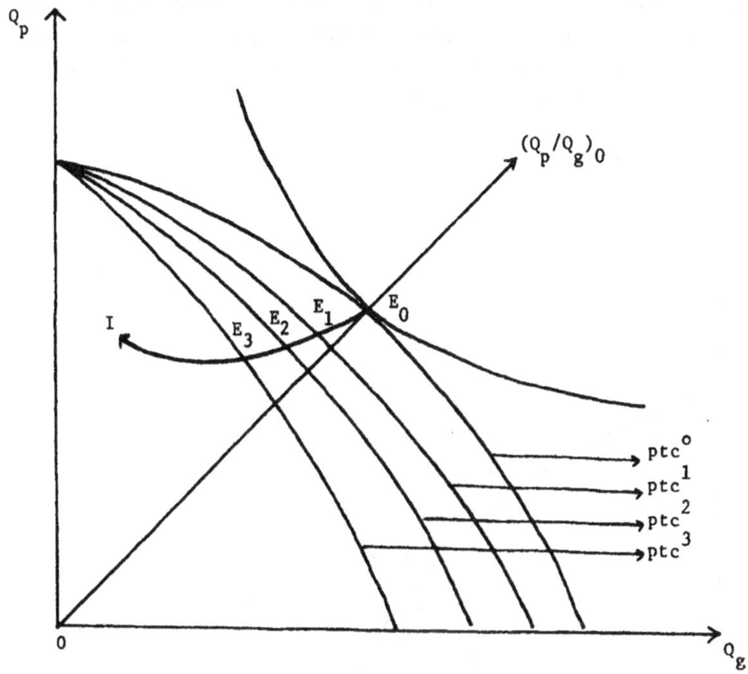

Figure 3

(4) $ptc^{c'}$: $Q_p = f_o(Q_g) - c' \cdot Q_g$, $c' =$ constant,

for various values of the (constant) marginal resource transfer cost, c′. Clearly $ptc^{c'} = ptc^o$ when $c' = 0$. The 'demand' curve for government production is now defined by:

(5) $Q_g = d(c') = \max U(Q_g, f_o(Q_g) - c' \cdot Q_g)$.

Along each ptc^c, the function d(c′) picks out the U-maximising value of Q_g. The function d(c′) is continuous, with $d' < 0$ if public services are not inferior goods. Analogous to the price-consumption curve in consumer theory, no generalisations can be made about the second derivative of d(c′). Path I in Figure 3 shows one possible configuration relating the desired Q_g to the marginal tax cost, c′.

Transforming units as we did for the cost function above, we get a relationship $G = D(C')$ having the same properties as $d(c')$. If we now assume that differences in social preferences between countries are systematically related to a set of economic, demographic and socio-political variables, S_d, we can define our demand function:

(6) $G \equiv F^d(C';S_d), \partial F^d/\partial C' < 0.$

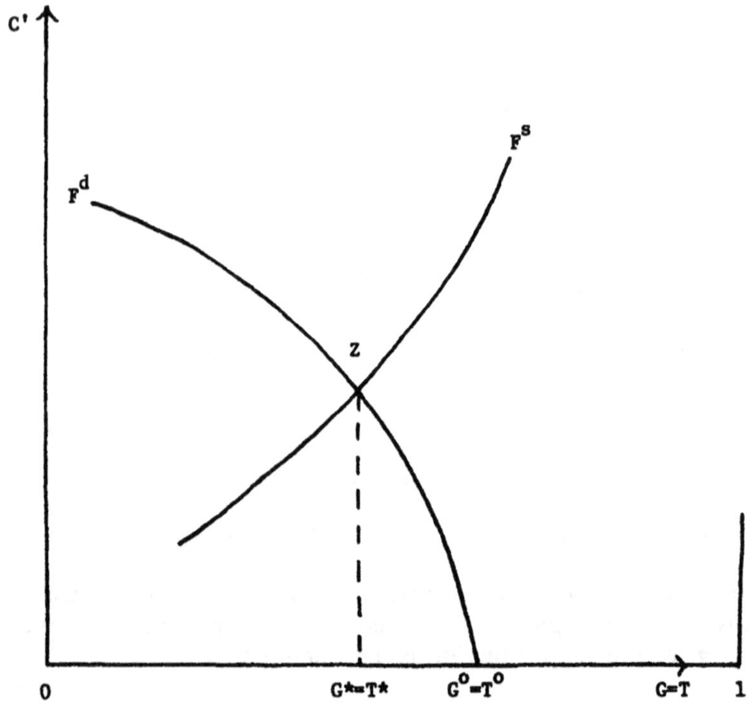

Figure 4

This function, shown in Figure 4 to conform with Path I of Figure 3, identifies 'the appropriate division of resource use between public and private goods' for each level of marginal tax cost, given the set of demand-relevant characteristics for each country.

The intersection of the F^s and F^d functions at point Z in Figure 4 thus determines the appropriate share of government in national product (G^*) and the appropriate tax ratio (T^*), applying our simplifying assumption that $G = T$. Government decision-making, of course, cannot generally be expected to achieve T^* (or G^*).[11] However, if we appeal to a 'tunnel effect' [*Hirschman, 1973*], operating on long-run budget determination such that the *actual* government share, G^a, is in a neighbourhood of G^* (or some linear transformation of G^* reflecting systematic institutional biases favouring sub-optimal Q_g,[12] or super-optimal Q_g[13]) then comparative inferences based on our model can provide useful information about the behaviour of the tax ratio between countries with different characteristics S_s and S_d.

Referring to Figure 4, we can provide answers to some of the questions raised at the end of section II. The value $G^o = T^o$ can be taken as a natural interpretation of Musgrave's notion of a 'desired revenue target' which, unhappily, will not be reached due to limitations on a country's 'ability to collect taxes'. The difference $G^o - G^*$ ($=T^o - T^*$) can be a measure of the *gap* between desired revenues and ability to collect. If there is an *absolute* tax constraint this would be reflected by a vertical positive asymptote of the F^s function, prohibiting completely any larger allocations to government.

More generally the intent of the term 'tax capacity constraint' is ambiguous. It can variously be taken as i) the marginal transference cost C' evaluated at either G^o or G^*, ii) the entire F^scurve, iii) the gap between G^o and G^*, or iv) the extent to which that gap would be narrowed by any favourable marginal shift of the F^s curve. It is conceivable that the ranking of countries according to severity of tax capacity constraints would differ with the measure being used.

IV THE MEANING AND MEASUREMENT OF TAX EFFORT

Ideally, tax effort should be related to the optimal allocation of resources between the public and private sectors, inclusive of tax cost considerations. Thus a pure measure would be $T^*_i - T^a_i$ for each country i, where T^a is the actual tax ratio. Note that a negative value would imply an over-zealous government; high T^a is not necessarily to be lauded in principle. Without information on T^*_i, we may compare observed tax ratios between countries after controlling for differences in the position of the F^s curve. Presumably this is the theoretical intent of attempts to measure tax effort. It has been widely acknowledged that this measure of 'effort' is really a hybrid concept capturing the combined effect of the position of F^d_i, which determines T^*_i, *and* the difference between T^*_i and T^a_i; as such it lacks a straightforward normative interpretation.

Accepting this hybrid concept as the target tax effort measure, serious problems afflict the econometric techniques used for its quantification. Basically the F^s curve cannot be identified with a single equation econometric model. The standard estimation techniques thus fail to control properly for supply differences.

The tax effort studies generally try to estimate the reduced equation derived from our structural model (equations 3 and 6):

$$(7)\ T^* = G^* = F\ (S_s, S_d).$$

This equation is then purged of the demand effects, S_d, in order to allocate their influences to the residual. The estimated equation is taken to measure tax capacity, and the residuals are considered as an index of effort. Proper choice of variables to be included is therefore the crucial problem. As Bahl remarks, 'the first step in the statistical analysis, and surely the most difficult in this approach, is estimating taxable capacity of a country by using only variables that may be properly classified as non-effort factors' [*Bahl, 1971: 582*]. Likewise Chelliah [*1971: 298*] states:

> The present analysis of tax ratio variations is deliberately intended to consider only the major factors that are presumed to affect the tax ratio through the side of ability to pay and collect taxes. Several sociopolitical and other factors affecting it through what has been termed the willingness to tax have been left out... [I]mplicit in the tax effort approach is the asssumption that the factors affecting willingness to tax are largely independent of the capacity factors whose effects have been estimated.

Three distinct difficulties are encountered using this reduced form methodology.

First, even if $S_s \cap S_d = \emptyset$ and for every pair (s_j, d_k), $s_j \in S_s$, $d_k \in S_d$, collinearity were absent, demand influences would remain in the reduced form parameter estimates due to simultaneous equations bias. Suppose that $S_s = (s_1, s_2)$ and $S_d = (d_1, d_2)$ satisfying the two conditions just stated, and that equation 7 were linearised to generate the econometric specification:

(8) $T = a_o + a_1 s_1 + a_2 s_2 + u,$

where $u = a_3 d_1 + a_4 d_2 + v$, and v is the true stochastic component of equation 7. Using (8), the estimated supply coefficient $\hat{a}_0$, $\hat{a}_1$ and $\hat{a}_2$ will still include demand effects.[14] As shown in Figure 5, the impact on T^* of any change in s_j will be determined by the extent of the shift in F^s *and* the shape of the F^d function in the relevant region. Depending on whether the

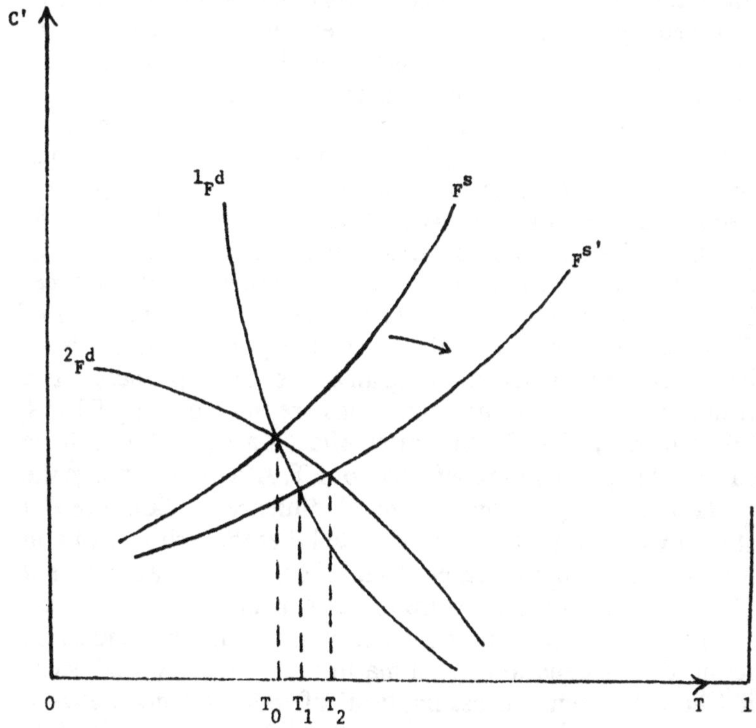

Figure 5

demand curve is ${}^1F^d$ or ${}^2F^d$ the impact of a shift in F^s to $F^{s'}$ will alternatively be T_1-T_0 or T_2-T_0.

Geometrically it is easy to see that the size of the demand influence in $\partial T^*/\partial S_j$ will be inversely related to the slope of the F^s curve. In the limiting case of a vertical F^s the factors which shift F^s will fully determine T^*, eliminating the simultaneous equations bias completely.[15] Notably, conditions approaching this limit are often *assumed* in the tax effort literature. For example Lotz and Morss declare that '...in developing countries, tax collection capabilities are especially likely to be *fully utilised* because public expenditure aspirations are especially likely to be high' (emphasis added).[16] In effect the simultaneous equations bias is presumed to be small for the sample being used. However this condition should not be an assumption. The degree to which supply constraints are absolute is an empirical issue, so this bias problem cannot be resolved by ignoring it.[17] Tests reported elsewhere by the author [*Bolnick, 1976*] suggest that demand influences do become important at intermediate stages of development.

A *second* bias may arise if any elements of S_s are collinear with elements of the set S_d. For example the size of the foreign trade sector (FT) is generally considered to be an important determinant of the strength of tax constraints[18] (i.e., the position of F^s), while population size (P) is often referred to as an important determinant of the desired division of resources between the public and private sectors[19] (i.e., the position of F^d). Yet it is also frequently noted that population size is an important argument explaining an economy's 'openness'. As a result, when tax capacity regressions are run including $FT \in S_s$ but excluding $P \in S_d$, the latter effect on tax ratios will be captured in part by the coefficient of FT. Attempts to purge the reduced form regression of demand influence will fail. A recent study by the author has demonstrated that the inclusion of P in a standard tax supply regression markedly alters the coefficient of FT, and thus the measure of tax capacity.[20]

The *third* important problem with using the truncated reduced form equation for estimating tax capacity would occur if Chelliah's 'implicit assumption' of independence between capacity and effort factors is violated; i.e., if $S_s \cap S_d \neq \emptyset$. Unhappily this is very likely to be the case. To the extent that any variable, such as per capita income (PCI) or urbanisation can be considered as an important determinant of the position of both F^s and F^d it is futile to try purging the reduced form equation of the demand influence.[21] By retaining the variable, measured capacity is overstated since the coefficient will include the combined effect of shifts in both curves caused by a change in the independent variable. Alternatively, excluding the variable eliminates its supply effect, thereby understating capacity and overstating effort.

The futility of trying to separate capacity from effort through a single equation model emerges in many of the discussions about the choice of independent variables. For example Chelliah notes that 'it is generally argued that high per capita income levels lead to high tax ratios because of both the correspondingly high capacity to pay taxes and the high income elasticity of demand for public goods' [*Chelliah, 1971: 280*]. Yet shortly thereafter he states that most studies take the level of per capita income

> to reflect the level of 'surplus' over subsistence out of which taxes could be paid as well as the level of economic development, which is accompanied by an increase in the literacy rate, monetization, urbanization, etc.—all of which facilitate tax collections ... It is fair to say that in most cases only factors assumed to operate on the supply side of funds have been taken into account. [*Ibid.: 291.*]

Bahl [*1971: 571–2*] is more candid about the contortions required:

> The tax formulation requires an a priori justification of the explanatory variables as factors affecting only taxable capacity. It is assumed that these explanatory variables are not proxy measures for those forces that affect the government's willingness to tax, e.g., an independent variable may not be included to reflect a higher level of demand for public expenditures. The problems associated with such an assumption may be illustrated by considering the possible interpretation of per capita income if included as an independent variable. In the tax effort approach it may be argued that a higher per capita income indicates a greater taxable surplus and therefore a potentially larger tax base. However, it may not be argued that a higher per capita income results in an increased demand for

public services and therefore a greater government share in national income.

Bahl recognises the contrived assumptions necessary before proper inferences about tax effort can be gleaned from a regression. Many other authors proceed with insufficient notice of the twists and turns to which their inference is subjected.[22]

V FUNCTIONAL FORMS

Acknowledging the problems discussed in the previous section, an additional bias is generated by the linearity assumption commonly employed in the regression analysis. Most *a priori* theorising about tax capacity determination suggests that capacity constraints ease at an accelerating pace during development. Empirical tests of non-linear relationships between T and PCI generally support this expectation.[23]

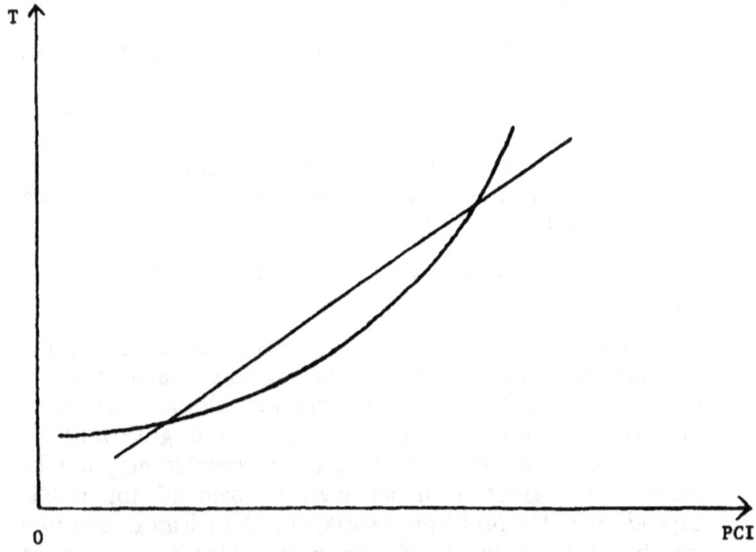

Figure 6

If the true path of tax capacity were a non-linear function of income, a regression which is linear in PCI would alternatively understate, overstate, and again understate the fitted value of the tax ratio, as shown in Figure 6. As a consequence the regression residuals would be systematically distorted, yielding tax effort measures with upward bias for higher and lower income countries, and downward bias for those in between. Even though there is no statistical difference between the overall tax effort measures or rankings using the alternative functional forms, the difference for individual countries may be large. The author tested this proposition by estimating the basic Lotz and Morss regression[24] with both linear and quadratic PCI effects on tax ratios. The sample included 37 LDCs with PCI < $800 in 1960. Letting the difference between linear and quadratic measures of tax effort be denoted by Δ, Figure 7 shows that our results conform to expectations. Furthermore the percentage discrepancy relative to the linear tax effort measure varies from nil to over 300 per cent. For any use of tax effort comparisons in which the quantitative value for individual countries may be important, regressions using linearity assumptions may provide systematically biased information.

VI CONCLUSIONS

In this paper we have tried to demarcate carefully the methodological problems encountered in using the regression approach to measuring tax effort among LDCs. The difficulties discussed here are not new, but they have not previously been examined within an explicit analytical framework. The primary advantage of this exercise is to provide a better basis for evaluating tax effort measures. As a by-product, our analysis allows us to clarify a number of ambiguous concepts that recur in the literature.

Our analysis has played by the rules of the tax effort game. Specifically, we have accepted comparison of observed tax ratios, after controlling for differences in tax collection capabilities (i.e. differences in the position of the F^s curve) as the legitimate object of study. However our model also demonstrates that such comparisons are actually hybrid measures which confuse (i) differences in performance relative to desires and (ii) differences in desires themselves across countries (i.e. differences in the position of the F^d curve). Only

Figure 7

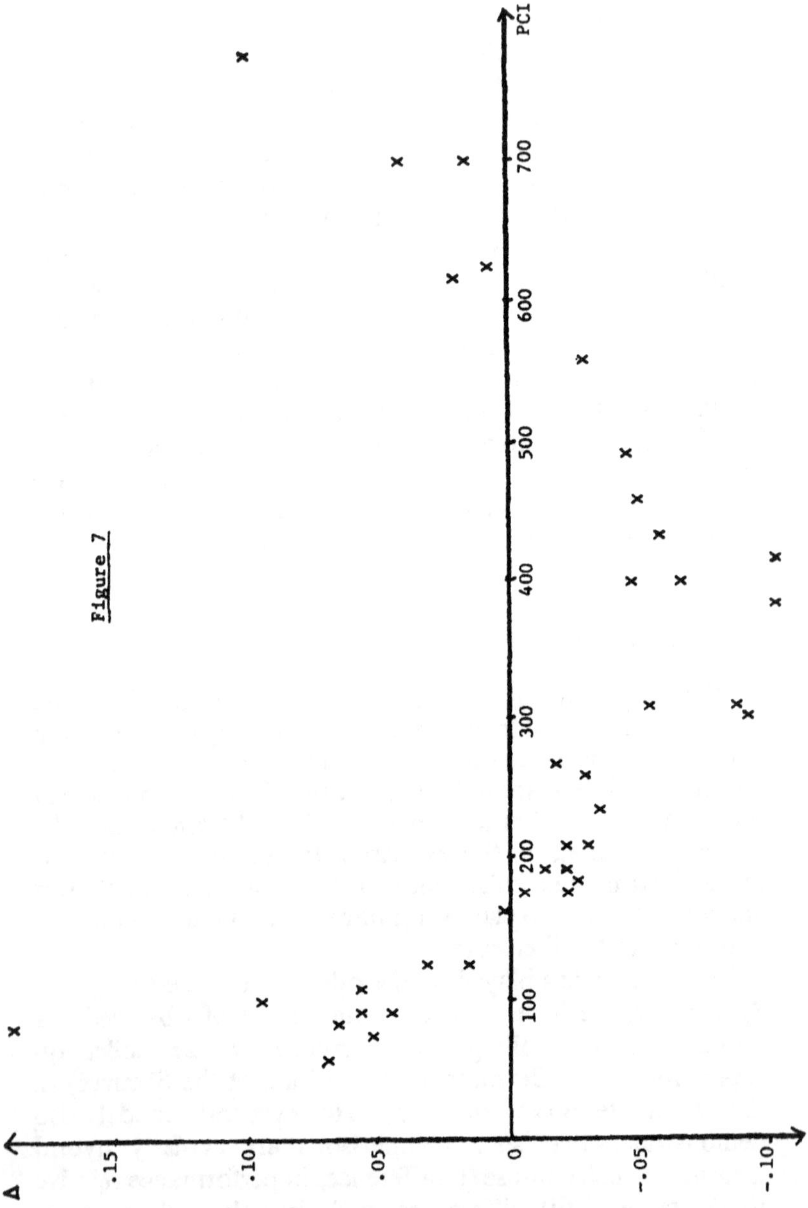

if the latter set of differences are assumed to be absent or unimportant (in the sense that they 'ought' not exist) can normative significance be attached to the tax effort measures—even if improved modelling minimises the types of methodological distortions we have enumerated.

NOTES

1. For example see Lotz and Morss [*1967*]; Bahl [*1971*]; Chelliah [*1971*]; Chelliah *et al.* [*1975*]; Musgrave [*1969*] and Shin [*1969*].
2. Notably in Bird [*1976*]; Musgrave and Musgrave [*1973*]; Chelliah [*1971*]; Morss [*1969*]; Peacock [*1969a*]; Prest [*1972*] and Bahl [*1971*].
3. As suggested by Bird [*1976*]; Peacock [*1969: 7*]; Prest [*1972: 142*]; and in Cline and Sargen [*1975: 385–6*].
4. Musgrave [*1969: 160*]. Similar remarks are made by Gupta [*1967, 1969*]; Morss [*1969*]; Bahl [*1971*]; Thorn [*1967*] and others.
5. Even very poor LDCs are unlikely to meet any absolute limits to raising taxes. The real world tax policy makers probably do not view their job as one of maximising revenues unconstrained by economic or political trade-offs. Bird [*1976: 253–4*] goes so far as to say that even specification of tax capacity (let alone measurement) 'seems conceptually impossible'.
6. In our normative model this cost includes resources used directly to levy taxes, plus loss of Q_p through dampened incentives and reduced efficiency in the private sector resulting from the tax policies. Finally, risks of social disorders may be affected by the tax structure.
7. It is easy to include debt, but by its omission nothing of substance is lost regarding tax effort comparisons; and the presentation is simplified.
8. These preferences can be based on Scitovsky social indifference curves, or on a policy-makers' Bergsonian social welfare function (as used by Gramlich [*1969*], Heller [*1975*] and others). In a democracy model we could envision alternative sizes of government put to a vote pairwise, in which case the median voters' preferences would determine policy.
9. At this point the model is simply that of Herber [*1975, chapter 1*].
10. It is possible for ptc^a to curve back to the left after some $\bar{Q}_g$ is reached, reflecting a situation where further increases in Q_g/Q_p, are so costly that both Q_g and Q_p must in fact be reduced. In this case we define $Q_g \in [0,\bar{Q}_g]$ as the relevant domain, and F^a will not be defined over the entire interval [0,1] since it approaches a vertical asymptote (an 'absolute tax constraint') from the left somewhere within that interval. We ignore this special case hereafter.
11. We are aware of the growing distaste in the profession for normative models of government, as recently expressed by Wagner [*1976*]. In discussing tax ratios we must therefore try to relate our simple model to actual processes, however crudely at this stage. A satisfactory positive theory of long run budget dynamics remains as a crucial research area.

12. As argued by Galbraith [*1960*] among others.
13. As suggested by the models of Buchanan and Tullock [*1962*] and Niskanen [*1971*].
14. Let the explicit form of equations 3 and 6 be:

$$(3')\quad C' = F^s(G;S_s) = b_o + b_1 s_1 + b_2 s_2 + b_3 G + e_s$$

$$(6\ )\quad G = F^d(C';S_d) = c_o + c_1 d_1 + c_2 d_2 + c_3 C' + e_d.$$

Solving for G in terms of S_s and S_d, and truncating the reduced form to allocate the demand influences to the residual, we find that the reduced form coefficients of s_1 and s_2 are:

$$a_1 = \frac{c_3 b_1}{1-c_3 b_3} \neq b_1 \qquad a_2 = \frac{c_3 b_2}{1-c_3 b_3} \neq b_2.$$

15. In this case we cannot express C′ as a single-valued function of G to define our F^s curve. However the proposition can be demonstrated by referring to the inverse functions of F^s and F^d, assuming they are well defined:

$$(3'')\quad G = F^{s^{-1}}(C', S_s) = r_o + r_1 s_1 + r_2 s_2 + r_3 C' + e_r$$

$$(6'')\quad C = F^{d^{-1}}(G, S_d) = p_o + p_1 d_1 + p_2 d_2 + p_3 G + e_p$$

Solving for the reduced form equation for G and allocating the direct demand effects to the residual we get:

$$(8'')\quad G = \frac{r_o}{1-p_3 r_3} + \frac{r_1}{1-p_3 r_3} s_1 + \frac{r_2}{1-p_3 r_3} s_2 + u.$$

As r_3 goes to zero, the coefficients of 8″ approach the true structural coefficients of 3″; the F^s curve approaches the vertical line at $G = r_o + r_1 s_1 + r_2 s_2 + u$; and the simultaneous equations bias approaches zero.
16. Lotz and Morss [*1970: 329*]. Similar remarks are made by Thorn [*1967*]; Bahl [*1971*]; and Hinrichs [*1966*] to some extent.
17. Lotz and Morss apply their regression to a low-income sample and then to a higher income sample of countries. They state that the higher R^2 in the former sample demonstrates the greater importance of supply constraints on the tax ratio for low income countries. This observation misses the point, though, since the problem may be that the explained variance itself includes demand effects through biases in the coefficients of the supply variables.
18. As in Hinrichs [*1966*] and Lotz and Morss [*1967*].
19. As discussed in Musgrave [*1969*] and Kelley [*1976*].
20. When demand-relevant demographic variables were added to a supply constraint regression, the coefficient for FT:

(i) dropped from 0·119 to 0·075 (both significant) for a sample of 36 LDCs with per capita income less than $1000 in 1960;

(ii) dropped from 0·118 to 0·060 and became insignificant for a sample of 28 countries with per capita income between $250 and $2250 in 1960.

21. Referring to the notation in note 14, we now let $s_1 \equiv d_1$. The reduced form coefficient of s_1 then becomes:

$$a_1 = \frac{c_3 b_1 + c_1}{1 - c_3 b_3} \neq b_1.$$

22. Even Bahl fails to acknowledge the demand influences which remain even if the condition $S_s \eta S_d = \theta$ is fulfilled.

23. For example see Gupta [*1968*] and Musgrave [*1969*]. Non-linear regressions generally produced significantly improved explanation of variance.

24. I.e., we estimated both:

$$T = a_o + a_1 PCI + a_3 FT + e$$

and,

$$T = a_o + a_1 PCI + a_2 PCI^2 + a_3 FT + e$$

and compared the residuals from the two regressions. Results qualitatively similar to those mentioned here are reproduced if the same test is conducted using Lotz and Morss' own data.

25. See the first paragraph of Section IV, above.

REFERENCES

Bahl, Roy W., 1971, 'A Regression Approach to Tax Effort and Tax Ratio Analysis', *IMF Staff Papers,* 18:3 November.

Bird, Richard M. 1976, 'Assessing Tax Performance in Developing Countries: A Critical Review of the Literature', *Finanzarchiv,* 34:2.

Bolnick, Bruce R., 1976, 'Demographic Effects on Tax Shares During Economic Development', WP. No. 35, Population and Employment Project, Geneva: ILO.

Buchanan, J. M. and G. Tullock, 1962, *The Calculus of Consent,* Ann Arbor, University of Michigan Press.

Chelliah, Raja J., 1971, 'Trends in Taxation in Developing Countries', *IMF Staff Papers,* 18:2, July.

Chelliah, Raja J., Hessel J. Baas and Margaret R. Kelly, 1975, 'Tax Ratios and Tax Effort in Developing Countries', *IMF Staff Papers,* 22:1, March.

Cline, William R. and Nicholas P. Sargen, 1975, 'Performance Criteria and Multilateral Aid Allocation', *World Development* 3:6, June.

Galbraith, John Kenneth, 1960, *The Affluent Society,* Boston, Houghton-Mifflin.

Gramlich, Edward M., 1969, 'State and Local Governments and Their Budget Constraints', *International Economic Review*, 10:2, June.

Gupta, S. P., 1969, 'Comment' in Peacock [*1969*].

Gupta, S. P., 1968, 'Public Expenditure and Economic Development—A Cross Section Analysis', *Finanzarchiv*, October.

Gupta, S. P., 1967, 'Public Expenditure and Economic Growth: A Time Series Analysis', *Public Finance*, 22:1, pp. 423–61.

Heller, P., 1975 'A Model of Public Fiscal Behaviour in Developing Countries: Aid, Investment and Taxation', *American Economic Review*, 65:3, June.

Herber, Bernard P., 1975, *Modern Public Finance*, 3rd Edition, Homewood: Irwin.

Hinrichs, Harley H., 1966, *A General Theory of Tax Structure Change During Economic Development*, Cambridge, Harvard Law School.

Hirschman, A. O., 1973, 'The Changing Tolerance for Income Inequality in the Course of Economic Development', *Quarterly Journal of Economics*, 87:4, November.

Lotz, Jorgen R. and Elliott R. Morss, 1970, 'A Theory of Tax Level Determinants for Developing Countries', *Economic Development and Cultural Change*, 18:3, April.

Lotz, Jorgen R. and Elliott R. Morss, 1967, 'Measuring "Tax Effort" in Developing Countries', *IMF Staff Papers*, 14:1, pp. 478–95.

Morss, Elliott R., 1969, 'Using Various Statistical Measures to Analyze the Size of the Public Sector', in Peacock [*1969*].

Musgrave, Richard A., 1969, *Fiscal Systems*, New Haven, Yale University Press.

Musgrave, Richard A., and Peggy B. Musgrave, 1973, *Public Finance in Theory and Practice*, New York, McGraw Hill.

Niskanen, W. A., 1971, *Bureaucracy and Representative Government*, Chicago: Aldine-Atherton.

Peacock, Alan T. (ed.), 1969, *Quantitative Analysis in Public Finance*, New York, Praeger.

Peacock, Alan T., 1969a, 'The Fiscal Economist and Quantitative Analysis' in Peacock [*1969*].

Prest, A. R., 1972, 'Government Revenue, the National Income, and All That', in R. Bird and J. Head, *Modern Fiscal Issues*, Toronto, University of Toronto Press.

Samuelson, Paul A., 1954, 'The Pure Theory of Public Expenditure', *Review of Economics and Statistics*, Vol. 36, November.

Shin, Kilman, 1969, 'International Differences in Tax Ratio', *Review of Economics and Statistics*, Vol. 51, pp. 213–20.

Thorn, Richard S., 1967, 'The Evolution of Public Finance During Economic Development', *The Manchester School of Economic and Social Studies*, Vol. 35, No. 1.

Wagner, Richard E., 1976, Review of Wilfred L. David (ed.), *Public Finance, Planning and Economic Development*, in *Economic Development and Cultural Change*, 24:2, January.

PART TWO

TAX REVENUE AND ECONOMIC GROWTH

The authors of Chapter 4 would like to express appreciation to the Secretaria Permanente de la Integracion Centroamericana (SIECA), Guatemala City, for its statistical support and an anonymous referee for incisive comments on an earlier draft. W. T. Wilford wishes to thank the University of New Orleans for sabbatical leave in San Salvador during which this project was initiated, and both authors acknowledge the Agency for International Development/El Salvador for a summer 1975 project which permitted completion of the manuscript. An earlier version of this paper was presented at the Robert Sidney Smith Memorial Session of the Southern Economic Association Annual Meeting, 13 November 1975, at New Orleans, Louisiana. Views expressed therein are solely those of the authors.

The author of Chapter 5 is indebted to Lawrence Schwartz and Stephen Reynolds for valuable comments on an earlier draft of his paper. He alone is responsible for any errors.

The author of Chapter 6 is indebted to Fernando-Henrique Cardoso, Michael Kuczinski, John Wells, Edgardo Floto and the editor of this volume for helpful criticism of an earlier draft.

Chapter 4

Estimates of Revenue Elasticity and Buoyancy in Central America 1955–74

D. SYKES WILFORD and W. T. WILFORD*

I. INTRODUCTION

One of the most important general hypotheses upon which most economists agree is that emerging nations must increasingly mobilise their own internal resources to promote economic growth, and perhaps the most important instrument by which resources may be marshalled is the implementation of an effective tax policy. N. Kaldor has pointed out that

> the importance of public revenue to the underdeveloped countries can hardly be exaggerated if they are to achieve their hopes of accelerated economic progress. Whatever the prevailing ideology or political colour of a particular government, it must steadily expand a whole host of nonrevenue-yielding services—education, health, communication systems, and so on—as a prerequisite to a country's economic and cultural development [*Kaldor, 1964: 255*].

As governments throughout the Third World implement mechanisms to capture internal financial resources, it is necessary that there be quantitative measures to evaluate success in stimulating public resources through tax policy. This analysis utilises the revenue-income elasticity methodology to measure the responsiveness of revenue structures to GDP in

*University of New Orleans.

the nations comprising the Central American Common Market (CACM), and to relate the theory of revenue-income elasticity of two fiscal policy criteria. The first issue in evaluating fiscal self-help performance is the ability of the tax structure to generate proportionately higher revenues both through discretionary action (tax rate and base changes, legislative enactment, improvement in collection techniques, etc.) *and* through revenue growth that is automatically generated through economic activity. This measure is traditionally identified as the *tax buoyancy* criterion. The second criterion relates to the responsiveness of revenue yields to movement in economic activity alone, or the *revenue-income elasticity* measure. Among the Third World regions in which sufficient data are available for a statistically accurate measure of these two criteria are the five nations comprising the CACM, including Costa Rica, El Salvador, Guatemala, Honduras, and Nicaragua. The five countries provide a statistical sample of 24 years in which to test the buoyancy and elasticity criteria, and to evaluate potential improvement in self-help performance of the five countries through the implementation of tax reform policies during the joint CACM-Alliance for Progress period 1961-74. Appendix I outlines the methodology used to estimate buoyancy and elasticity characteristics.

II CENTRAL AMERICAN BUOYANCY AND ELASTICITY MEASURES

(a) *The Literature*

The five countries comprising the CACM have, since 1960, espoused the goal of harmonising the tax structure throughout the isthmus. It has been, however, among the thorniest objectives to implement, and the 1972 *Decade Study* by the Secretariat of Central American Economic Integration (SIECA), in reviewing the progress toward economic integration, emphasised the lethargic movement toward fiscal harmonisation as follows [*Secretariat de la Integración Económica Centroamericana (SIECA), 1972: 1* (translation by authors)]:

> One of the most unattended areas within the march of Central American economic integration during the decade of 1960 was tax harmonisation. The preceding undoubtedly owes, at least in part, to the fact that the five countries have authorised liberal exemptions in the payment of taxes on income of firms that are sheltered by fiscal incentives laws which in practice harmonise the taxes on corporate incomes of firms participating in free trade with a single tax of zero, at least during some years.

The system of incentives for industrial development, including exemptions on corporate income and import duties on intermediate capital goods, was analysed in a 1971 study by C. Joel [*Joel, 1971: 229–52*]. Joel concludes that the income tax exemption has not been especially effective in stimulating foreign capital flow, but tariff exemption for capital goods has been important in investment decisions. H. Hinrichs hypothesises that tax incentives in Guatemala have been a major cost as measured by revenue loss compared with investment stimulation. Pointing to the fact that total exemptions equalled or exceeded the value of increased investment in Guatemala in 1970, he concludes that the costs of the incentives exceeded the benefits [*Hinrichs, 1974*].

The SIECA Decade Study makes two additional salient comments on the CACM tax structure. It points out that [*SIECA, 1972: 1* (translation by authors)]:

> one of the most important and persistent obstacles to the development of the region during the decade was the lack of tax systems to finance the level of public expenditures consistent with regional needs. [The result has been that] the levels of public investment and state services provided to the Central American population have been much less in comparison with the levels achieved in other Latin American countries with a social structure similar to those of the Central American economies:

The final SIECA observation is a general indictment of a revenue system which it characterises as regressive and undynamic. The report comments (translation by authors):

> ... the tax systems in all the countries are characterised by regressivity and little dynamism. The administration and collection of the taxes is difficult and deficient, and, in some aspects, the legal statements contained in national legislation are contrary to the principles and objectives of integration.

The thrust of the SIECA study on fiscal harmonisation is that the tax system in Central America is (1) discriminatory between countries and, therefore, inconsistent with the working of comparative advantage within the Common Market, and (2) inadequate in terms of its ability internally to generate the required public resources for development, i.e. the revenue income elasticity of the isthmus is low.

On the other hand, a 1970 study by Montrie, Fedor, and Davis in the *National Tax Journal* suggests that, throughout Latin America, the tax structures were encouragingly income-responsive during the 1960s. The purpose of their analysis was to 'present an operationally meaningful method of evaluating self-help performance indicators through intercountry comparisons of the level and trends of revenue collection' [*Montrie, Fedor, and Davis, 1970: 325–34*].

In an effort to measure the impact of self-help performance through tax and revenue improvement during the period of the Alliance for Progress, Montrie, *et al.* postulated a number of tests to rank countries on the basis of revenue performance indicators. They computed the revenue-income elasticity coefficients for eighteen Latin American countries over the period 1961–67, ranging from a high of 2·28 for Chile to a low of −28·4 for Uruguay. The surprisingly high elasticities during the Alliance six-year period led them to conclude that:

> The assumption that poor countries can't be expected to raise levels of revenue to finance development programs has seldom been questioned. The data presented here imply that, while the level of per capita income is an important influence on revenue levels, many relatively low-income countries can surpass more advanced countries. This is especially true in respect to revenue-collecting ability at the margin. Seven Latin American countries show income elasticities in excess of 1·5 for the period.

For the five countries in the CACM the reported elasticities were[1]

Costa Rica	1·83
El Salvador	0·49
Guatemala	1·01
Honduras	1·32
Nicaragua	1·75

TABLE 1

BUOYANCY COEFFICIENTS IN CENTRAL AMERICA*

(t statistics in parenthesis)

Revenue Source	CACM *1955–74*	CACM *1961–74*	*Guatemala* *1955–74*	*Guatemala* *1961–74*	*Honduras* *1951–74*	*Honduras* *1961–74*	*Nicaragua* *1955–74*	*Nicaragua* *1961–74*	*Costa Rica* *1955–74*	*Costa Rica* *1961–74*	*El Salvador* *1955–74*	*El Salvador* *1961–74*
Total Current Revenue	·97	1·13	·86	1·02	1·10	1·20	·96	1·00	1·02	1·15	·86	1·06
	(25·5)	(60·0)	(10·8)	(16·8)	(28·8)	(34·2)	(24·3)	(16·4)	(21·9)	(38·4)	(8·9)	(23·7)
Total Tax Revenue	1·03	1·14	·89	1·06	1·13	1·25	·99	1·03	1·04	1·13	·94	1·09
	(15·4)	(5·1)	(10·1)	(16·0)	(25·3)	(41·9)	(15·2)	(10·8)	(37·3)	(35·3)	(17·1)	(23·6)
Total Direct Taxes	1·39	1·41	1·30	1·31	1·51	1·95	1·30	1·23	1·26	1·27	1·59	1·53
	(12·6)	(9·4)	(9·9)	(7·4)	(9·6)	(8·9)	(7·8)	(6·4)	(19·3)	(13·3)	(20·8)	(13·5)
Personal amd Corporate Taxes	1·43	1·45	1·33	1·41	1·58	1·98	1·14	1·05	1·45	1·52	1·63	1·34
	(12·7)	(9·8)	(11·1)	(9·2)	(14·6)	(8·5)	(7·8)	(5·5)	(17·4)	(15·6)	(11·3)	(11·1)
Net Worth Taxes	1·39	1·31	1·20	1·12	·64	1·30	1·56	1·44	·05	·40	1·42	1·38
	(12·1)	(7·5)	(4·9)	(4·2)	(3·2)	(9·7)	(6·7)	(6·3)	(0·2)	(1·0)	(9·5)	(3·8)
Total Indirect Taxes	·96	1·06	·86	1·01	1·00	1·02	·95	1·01	·98	1·10	·66	·95
	(10·6)	(20·9)	(8·7)	(15·7)	(40·8)	(26·3)	(9·6)	(7·7)	(20·5)	(21·9)	(5·7)	(9·2)
Import Taxes	·37	·40	·12	·20	·60	·46	·26	·14	·25	·16	·44**	·54
	(8·4)	(5·4)	(2·1)	(2·35)	(10·5)	(10·5)	(2·9)	(1·2)	(3·9)	(1·45)	(4·6)	(3·8)
Export Taxes	·81	1·24	·69	1·05	1·32	1·28	1·23	2·03	1·11	1·27	·64	1·42
Excise, Consumption, and	(1·86)	(4·2)	(1·6)	(2·8)	(9·2)	(5·4)	(1·2)	(2·0)	(12·9)	(7·7)	(1·8)	(6·8)
Sales Taxes	1·46	1·55	1·36	1·38	1·42	1·53	1·57	1·55	1·72	1·96	1·19**	1·11
	(18·8)	(15·7)	(10·6)	(8·4)	(24·0)	(14·7)	(18·2)	(15·5)	(12·5)	(16·9)	(30·5)	(10·7)
Non-tax Revenue	·74	·97	·81	·86	·88	·72	·85	·94	·72	·97	n/a	·77
	(6·1)	(8·9)	(7·9)	(8·6)	(5·9)	(1·9)	(7·8)	(5·1)	(3·2)	(3·7)		(3·6)

*First order autocorrelation adjustment where required.

**Data for 1951–74 period.

While the Montrie study is an excellent first step at estimating Latin American self-help performance, it is doubtful that the results, at least for the CACM, are valid over the entire period since 1961.

(b) *Buoyancy Estimates, 1955–74*

Revenue data for 1955–74 were fitted to a regression of equation form (5) in Appendix I.

The ξs generated therefrom are given in Table 1 along with t statistics, and are calculated for 1955–74 and the CACM-Alliance years of 1961–74. The ξs for the two periods are presented in order to permit some measure of improvement in self-help performance during the 1961–74 Alliance-CACM period. Several general observations on the ξs are in order. *First*, the ξs were, in almost every case, higher during the Alliance period than for the 1955–74 years. *Second*, the t statistics associated with the ξs are highly significant for almost all revenue sources, the only exception being the t statistic for some of the import and export coefficients. *Third*, the equation fits were excellent for almost all equations as measured by the t statistics, the F levels, and the R^2s. While the R^2s are not presented in the table, they were in most cases from 0·90 upward. *Fourth*, all equation fits were adjusted for first order autocorrelation where required.[2]

(i) *Total Current Revenue*. One would hypothesise *a priori* for developing economies an overall ξ greater than unity. That is, given the need for marshalling public resources during development, those countries that are experiencing growth should be expected to exhibit a growth-elastic revenue base. However, contrary to the conclusions reached in the Montrie, Fedor, and Davis data on Latin America, our results for the nineteen-year period 1955–74 show that the revenue structure in Central America has barely been able to keep pace with economic growth, and that the overall ξ for total current revenue has been approximately unity. While there have been minor differences in revenue performance between countries, the ξs for all five nations hovered at unit elasticity or less. For example, the *total current* revenue ξ for the CACM during the 1955–74 period is 0·97 with a t statistic of 25·5 (Table 1). The most elastic structure as measured by the revenue performance criterion was Honduras at 1·10, followed by Costa Rica (1·02), Nicaragua (0·96), with El Salvador and Guatemala exhibiting highly inelastic structures at 0·86. This most comprehensive of revenue self-help measures is most discouraging for policy-makers who view the marshalling of public sector resources as critical to Central American economic development.

The total current revenue ξ for 1961–74 in Table 1 does show improvement for all five countries as compared with the 1955–74 data. The higher elasticity is perhaps the result of increased emphasis of all five countries on both tax reform and collection techniques which were initiated with the Alliance for Progress in 1961. While performance has clearly improved since 1960, the fiscal structure remains relatively lethargic in that, even with self-help emphasis since 1961, the ξ for the CACM was only 1·13, and the highest country ξ was recorded by Honduras at 1·20, followed by Costa Rica (1·15), El Salvador (1·06), Guatemala (1·02), and Nicaragua (1·00). Thus the overall ξ for the five countries has been, since 1961, only slightly above unity.

(ii) *Total Tax Revenue*. The total *tax* revenue ξs in Table 1 follow closely those of total *current* revenue, although in each case the former are somewhat more elastic. The ξ for total *tax* revenue in the CACM was 1·03 for 1955–74 and 1·14 during the Alliance-CACM years. Again, as with total *current* revenue data, the total *tax* equations were highly significant with t statistics ranging from a low of 5·1 to a high of 49·1 (Table 6).

(iii) *Total Direct Taxes*. One would *a priori* expect total direct taxes to exhibit a relatively high ξ, and those for Central America are no exception. Direct taxes, including personal and corporate as well as net worth levies, recorded a ξ of 1·39 for 1955–74 and 1·41 for the CACM-Alliance period. We conclude that total direct tax ξ for the CACM during the past fifteen years has not increased materially, a conclusion that is most unexpected since much of the effort at tax reform and improved collection in each of the five countries during the decade of the 1960s focused upon personal and corporate yields.

As the potentially most elastic source, direct revenues are among the few levies that can build in significant long-term flexibility. As indicated in Table 1, the only nation materially improving its ξ during the CACM-Alliance period was Honduras, whose ξ rose from 1·51 to 1·95. Costa Rica's *direct* tax ξ remained virtually unchanged (1·26 and 1·27) as did Guatemala's (1·30 to 1·31), while both El Salvador and Nicaragua experienced an absolute *decline* in the ξ for direct taxes during the CACM-Alliance period. At a time when import levies were being slashed with the elimination of intra-area trade, one would have expected tax reform measures to have been focused upon direct taxes and, therefore, the overall ξs to have increased. They did not.

(iv) *Personal, Corporate, and Net Worth Taxes.* One of the most elastic revenues in the CACM since 1955 has been personal and corporate levies with an ξ of 1·43 for the 1955–74 period and 1·45 for the Alliance years. Honduras, Guatemala, and Costa Rica showed improvement in this category during the Alliance, while the El Salvador and Nicaragua ξs absolutely declined. The ξ for net worth taxes varied from a high of 1·56 for Nicaragua to a low of 0·05 for Costa Rica for 1955–74, with overall CACM ξ recorded at 1·39. The net worth ξ absolutely *declined* to 1·31 during the Alliance. In short, the two major components of direct taxes in the CACM exhibited relatively elastic ξs, but the ξs did not increase during the Alliance.

(v) *Total Indirect Taxes. Indirect* taxes constituted around 79 per cent of total revenues for the CACM in 1975 (Appendix II). The toal *indirect* tax ξ for 1955–74 was 0·96, increasing to 1·06 for the Alliance. As indicated in Table 1, the indirect tax revenue structure least responsive to economic growth was El Salvador with ξs of 0·66 and 0·95 for the two periods. Almost all other countries recorded ξs of approximately unity. Much of the Central American discretionary intervention in tax rate and base alterations was associated with indirect levies during the 1960s and, even with those revenue-generating improvements, the ξ still remained around unity. While indirect taxes as a whole were unit elastic, the ξs of the two major categories, including taxes on foreign trade and excise and sales levies, differed markedly in revenue performance. For example, import taxes were the least elastic of all levies in the CACM revenue base for 1955–74. While import revenues have contributed as high as 50 per cent of the total as recently as

1960, the ξ was only 0·37 for 1955–74, increasing to 0·40 during the Alliance. Not only were the import ξs very low, a number of them failed the test of statistical significance at the 0·05 level (Table 1). The revenue responsiveness of import levies for Guatemala was only 0·12 and 0·24 for the 1955–74 and 1961–74 periods respectively, followed by Nicaragua (0·26 and 0·14), Costa Rica (0·25 and 0·16), El Salvador (0·44 and 0·54), and the most elastic was Honduras (0·60 and 0·46). The import revenue ξ was *lower* in almost every case during the CACM period, evidencing the negative impact of import-substitution policies on the tax structure.

The revenue-income elasticity which has been introduced into the CACM fiscal structure during the past twenty years appears to have been largely in the form of levies on excisable consumption, and sales. Constituting 43 per cent of isthmus revenue in 1974, the revenue performance ξ was a very high 1·46 for 1955–74 and 1·55 for 1961–74. It is evident from the data that these levies are far more progressive than is typically the case in developed countries. Indeed, analysis of the sources of the high elasticity suggests that they resulted not from the addition of new taxes or increased tax rates, but rather because of the progressive nature of the taxes themselves. In short, such indirect taxes are imposed upon goods which are, by and large, purchased by higher income groups and, as per capita income increases, the yield from these sources apparently tends to increase more than proportionately. The data suggest that Third World countries can perhaps look to specific forms of sales and excise taxes to significantly improve the elasticity of the revenue structures.

Those countries exhibiting the highest excise and sales ξs were Costa Rica (1·96 for 1961–74) and Nicaragua (1·55), followed by Honduras (1·53), Guatemala (1·38), and El Salvador (1·11).

Non-tax revenues, which contribute less than ten per cent of CACM revenues, showed a ξ considerably less than unity (Table 1).

(c) *The Stability/Flexibility Criterion: Revenue Elasticity Estimates*

The ξs in Table 2 are derived from data fitted to a regression of equation form (6) in Appendix I. For each of the five countries

TABLE 2

REVENUE-STABILITY/FLEXIBILITY CRITERION: CENTRAL AMERICA'S REVENUE-INCOME ELASTICITY COEFFICIENTS ADJUSTED FOR EXOGENOUS RATE, BASE AND OTHER ALTERATIONS*

(t statistics in parenthesis)

	Guatemala		*Honduras*		*Nicaragua*		*Costa Rica*		*El Salvador*	
Revenue Source	1955–74	1961–74	1951–74	1961–74	1955–74	1961–74	1955–74	1961–74	1955–74	1961–74
Total Current Revenue	·89	1·05	1·13	1·17	·86	·88	·99	1·12	·87	·95
	(36·9)	(16·0)	(25·3)	(23·6)	(15·7)	(12·3)	(12·6)	(3·0)	(6·9)	(20·0)
Total Tax Revenue	·78	·93	1·13	1·25	·99	1·03	1·02	1·16	·95	1·13
	(8·6)	(35·6)	(25·3)	(41·9)	(15·2)	(10·8)	(13·3)	(18·3)	(8·0)	(14·9)
Total Direct Taxes	1·06	1·08	1·13	1·43	1·30	1·23	1·06	1·19	1·76	1·53
	(16·0)	(16·2)	(25·2)	(10·2)	(7·8)	(6·4)	(7·3)	(10·5)	(8·6)	(13·5)
Personal and Corporate Taxes	1·01	1·12	1·48	1·83	1·14	1·05	1·43	1·56	1·67	1·46
	(12·7)	(25·8)	(7·2)	(9·1)	(7·8)	(5·5)	(7·3)	(19·0)	(7·3)	(11·5)
Net Worth Taxes	1·20	1·12	·64	1·30	1·56	1·44	1·31	1·87	·80	1·64
	(4·9)	(4·2)	(3·2)	(9·7)	(6·7)	(6·3)	(6·0)	(4·9)	(2·1)	(4·1)
Total Indirect Taxes	·81	·89	1·00	1·02	·75	·78	·82	·98	·75	·83
	(7·3)	(15·7)	(40·8)	(26·3)	(9·9)	(8·3)	(15·0)	(8·7)	(4·7)	(6·2)
Import Taxes	·12	·20	·60	·46	·26	·14	·25	·16	·44 **	·54
	(2·1)	(2·3)	(10·5)	(10·5)	(2·8)	(1·2)	(3·8)	(1·4)	(4·6)	(3·8)
Export Taxes	·01	·42	1·32	1·28	·81	·22	1·11	1·27	·54	·98
	(·1)	(1·1)	(9·2)	(5·4)	(1·6)	(·5)	(12·9)	(7·7)	(1·4)	(2·6)
Excise, Consumption, Sales Taxes	1·09	1·08	1·42	1·53	1·47	1·47	1·41	1·51	1·09 **	·98
	(7·5)	(8·2)	(24·0)	(14·7)	(10·7)	(8·9)	(8·9)	(8·5)	(5·5)	(11·9)
Non-tax Revenue	·81	·86	·89	·72	:85	·94	·72	·97	n/a	·77
	(7·9)	(8·6)	(5·9)	(1·9)	(7·8)	(5·1)	(3·2)	(3·7)	n/a	(3·6)

*First Order autocorrelation correction adjustment where required.

**Data for 1951–74 period.

revenue data for the two periods were corrected for major discretionary alterations in rates or bases through introduction of a dummy variable in those years where exogenous influence occurred. Only those exogenous actions which significantly influenced revenue generation were assigned a dummy, and so a number of the less important legislative actions by the five governments were not filtered through dummy analysis. As a result, the ξs are probably slightly higher than those assuming all discretionary actions filtered.[3]

The data in Table 2 report the same basic information as in the previous table, including the $\hat{\xi}$ (adjusted for exogenous discretionary actions), and the relevant t statistic. On the assumption that the purpose of an exogenous government action is to generate revenue, we expect the stability/flexibility $\hat{\xi}$ to be lower than the buoyancy statistic. As it turns out, however, some of the $\hat{\xi}$s after adjustment were slightly higher than their buoyancy counterparts, suggesting that the effect of at least some of the discretionary actions by legislatures in Central America was to reduce, rather than increase, revenues. It should be noted that there were not a large number of discretionary actions during 1955–74, certainly less than one would expect for a developing region in which self-help is an adjunct to attracting loans and grants from international agencies.

Some observations on the stability/flexibility $\hat{\xi}$s in Table 2 are in order. The total current revenue $\hat{\xi}$s for Nicaragua and El Salvador are highly inelastic at 0·88 and 0·95 respectively for the Alliance period, followed closely by Guatemala and Costa Rica. Honduras registered the most elastic $\hat{\xi}$ at 1·13 for 1951–74 amd 1·17 for 1961–74. In most cases the direct tax $\hat{\xi}$s adjusted for exogenous influences (Table 2) were lower than their counterparts in Table 1, a conclusion which confirms our earlier finding that the revenue structures for the five countries are relatively income insensitive and, therefore, cannot be relied upon to generate proportionately greater public resources during the development process.

An approximation of the *total current revenue* stability/flexibility $\hat{\xi}$ for the CACM as a whole may be estimated as a weighted average of the individual $\hat{\xi}$s as follows:

Country	% CACM Revenue	$\hat{\xi}$ 1961–74	Weighted Country $\hat{\xi}$, 1974
Guatemala	29	1·05	·30
Honduras	12	1·17	·14
Nicaragua	17	·88	·15
Costa Rica	23	1·12	·26
El Salvador	19	·95	·18
Total	100%		Regional $\hat{\xi}$ = 1·03

The 1·03 elasticity suggests that planners may expect the growth rate in GSP and central government revenues to increase at approximately the same rate over time. Given the already very low tax burden for Central America, such a revenue growth path will not be adequate to service demands for social goods and services during the development process.

Total *direct* taxes and *sales and excise* levies remained the most income-elastic as measured by the stability/flexibility criterion. The total *direct* tax $\hat{\xi}$ for El Salvador was high at 1·76 for 1955–74, while both the Guatemalan and Costa Rican $\hat{\xi}$s remained slightly above unity. The *excise and sales* taxes approached 1·5 for Honduras, Nicaragua, and Costa Rica and was close to unity for El Salvador and Guatemala. Both *import* and *export* taxes remained highly inelastic with the latter exhibiting the most dramatic decline after adjustment for exogenous influence to 0·42 for the Alliance period.[4]

(d) *Total Tax Revenue Buoyancy Estimates: Illustrative Regression Fit*

While we do not report all of the regression data for each of the ξs presented in Tables 1 and 2, it is useful to review one example of the statistical fits associated with the buoyancy estimates. Table 3 gives $\hat{\xi}$s, t statistics, δ significance levels, R^2s, F level, Durbin–Watson statistic, and autocorrelation adjustment (rho) for *total tax revenues.* The $\hat{\xi}$s ranged from 1·13 for Costa Rica to 0·94 for El Salvador, and the t statistics as well as δ were all significant at the 0·05 level. The R^2s ranged from 0·93 to 0·99, and satisfactory F levels were recorded. Six of the regressions required first order autocorrelation adjustment. The highly satisfactory equation fits suggest that the Central American tax revenues are closely related to GDP.

TABLE 3
CENTRAL AMERICA: TOTAL TAX REVENUES G.D.P. ELASTICITY COEFFICIENT: MEASURE OF BUOYANCY

	CACM		*Guatemala*		*Honduras*	
	1955–74	*1961–74*	*1955–74*	*1961–74*	*1955–74*	*1961–74*
Elasticity Coefficient	1·03	1·14	·89	1·06	1·13	1·25
t Statistic	15·36	5·12	10·14	16·00	25·27	41·90
δ Significant at ·05 level	yes	yes	yes	yes	yes	yes
$\bar{R}^2$	·99	·99	·99	·99	·99	·99
F level	23322·8	2621·9	8282·0	12397·8	11291·5	1756·2
D.W.	1·62	1·25	1·08	1·70	1·70	1·22
rho	·81	—	·80	·55	·66	—

	Nicaragua		*Costa Rica*		*El Salvador*	
	1955–74	*1961–74*	*1955–74*	*1961–74*	*1955–74*	*1961–74*
Elasticity Coefficient	·99	1·03	1·04	1·13	·94	1·09
t Statistic	15·21	10·75	37·30	35·28	17·06	23·59
δ Significant at ·05 level	yes	yes	yes	yes	yes	yes
$\bar{R}^2$	·99	·99	·98	·99	·93	·97
F level	3972·5	2799·0	1391·2	1244·4	291·0	556·2
D.W.	1·85	1·76	1·39	2·40	1·13	1·38
rho	·59	·54	—	—	—	—

III. CONCLUSIONS

Analysis of the *revenue buoyancy* of the Central American countries points to a revenue-GDP ξ of approximately unity over the 1955–74 period, with some minor improvement since 1961. The elimination of intra-regional tariffs combined with fiscal incentives tax concessions have reduced the contribution of import levies in the CACM from 50 per cent in 1960 to 23 per cent in 1974. The reduced weight of this highly inelastic source combined with greater reliance upon the more elastic sales and excise levies contributed to the slight rise in overall revenue performance of the isthmus between 1961 and 1974. The data show that the Alliance period did not significantly improve the ξ of direct taxes and, indeed, the direct tax ξ for some countries actually declined.

We may characterise the revenue structure in Central America as relatively *stable*, i.e. the $\hat{\xi}$s with adjustment for exogenous influences are in most case less than unity. It would appear that, if the CACM is to rely upon fiscal revenues as a source for marshalling resources it must, given its current fiscal structure, resort over time to discretionary alteration of the rate/base structures. The alternative is, of course, to weight the tax system more heavily with income-elastic direct and excise sources.

Stability is not a desirable feature of revenue structures for emerging nations where the demands for social goods and services, as well as for infrastructure capital, are highly GDP-elastic. Countries whose revenue structures are GDP-inelastic will encounter a recurring need to resort to discretionary legislative action in order to meet fiscal deficits during the growth process or, more likely, to turn to international lending agencies for support and, in the absence thereof, internally to monetise the debt. Politically unpopular at both the legislative and executive levels in all countries, discretionary alterations in tax structures which result in higher burdens are rarely implemented in emerging nations. For this reason, an inflexible revenue strucuture is especially undesirable in emerging countries. Faced with fiscal deficits and the near impossibility of increasing short-term revenues through discretionary action, governments often resort to the printing presses. The creation of a flexible structure provides increased revenues during the growth process without the need for continuous discretionary policy—be it higher tax rates or printing presses.

APPENDIX I

The following procedure is used to estimate buoyancy for both aggregated and disaggregated revenue sources. Define a log-linear relationship between revenue (R) and income (Y) such that R is a dependent function of Y

$$R = e^{\delta}Y^{\xi} \qquad (1)$$

where e = exponential,
δ = constant term, and
ξ = revenue-income elasticity coefficient.

Equation (1) yields a convenient method for determining ξ. Since ξ may be defined as

$$\xi = \frac{d \ln R}{d \ln Y} \tag{2}$$

equation (1) may be derived from (2) as follows

$$\xi d \ln Y = d \ln R.$$

Now integrating

$$\xi \int d \ln Y = \int d \ln R \tag{2b}$$

$$\xi \ln Y + C = \ln R + C', \tag{2c}$$

where C and C′ are constants.

Taking antilogs, $$Y^{\xi} e^{(C-C')} = R. \tag{3}$$

Defining (C–C′) as δ, then (3) is reduced to equation (1).

If the revenue data (R) in equation (1) are defined to include all collections whether income or non-income related, the ξ calculated therefrom is the buoyancy measure.

Suppose that R shifts over time due to changes in exogenous factors. The revenue data may be adjusted for such non-income-related influences by respecifying equation (1) as

$$R = e^{\sum_{i=1}^{m} \delta_i x_i Y^{\xi}} \tag{4}$$

where x = 0 is preshift, and x = 1 is postshift. Then m − 1 is the number of shifts in R, and the $\hat{\xi}$ measures the revenue-income elasticity, or stability characteristic.

DERIVATION OF THE ESTIMATING EQUATIONS FOR THE CRITERIA

Equations (1) and (4) answer quite different questions. Equation (1) estimates an ξ which may be interpreted as the historic buoyancy criterion, while equation (4) estimates an $\hat{\xi}$ which permits evaluation of the stability/flexibility characteristic as revenue-inelasticity.

The estimating equations for ξ and $\hat{\xi}$ may be derived as follows. Referring to (2c) $\ln R = \delta + \xi \ln Y$.

Taking the logarithm of (4) $\ln R = \sum_{i=1}^{m} \delta_i x_i + \hat{\xi} \ln Y,$ (4a)

and introducing error terms γ and $\hat{\gamma}$ for (2c) and (4a) respectively, the estimating equations are

$$\ln R_j = \delta_{=} + \xi_j \ln Y + \gamma_j \quad (5)$$

and

$$\ln R_j = \sum_{i=1}^{m} \delta_{ij} x_i + \hat{\xi}_j \ln Y + \gamma_j \quad (6)$$

where R_j is the revenue from the j_{th} source.

Clearly ξj and $\hat{\xi} j$ are easily derived from the estimating equations. They are the coefficients of $\ln Y$ for the *buoyancy* and *revenue stability* characteristics respectively.

THE ξ COEFFICIENT VALUES

It is clear that $\xi \gtreqless 1$ depending upon the rate and base definition of the revenue source. Further,

$\sum_{i=1}^{m} \delta_{ij} x_i > \delta_j$	with a net increase in the base and/or rate (an upward shift of the constant); and
$\sum_{i=1}^{m} \delta_{ij} x_i < \delta_j$	with a net decrease in the base or rate (a downward shift of the constant); and
$\sum_{i=1}^{m} \delta_{ij} x_i = \delta_j$	with offsetting rate or base changes or no significant dummy changes (no shift in the constant).

Therefore,

$$\hat{\xi}_j \gtreqless \xi_j \qquad \text{when} \qquad \sum_{i=1}^{m} \delta_{ij} x_i \gtreqless \delta_j.$$

Assuming that most rate or base adjustments have as their purpose revenue creation, we can assume that, in general, $\hat{\xi} < \xi$ and that

$\sum_{i=1}^{m} \delta_{ij} x_i > \delta_j$ will be the usual situation.

APPENDIX 2

TABLE 1

TAXES AS A PERCENTAGE OF GROSS DOMESTIC PRODUCT, CENTRAL AMERICA, 1960–74

Region and Measure	*1960*	*1974**	*Region and Measure*	*1960*	*1974**
CACM			Guatemala		
Total	9·2	10·3	Total	7·6	8·2
Direct	1·2	2·2	Direct	0·8	1·3
Indirect	8·0	8·1	Indirect	6·8	6·9
Costa Rica			Honduras		
Total	10·7	12·6	Total	9·8	11·2
Direct	1·7	3·2	Direct	1·6	3·5
Indirect	9·0	9·4	Indirect	8·2	7·7
El Salvador			Nicaragua		
Total	10·9	10·7	Total	8·8	10·3
Direct	1·4	2·6	Direct	1·2	1·7
Indirect	9·5	8·1	Indirect	7·6	8·6

*Preliminary Data
Source: SIECA data.

TABLE 2

TAX COLLECTIONS IN CENTRAL AMERICA, SELECTED YEARS 1960–1974
(million $)

Year	*CACM*	*Costa Rica*	*El Salvador*	*Guatemala*	*Honduras*	*Nicaragua*
1960	255·3	48·5	61·9	79·5	33·8	31·6
% of CACM	100	19	24	31	13	13
1965	365·8	66·4	84·5	107·7	49·4	57·9
% of CACM	100	18	23	29	14	16
1968	423·9	86·3	86·4	122·9	68·2	60·1
% of CACM	100	20	20	30	16	14
1970	526·0	119·5	105·8	147·9	80·8	71·9
% of CACM	100	23	20	28	15	14
1974*	876·3	203·0	169·0	251·3	108·5	145·0
% of CACM	100	23	19	29	12	17

*Preliminary data
Source: Data derived from information provided by I SIECA.

TABLE 3
DIRECT TAXES AS PERCENTAGE OF TOTAL TAX REVENUE

Year	*CACM*	*Costa Rica*	*El Salvador*	*Guatemala*	*Honduras*	*Nicaragua*
1957	13	20	11	10	20	11
1960	13	16	12	10	17	14
1966	21	23	19	15	26	24
1969	25	29	30	16	31	22
1972	23	24	24	18	27	22
1974*	21	26	25	16	31	16

*Preliminary Data
Source: Derived from data provided by SIECA

NOTES

1. Since no tests on significance of the elasticities are reported it is doubtful that they are, with only six observations, statistically meaningful. Further, it is not clear whether the elasticities were calculated on the basis of beginning and end points over the 1961–67 period, or whether they were based upon log-linear regression analysis.
2. The regression package utilised was the Brookings Institution PLANETS program for the PDP 10 computer.
3. Very few of the exogenous influences were regional in their effect, and it was not possible to calculate a meaningful stability/flexibility for the CACM as a whole by use of dummy variable analysis.
4. The import tax ξs were not changed with the stability/flexibility criterion since no important rate or base alterations were introduced except those announced in the San Jose Protocol agreement of 1968. The revenues collected on the basis of the Protocol are reported separately in the regional revenue statistics, thus mitigating the necessity of introducing a dummy.

REFERENCES

Banco Central de Honduras, 1965–73, (various issues), *Memoria Anual.*

Banco Central de Reserva de El Salvador, 1960–75, (various issues), *Revista Mensual.*

Consejo Monetaria Centroamericano, 1968–74 (various issues), *Boletin Estadistico.*

Consejo Nacional de Planificación y Coordinación Económica, Government of El Salvador, 1975, *Indicadores Económicos y Sociales, Enero—Deciembre, 1974,* San Salvador.

Hinrichs, H., 1974, 'Tax Reform Constrained by Fiscal Harmonisation within Common Markets: Growth without Development in Guatemala', *Fiscal Policy for Industrialisation and Development in Latin America*, Gainesville: University of Florida Press.

International Bank for Reconstruction and Development, 1967, *Economic Development and Prospects of Central America,* Statistical Appendix, Vol. 2, Washington, D.C.

Joel, Clark, 1971, 'Tax Incentives in Central American Development', *Economic Development and Cultural Change,* 19 (2), January, pp. 229–52.

Kaldor, Nicholas, 1964, 'Will Underdeveloped Countries Learn to Tax?', *Essays on Economic Policy,* Vol. 1, London: Gerald Duckworth & Co. Ltd.

Montrie, Charles, Kenneth J. Fedor and Harlan Davis, 1970, 'Tax Performance Within the Framework of the Alliance for Progress: A Comparative Evaluation', *National Tax Journal,* Vol, XXIII.

Secretaría de Economía y Hacienda, 1967, *Sales Tax in Honduras,* Tegucigalpa.

Secretariat de la Integración Económica Centroamericana (SIECA), 1972, *El Desarrollo Integrado de Centroámerica en la Presente Decada: Bases y Propuesta Para el Perfeccionamiento y la Reestructuración del Mercado Común Centroamericano, Vol. 10, Las Finanzas Públicas y La Integración* (Programa de Armonización Tributaria), Guatemala City.

Secretaría Permanente de Tratado General de Integración Económica Centroamericana, 1973, *Series Estadísticas Seleccionadas de Centroámerica y Panamá, Guatemala City.*

Secretaría Permanente de Tratado General de Integración Económica Centroamericana, 1963, *Tercer Compendio Estadístico Centroamericano,* Guatemala City.

Chapter 5

Exports, Taxes and Economic Growth: the case of El Salvador

LUIS RENE CACERES*

I. INTRODUCTION

The advent of the Central American Common Market (CACM) in 1961 saw the beginning of a new economic era for El Salvador. This era was hoped to be the one of industrialisation and rapid economic growth based on the investment opportunities and economies of scale that the larger market would offer. El Salvador had been one of the most ardent supporters of the formation of the Common Market and had even established bilateral free trade agreements with Guatemala and Honduras in the 1950s. This interest was due to the economic authorities' realisation that, given El Salvador's lack of natural resources, small territory and large population, an increase in trade appeared to be a promising path toward economic development. In retrospect, two periods can be distinguished: one of impressive growth between 1960 and 1966, during which its Gross Domestic Product (GDP) grew at one of the highest rates in the developing world; and one of relative stagnation from 1966 to 1971, during which annual GDP growth rate was barely higher than the 3·65 per cent rate of population growth (see Table 1).

*Department of Economics, University of Utah.

TABLE 1
SUMMARY OF EL SALVADOR'S ECONOMIC GROWTH
DURING 1960-71

Sector	*Average Annual Growth Rate (%)*		*Share of GDP (%)*	
	1960-66	*1966-71*	*1960*	*1971*
Gross Domestic Product	8·10	3·71	100·0	100·0
Imports	12·96	1·25	24·1	27·1
Private Investment	7·81	3·15	11·0	12·1
Private Consumption	7·23	3·51	80·4	77·6
Public Consumption	4·79	5·00	10·0	10·9
Public Investment	23·17	–4·50	3·0	3·2
Exports	13·40	2·46	20·5	23·2

Source: CONAPLAN, *Indicadores Ecónomicos y Sociales*, various issues [see text, note 3].

II. THE MODEL

The model consists of ten linear behavioural equations and eight identities. These were estimated using annual observations for the same period 1960-71 by the method of Ordinary Least Squares (OLS). Other methods of estimation were not used because since the sample is so small, it would be difficult to establish how much of the coefficient's bias is due to simultaneous equation bias and how much of it is due to small sample bias.[1] But since most of the stochastic equations have a high coefficient of determination (R^2), the correlation between the random errors and the endogenous variables is small and thus the simultaneous equation bias can be expected to be weak.[2]

The main source of data is *Indicadores Económicos y Sociales*, the bi-annual publication of the Consejo Nacional de Planificación y Coordinación Económica (CONAPLAN), El Salvador's public planning agency. All annual data has been deflated and expressed in constant 1963 millions of colones.[3] The endogenous variables used in the model are:

Cd = consumer expenditure on durable goods
Cnd = consumer expenditure on non-durable goods
Cs = consumer expenditure on services
Cpt = total private consumption

Cg = public consumption
Mc = import of consumer goods
Ms = import of services
Mk = import of capital goods
Mi = import of intermediate goods
Mt = total imports
Iph = private investment in plant, machinery and housing
Ig = public investment
It = total investment, private and public
D = depreciation
Kt = capital stock
T = total tax revenues
Y = gross domestic product
Yd = disposable income

The exogenous variables used in the model are:
E = total exports, commodities and services
Z-1 = terms of trade effect, lagged one year
Ii = investment in inventories
Tr = public transfer payments and interest on public dept
Fi = internal public borrowing
Fe = external public borrowing
Di = statistical discrepancy
O = factor payment abroad
w = marginal tax ratio
G = funds provided by public enterprises
Mk-1, Mi-1, K-1 = lagged endogenous variables

In the estimated model presented in Table 2, the 't' ratios are shown underneath their corresponding regression coefficients, R^2 is the coefficient of determination, D.W. is the Durbin–Watson statistic and the symbols * and ** denote that the D.W. test reveals positive autocorrelation of residuals or that it is inconclusive at the 5 per cent level respectively.

(a) *Consumption*

Private consumption expenditure on durable and non-durable goods is made dependent on current disposable income. Consumption of services is dependent on current income and a weighted sum of past levels of incomes, the weights declining exponentially over time. This function is of the form:

$$Cs = a + b \sum_{i=0}^{i=\infty} \lambda^{i} Yd$$

This, by the Koyck transformation,[4] becomes

$$Cs = a\,(1\text{-}\lambda) + b\,(1\text{-}\lambda)Yd + \lambda Cs\text{-}1$$

TABLE 2
THE ECONOMETRIC MODEL

Stochastic Equations

		Equation	R^2	D.W.	
Cnd	=	177·4360 + 0·5421 Yd			
		(5·95) (30·13)	0·989	1·68	(1)
Cs	=	−22·5263 + 0·0699 Yd			
		1·38 (2·38) + 0·7871Cs–1	0·991	2·11	(2)
		(6·96)			
Cd	=	−21·5263 + 0·765 Yd	0·909	1·96	(3)
		(1·70) (10·01)			
Mc	=	35·5140 + 0·0701 Yd	0·829	1·21**	(4)
		(2·13) (6·97)			
Mk	=	-24·79 + 0·442 Iph + 0·391 Ig	0·868	0·65*	(5)
		1·68 (3·87) (2·01)			
Mi	=	1·6479 + 0·3182 It + 0·6291 Mi–1	0·934	2·42	(6)
		(0·71) (2·69) (5·42)			
Ms	=	5·4119 + 0·0403 Y	0·916	1·93	(7)
		(0·71) (10·46)			
Iph	=	−59·3774 + 0·2797E–1 + 0·3580Z–1	0·802	1·62	(8)
		(2·19) (4·71) (2·49)			
D	=	-7·8677 + 0·0198 K–1	0·982	1·92	(9)
		(1·69) (2·35)			
Cg	=	0·896 T	0·866	1·52	(10)
		(20·11)			

Identities

Cpt	=	Cnd + Cs + Cd	(11)
Mt	=	Mc + Mk + Mi + Ms	(12)
T	=	wY	(13)
Ig	=	T – Cg – Tr + Fe + Fi + G	(14)
It	=	Iph + Ii + Ig	(15)
K	=	K–1 + It – D	(16)
Y	=	E + Cpt + It – Mt + Cg + Di	(17)
Yd	=	Y – O – T –D	(18)

which is the form estimated here. This function was also estimated for durable and non-durable goods but the distributed lag coefficients were statistically insignificant. However, Cáceres [*1973*] in a recent paper found that El Salvador's aggregate consumption function does have a significant lagged coefficient, a behaviour confined to the Central American countries in Latin America.

The constant terms or intercepts of the consumption functions are statistically significant at the 0·01 level only for the consumption of non-durable goods. This means that the Cnd/Yd ratio is not stable in the long run and that as income grows more expenditures will be shifted to durables, services or saving. This is consistent with the fact that Cnd is composed mainly of food and other normal goods whose income elasticity declines as income increases.[5] The income elasticity of Cnd was calculated[6] to be 0·87 in accordance with Engel's Law, and this value is higher than the estimates reported for developed countries [*Houthakker, 1957*] and very close to those calculated for other developing countries [*Weisskopf, 1971*]. The income elasticity of Cd and Cs were calculated to be 1·21 and 1·10 respectively, values lower than those found in developed countries. The marginal propensities to consume non-durable and durable goods are 0·5421 and 0·0765 respectively. For consumption of services, the short-run and long-run marginal propensities are 0·0699 and 0·8463 respectively.[7] The mean lag for the consumption of services is 3·5 years.[8]

The changes in the structure of private consumption indicate a tendency for the share of non-durable goods to decrease while services and durables have increased their percentage share of private consumption (see Table 3). Note that while the

TABLE 3
CHANGES IN STRUCTURE OF PRIVATE CONSUMPTION

	Percentage Share of Private Consumption (%)		*Average Annual Rates of Growth*	
	1962	*1971*	*1960–66*	*1966–71*
Non-durables	71·92	67·37	6·93	2·21
Durables	5·87	7·27	12·75	3·00
Services	22·21	25·36	6·88	7·02

Source: CONAPLAN, *Indicadores Economicos y Sociales*, various issues.

consumption of durables increased by 12·74 per cent annually during 1960–66, its annual growth was only 3·00 per cent during 1966–71. The annual growth rates of exports during these periods were 13·40 and 2·46 per cent respectively. This raises the possibility that the consumption of durables is dependent on the credit conditions and import restrictions derived from the situation in the external sector.[9]

(b) *Investment*

Total investment has been divided into three components: (1) government investment, (2) inventories, and (3) investment in construction, plant and equipment.

Current investment in construction, plant and equipment is a function of exports and the terms of trade effect,[10] both lagged one year.[11] A causation chain may occur, in that export earnings enable the banking authorities to increase the money supply and lower the interest rate which in a Keynesian fashion increases the demand for investment.[12] Another explanation is that, as several studies have indicated, investment is related to the level of business profits.[13] Therefore, the level of exports can be interpreted as a proxy for profits and thus explain private investment.[14]

Equation (8) suggests that El Salvador's investment sector and economic growth depend on the growth of its export sector. This is an obstacle to economic development. For, on the one hand, the export sector suffers fluctuations that give a zig-zag trajectory to private investment. A consequence is that the rapid growth in the labour supply is met with an investment sector whose activity increases, decreases or stays constant according to the whims of the external sector.[15] In effect, the period of relative economic stagnation that set in after 1966, is one during which exports have grown very slowly (see Table 1). But in addition to this, the private investment sector faces other constraints. Higgins [*1968*] has indicated that in a densely populated country the returns to both capital and labour are low. This would be a severe constraint on El Salvador since it is the smallest and most densely populated country in the American continent. This fact plus the risk-averse attitude of the private investors would lead them to direct their investments in areas of large and safe returns such as in the tertiary sector or abroad.

Several alternative forms were tried to estimate separate functions for housing and plant and equipment investments, but the fit was always inferior than the one obtained when they were combined. To explain this fact, note that investment in plant and equipment increased from 105 millions in 1960 to 163 millions in 1965, while investment in construction declined from 57 millions to 48 millions in the same period (a period of rapid export growth). But the reverse trend occurred afterwards (when exports experienced a slow growth) plant and construction investments increasing to 171 millions and 64 millions, respectively, in 1971 (see Table 4). It appears that

TABLE 4

CHANGES IN THE STRUCTURE OF PRIVATE INVESTMENT

Sector	*Percentage Share of Private Investment (%)* 1962	1971	*Average Annual Rates of Growth* 1960–65	1965–71
Plant and Equipment	60·76	58·58	11·05	1·12
Construction	25·95	21·22	−3·16	5·21
Inventories	13·29	20·20	−5·33	74·24

Source: CONAPLAN, *Indicadores Economicos y Sociales*, Enero-Junio 1972.

businessmen, not reckoning with the foreign exchange necessary to import the capital goods required by their plant and equipment projects, invested their funds in housing, a sector that demands much less imports. Thus, it can be seen that construction investment is of a countercyclical nature relative to plant investment. A similar countercyclical behaviour, due to other reasons, has been found in the U.S. by Guttentag [*1961*].

Inventory investment has been treated as an exogenous variable. However, its fluctuations seem to follow the electoral calendar (see Table 5). It can be seen that inventories build up one year before presidential elections and in the year of congressional elections. It seems that businessmen, fearing that

TABLE 5
FLUCTUATIONS IN INVENTORY INVESTMENT

Year	*Inventory Investment (Millions of colones, 1963 prices)*	*National Election*
1960	15	
1961	25	
1962	21	President
1963	12	
1964	54	Congress
1965	11	
1966	36	Congress
1967	3	President
1968	7	Congress
1969	29	
1970	43	Congress
1971	61	
1972		President

Source: CONAPLAN, *Indicadores Económicos y Sociales*, Enero-Junio 1972.

national elections may spark a wave of violence and disturbance in the country, increase their stocks at intervals delineated by political events.

(c) *Imports*

Imports have been disaggregated in four categories: (1) consumer goods, (2) raw materials and intermediate goods, (3) capital goods and (4) services. They are explained by equations (4)–(7).

In equation (4) for the import of consumer goods, the explanatory variable is disposable income. The marginal propensity to import consumer goods is 0·0701 and the income elasticity is 0·64. The share of consumer goods as a percentage of total imports has declined from 33·50 per cent in 1962 to 25·94 per cent in 1971 (see Table 6).

Its composition has been altered also. While non-durable and durable goods represented 31·54 and 7·82 per cent of total imports, respectively, in 1960, the shares had changed to 17·40 and 8·20 per cent in 1971. Also, the import of foodstuffs was only ten per cent of total imports in 1962, changing to 17 per cent in 1971.

TABLE 6
STRUCTURE AND GROWTH OF IMPORTS

	Percentage of Total Imports (%)		*Annual Growth Rate*	
	1962	*1971*	*1960–66*	*1966–71*
Consumer Goods	33·50	25·94	7·37	–0·45
Services	14·89	14·89	0·40	3·25
Capital Goods	16·01	16·00	21·33	–1·40
Intermediate Goods	35·60	44·04	25·25	3·61

Source: CONAPLAN *Indicadores Económicos y Sociales*, various issues.

Equation (7) explains imports of services as a function of GDP. The marginal propensity to import services is 0·0402. This sector's share of total imports has shown only a small variation in the sample period. However, the factor payments abroad have shown a fast rise during the sample period, growing at an average annual rate of 21 per cent. In 1960 factor payments abroad represented 0·5 per cent of GDP whereas in 1971 the percentage had risen to 0·95 per cent.

The import of capital goods is a function of private and public investment. Equation (5) indicates that the private sector requires more imported capital goods than the public sector. Most of the imported capital goods are destined for industrial projects while the share of capital imports destined for agriculture has shown a declining tendency.

The imports of intermediate goods are explained by a Koyck-type equation. Equation (6) shows that the short- and long-run marginal propensities to import intermediate goods out of total investment are 0·3182 and 0·8570 respectively. The regression coefficient of Mi–l and its 't' ratio are nearly twice as large as those of It indicating that the installed stock of capital (and its rate of utilisation) is the main determinant of intermediate good imports.[16]

A distributed lag function was also estimated for Mk,[17] and the short- and long-run marginal propensities to import capital goods out of total investment were 0·24 and 0·49 respectively. Adding these values to those calculated for import of intermediate goods, it turns out that the total short- and long-run marginal propensities to import out of total investment are 0·56 and 1·24 respectively. The important result is that, in the long run, one Colón of investment produces an increase of 1·24 Colón in imports.

The share of total imports of intermediate goods has increased from 35·6 per cent in 1962 to 44·0 per cent in 1971. This is derived from the type of manufacturing industry established in El Salvador, which uses little native raw materials and consists mainly of foreign firms that mix imported raw materials, thus adding little or negative value to the economy, with no spread effects or backward linkages to the rest of the economy.[18] This class of 'import substitution' industrialisation requires a continuous supply of foreign imports, thus increasing the vulnerability and dependence of the economy. The implementation of import substitution policies in El Salvador may lead one to expect that such policies have caused a reduction in total imports or even that El Salvador has enjoyed balance of trade surpluses during the CACM years. But in reality the contrary has happened. The Common Market years have coincided with a drastic deterioration of El Salvador's (as well as other Central American countries') balance of trade. The deficit in goods and services account has risen steadily from US $2·6 million in 1961 to US $50·8 million in 1966, decreasing slightly in the 1967–70 period, to reach the sum of US $45·8 million in 1971.

It appears that while the share of total imports of capital goods and services has remained constant, the decrease in the consumption sector's share has been more than offset by an increase in the share of intermediate goods. Consequently, the contribution of total imports to the national product increased from 24 per cent in 1962 to 27 per cent in 1971. Given that the import elasticity of GDP is 1·22, it can be expected that in the future the import percentage will continue to increase unless the present economic structure is altered. It appears then that the import substitution policy pursued in El Salvador since 1960 has actually increased its dependence on imports.

(d) *Public Sector*

Public consumption is made dependent on total tax revenues. Public investment is defined by identity (14) as total tax revenues less government consumption, less public transfers, plus public internal and external borrowing, plus funds from the public agencies. The percentage shares of GDP of these two sectors have remained nearly constant at 10 per cent and 3 per cent, respectively, throughout the sample period. The annual rate of growth of Cg has also remained fairly constant. Ig, however, has shown a marked contraction since 1966. The reason may be found in the sluggish growth in public revenues after 1966, caused by a decline in coffee export taxes, which account for 15 per cent of total taxes. This has been aggravated by the loss of import duties from intra-regional trade and by the generous tax concessions granted to foreign investors as a device to attract foreign investment.

Given the severe constraints to private investment and the existing high demand for public services, a case for enlarging the public sector emerges. There are several reasons why the expansion of the public sector is desirable if not urgent. First, there is evidence that public investment acts as a stimulant of the modernising forces in the country [*Adelman and Morris, 1968*]. Second, an increase in the level of public participation in the economy tends to decrease the inequality of income distribution [*Adelman and Morris, 1971*]. This is especially important since the CACM has attracted much foreign investment to El Salvador, which is known to contribute to more inequality [*Adelman and Morris, 1971*]. And third, there is evidence that some public undertakings, such as education, contribute greatly to economic growth [*Selowsky, 1969; Hayami and Ruttan, 1970; Pscharopoulous, 1971*]. Also, there are studies [*Tricart, 1964*] which suggest that the extreme *laissez-faire* method of industrialisation pursued in El Salvador has contributed very little to the welfare of the population.

But an increase in the public sector requires an adequate supply of public revenues, and the situation here is dismal. In effect, the ratio of tax revenues to GDP has declined in the 1960–71 period. There are studies which place El Salvador and other Central American countries among those with the lowest 'tax-effort' in the developing world.[19] El Salvador's poor performance in the fiscal field becomes more alarming when it is recalled that a tax reform law was enacted in 1964 which raised income tax rates to 67·5 per cent on incomes over US $78,000. Besides, there are many developing countries with lower GNP per capita and higher tax efforts than those of El Salvador.[20]

The precarious tax situation can be explained in part by the widespread tax evasion and the lack of collection efficiencies of the fiscal authorities.[21] Moreover, since the formation of the CACM, El Salvador and the other Central American countries have offered generous income and import tax concessions to local and foreign investors. This tax incentive programme caused bitter disputes among the five countries, as the less developed ones insisted on authorisation to grant even more liberal fiscal incentives. Regretfully, a study by Joel [*1971*] indicates that fiscal incentives were the least influential location factors in Central America.[22] Similar conclusions were reached by McClelland.[23] Another study [*Bickey and Aubey, 1971*] suggests that the primary reason for foreign firms to invest in El Salvador was market penetration. Faced with a shortage of public revenues, the governments of El Salvador have tried to implement tax reforms but with very little success. Given the socio-economic and political structure of El Salvador, it seems that to the ruling party the political losses of tax reform outweigh the economic gains that may be derived from it.[24]

(e) *Export Sector*

There has been a marked change in the commodity composition of the export sector, the most striking feature being the phenomenal increase in the manufacturing share of total exports from 5·3 per cent in 1962 to 23·9 per cent in 1971. This was accompanied by a marked reduction in the cotton share, from 21·7 to 12·7 per cent. Coffee continues to be El Salvador's main export, however. The coffee export share increased by 2·9 per cent during the period (to 40·7 per cent in 1971), but this is still lower than its share of exports (around 70 per cent) during the 'fifties. It should be added that the slow growth of exports since 1966 has been due to a contraction in the exports of primary products to non-Central American markets; neither the exports to Central America nor the internal market have been able to stimulate a rapid growth of the economy. El Salvador's dependence on the export of primary products continues while its dependence on imports has increased.[25]

(f) *Identities*

Equation (9) describes depreciation as a linear function of the stock of capital lagged one year. The model is closed with the help of eight national accounting identities which express consumption, imports, investments, GDP, capital stock and disposable income as a sum of their component parts. The identity for public investment was explained before. Identity (13) makes total public revenues dependent on the policy variable w, which is the same as the tax ratio.

(g) *Impact Multipliers*

The reduced form of the model was calculated and its most important components are shown in Table 7. The coefficients of this matrix are the impact multipliers that the exogenous variables exert on the endogenous variables. Thus, for example, an increase of 1 Colón in exports produces an increase of 0·273 Colón in public consumption; an increase of 1 Colón in inventory investment produces an increase of 0·325 Colón in import of raw materials, etc. Since the ratio of tax revenues to GDP is a policy variable whose value changes from year to year, a different multiplier matrix corresponds to each year of interest. The matrix shown in Table 7 corresponds to w = 0·11, as in 1971, but it was also calculated for each year of the sample and it was found that the multipliers are not radically affected by the tax ratio. Note that all the multipliers have signs which agree with our *a priori* expectations, this being an indication that the model is consistent and properly specified. Note also that exports produce the largest multiplier in GDP.

(h) *Forecasts*

Using the multiplier matrix, the values of the endogenous variables were forecast for the 1972–80 period. In these forecasts, some exogenous variables were held constant throughout the period at the following values:

TABLE 7
IMPACT MULTIPLIERS

Endogenous Variables	*Exogenous Variables*							
	Cs–1	*Mi–1*	*E–1*	*Z–1*	*Ii*	*Fe*	*E*	*O*
Cnd	0·976	–0·780	0·083	0·106	0·845	0·360	1·238	–1·309
Cs	0·916	–0·101	0·011	0·014	0·109	0·046	0·160	–0·169
Cd	0·138	–0·110	0·012	0·015	0·119	0·051	0·175	–0·185
Mk	0·010	–0·008	0·125	0·160	0·009	0·395	0·013	–0·008
Mi	0·008	0·625	0·090	0·115	0·325	0·321	0·010	–0·006
Mc	0·126	–0·101	0·011	0·014	0·109	0·047	0·160	–0·169
Ms	0·082	–0·066	0·007	0·009	0·071	0·030	0·105	–0·065
Iph	0·000	0·000	0·280	0·358	0·000	0·000	0·000	0·000
Cg	0·220	–0·176	0·019	0·024	0·190	0·080	0·279	–0·173
Cpt	2·026	–0·990	0·105	0·135	1·073	0·458	1·574	–1·662
Mt	0·227	0·448	0·232	0·297	0·514	0·793	0·288	–0·224
It	0·026	–0·020	0·282	0·361	1·001	1·001	0·032	–0·020
T	0·245	–0·196	0·021	0·027	0·213	0·091	0·312	–0·193
Ig	0·026	–0·020	0·002	0·003	0·022	1·000	0·032	–0·020
Y	2·045	–1·635	0·174	0·222	1·771	0·755	2·598	–1·607

Di = 18	Fi = 25
Z–I = 21	Fe = 25
Ii = 40	Tr = 50
O = 25	G = 50

Five projections were run with the annual rate of growth of exports and the tax ratio taking alternate values. The results are shown in Table 8.

The results indicate that the effect of increasing the tax rate from 0·12 to 0·20 is to increase the average annual GDP growth rate by approximately 0·50 per cent. Other effects of increasing the tax ratio are to reduce the growth of private consumption and increase the growth of public consumption and investment. As a consequence, the saving ratio increases modestly.[26] Also, the projections indicate that the main source of growth is the export sector, such that doubling the rate of growth of exports more than doubles the rate of GDP growth.

A fifth projection was conducted with all the variables as in run 1, the only difference being that Fe was increased by 20 million every year. In this case, the resulting GDP are higher than those of run 1 in 1972 and 1973. But after 1973 the reverse occurs, the new GDP values becoming progressively smaller than those of run 1. The resulting average annual GDP growth rate for this last projection was 2·35 per cent, lower than that of run 1 (see Table 9).

To explain this paradoxical result that increasing foreign loans to finance public investment reduce the rate of economic growth, notice that although run 5 has values of Ig that are 20 million higher than those of run 1, it also has higher values of Mk and Mi which more than offset the increase in Ig after 1973. It should be recalled that the Mi function is a distributed lag function whose level depends on present and past investment levels. Thus, investment that takes place today contributes to the future demand of imported raw materials. An investment boom, derived from either higher levels of foreign loans or from higher export earnings, increases the stock of capital, but once the boom is over the increase capital stock requires a higher inflow of imported intermediate goods, thus accentuating the depression.[27] This is a process of economic growth with a built-in depressive force.

TABLE 8
PROJECTIONS

Run	Tax Rate	Export Growth %	Resulting Average Annual Growth Rate (%)							Saving Ratio (in 1980)
			Iph	*Cg*	*Cpt*	*Mt*	*It*	*Ig*	*Y*	
1	0·12	3	1·61	2·25	2·84	2·45	0·59	1·13	2·76	0·125
2	0·12	6	4·37	5·57	6·01	5·18	5·18	2·65	6·54	0·131
3	0·20	3	1·61	11·72	1·81	2·90	2·90	5·46	3·18	0·122
4	0·20	6	4·37	17·51	5·14	5·73	5·73	7·91	7·14	0·134
5	0·12	3	1·61	2·13	2·78	2·61	1·31	3·89	2·35	0·123

TABLE 9
COMPARISON OF RUNS 1 AND 5

	Run 1					Run 5				
Year	*Mk*	*Mi*	*Mt*	*Ig*	*Y*	*Mk*	*Mi*	*Mt*	*Ig*	*Y*
1972	108	295	676	80	2435	116	301	692	101	2450
1973	110	298	688	81	2502	118	309	707	101	2508
1974	113	302	702	82	2571	121	315	722	102	2507
1975	115	307	716	82	2641	123	321	737	103	2635
1976	118	311	730	84	2714	126	327	752	104	2703
1977	121	316	745	85	2789	129	332	767	105	2775
1978	124	322	761	86	2867	131	338	783	106	2749
1979	127	327	777	87	2948	134	344	799	107	2927
1980	130	333	794	88	3031	137	350	816	108	3007

III CONCLUDING REMARKS

This study suggests that the import substitution type of industrialisation pursued in El Salvador since 1960 has distorted the economy, making it more dependent on imports. The vulnerability of the economy has been enhanced by its crucial dependence on external forces, in the form of a higher reliance on imported raw materials, and in addition, an alarming number of enterprises are being bought up by foreign firms.[28]

This has taken place when the need for rapid economic growth and development is now more urgent than ever. The latest census figures indicate that 46 per cent of El Salvador's population is fifteen years old or younger and it is expected that the labour supply will grow by 4·46 per cent annually during the period 1972–85. If labour productivity remained constant at the 2·6 per cent annual increase as in the past decade, and if the existing marginal capital–labour ratio remained unaltered, the annual increase in GDP required to absorb the increase in labour-supply is 11·72 per cent, by far higher than the most optimistic projections indicate. Under these formidable constraints the only options seem to be radical structural changes in the economy, involving tax credit and above all, land reforms. Equally strongly desirable are policies designed to bring the benefits of economic growth to all the people[29] and stop the current process of economic growth without economic development.

NOTES

1. The equations for depreciation and private investment use only exogenous variables and are free of the simultaneous equation bias. The remaining equations, though, are over-identified and subject to this bias. However, it has been suggested that OLS may be a desirable estimation method in cases where the explanatory variables are lagged endogenous variables, as in equations (2) and (6), since the biases due to simultaneity and to the distributed lag tend to counteract each other. See Evans [*1969: 53*].
2. Smith [*1970*] using Monte Carlo methods, found that OLS was the most appropriate estimating technique for a 34 equations model.
3. One Colón = 0·40 US dollar. CONAPLAN, in conjunction with the Central Bank (Banco Central de Reserva) started to compile the

national income accounts of El Salvador in 1950. It is the Central Bank's policy to revise, and amend if necessary, the national accounts of a given year during the following two years. The data employed in this study had been amended by the Central Bank in 1972 and 1973. At a higher aggregation level this data can be found in the national accounts section of the IMF's International Financial Statistics.

4. Koyck [*1954*].
5. Leser [*1963*] has suggested that consumption functions should be in a form that reflect the changing income elasticities over time.
6. All elasticities reported in this paper were computed at the mean values of the sample.
7. The long-run propensity is equal to the coefficient of Yd divided by one minus the coefficient of Cs–1. For a derivation see, for example, Aigner [*1971: 114*].
8. The mean lag is defined to be the average number of years during which a change in Yd has an effect on Cs. It is equal to the coefficient of Cs–1 divided by one minus the coefficient of Cs–1. For a discussion of mean lags in the context of the consumption function see Kuh and Schmalensee [*1973: Ch. 3*].
9. The importance of credit conditions for the purchase of durable goods has been shown by Lee [*1967*].
10. A similar equation was used to explain private investment behaviour in Peru by Thorbecke and Condos [*1966*].
11. The form of this equation is in accordance with several studies which indicate that there exists a lag of one year or more between private investment response and changes in the relevant economic variables. See Eisner [*1960*], deLeeuw [*1962*] and Almon [*1965*].
12. When discussing the efficacy of monetary policy in developing countries, Eshag [*1971: 304*] concludes that 'one may venture the opinion that business investment would generally be relatively more sensitive to monetary measures in the less-developed countries than in the industrial countries'.
13. See, among others, Klein and Goldberger [*1955*]; Kuh [*1953*] and Eisner [*1967*].
14. Some models of developing countries [*Schotta, 1966; Baker and Falero, 1971*] have presented cases where monetary variables such as the money supply and long-term capital liabilities to foreigners explain a higher percentage of the variance in national income than real variables do. In fact, exports have turned out to be statistically insignificant in these models. But this may be due to the fact that, as equation (8) indicates, the effect of exports on income is felt after a lag of one year and those models use only current exports.
15. In recent years there has been a debate on the effect that export instability exerts on investment in the less developed countries. In a well-known work, MacBean [*1966: Ch. 3*] reported that his studies found no evidence of a relationship between exports and investment. This may be explained by the fact that MacBean uses values of total investment which are influenced by political and speculative factors just

as these factors influence public and inventory investment. Under this condition a significant correlation between exports and investment may be difficult to detect.

16. Siri [*1975*], using the trend through the peaks method, has calculated the rate of capacity utilisation in the Central American countries' industrial sectors. His estimates for El Salvador indicate the absence of wide fluctuations in idle capacity:

Percentage of idle capacity in industrial sector

Year											
1960	1961	1962	1963	1964	1965	1966	1967	1968	1969	1970	1971
10·6	10·0	8·0	10·2	10·0	10·3	9·0	10·5	11·0	13·2	13·0	11·0

17. The estimated function is:

$$Mk = -1{\cdot}2387 + 0{\cdot}2408It + 0{\cdot}3714\ Mk\text{–}1$$
$$(0{\cdot}87)\quad (3{\cdot}58)\quad (2{\cdot}37)$$
$$R^2 = 0{\cdot}87\ \text{D.W.} = 1{\cdot}64$$

18. A sample of twenty industries in El Salvador reveals that the average percentage of imported raw materials is 91 per cent, see Molina Chocano [*1971*]. This situation is common to the other Central American countries, see Hansen [*1967: 50*].
19. See Lotz and Morss [*1967*], Chelliah [*1967*], Bahl [*1971*].
20. Chenery's [*1971*] model of socio-economic transformation assigns a tax ratio of 0·175 to El Salvador contrary to its 0·11 actual value.
21. Hart [*1970*] contends that those are the main obstacles to effective fiscal policy in Latin America.
22. The importance of the Central American countries' infrastructure in determining the spatial pattern of industrial location in Central America are discussed by Odel and Preston [*1973*]. For results of tax exemptions programmes in other countries see Bilsborrow and Porter [*1972*], Lent [*1967*].
23. McClelland [*1972, 158*] also reports that 'the greatest [fiscal] incentives, in other words, went to those importing most and contributing least to value added domestically'.
24. Wynia [*1972: 93*] tells us that 'by 1963 [the president] succeeded in his campaign to gain elite support, but it came at the expense of new social reforms and most of his tax reforms.' When another attempt at tax reform took place in 1967, Wynia tells us that a 'loud opposition attack on the president's reforms rose in El Salvador . . . he hastily decided to preserve his upper and middle class support by similarly rescinding his tax reforms in early 1968'.
25. An analysis of the dependence of the Central American countries' intraregional (Common Market) trade on their exports of traditional products to areas outside Central America, can be found in Caceres [*1975*].
26. This can be compared to Singh's [*1971*] cross-sectional study which indicates that in underdeveloped countries in order to increase the saving ratio by 1 per cent the tax ratio has to increase by 6 per cent.
27. It may follow that an inflow of foreign aid creates a demand for even higher inflows of aid in the future. El Salvador's external debt was 31·55

million dollars in 1951 which increased to 63·74 million in 1961 and to 228·65 in 1971. Dos Santos [*1970: 233*] concludes that 'Foreign capital and foreign "aid" fill up the gaps that they themselves created.'

28. This situation is taking place in all Central American countries, see [*Committee of Nine, Alliance of Progress, 1966*]. Wilmore [*1973: 303*] observes that 'the program of economic integration . . . is paradoxically contributant to the decline of the Central American industrialist'.
29. CONAPLAN's Third Development Plan 1973–77, acknowledges that in 1971 there were 17 hospital beds per 10,000 inhabitants, a decrease from 23 per 10,000 inhabitants, in 1961. Also, the daily calories intake per capita decreased from 2030 in 1961 to 1914 in 1971. And, the wage to industrial workers increased by only 9·2 per cent from 1964 to 1970 while the productivity per worker increased by 20·12 per cent.

REFERENCES

Adelman, I. and C. T. Morris, 1968, 'An Econometric Model of Socio-Economic and Political Change in Underdeveloped Countries', *American Economic Review*, LVIII, December.

Adelman, I. and C. T. Morris, 1971, 'An Anatomy of Income Distribution Patterns in Developing Nations', *Development Digest*, October.

Aigner, D. 1971, *Basic Econometrics*, Englewood Cliffs: Prentice Hall.

Almon, S., 1965, 'The Distributed Lag Between Capital Appropriation and Expenditures', *Econometrica*, 33, January.

Bahl, R. W., 1971, 'A Regression Approach to Tax Effort and Tax Ratio Analysis', *International Monetary Fund Staff Papers*, 18.

Baker, A. B. and F. Falero, 1971, 'Money, Exports, Government Spending, and Income in Peru, 1951–66', *The Journal of Development Studies*, July.

Bickey, W. J. and R. T. Aubey, 1971, 'A Behaviour Approach to Industrial Simulation Analysis', *Economic Development and Cultural Change*, 18, January.

Bilsborrow, R. E. and R. C. Porter, 1972, 'The Effects of Tax Exemptions on Investment by Industrial Firms in Columbia', *Weltwirtschaftliches Archiv*, 108.

Caceres, L. R., 1973, 'Consumption Functions for Latin America', *Intermountain Economic Review*, 4, Fall.

Caceres, L. R., 1975, 'Export Instability in a Common Market: The Case of Central America', Paper presented at the annual meeting of the Western Economic Association, San Diego.

Chelliah, R. J., 1971, 'Trends in Taxation in Developing Countries', *International Monetary Fund Staff Papers*, 18, July.

Chenery, H., 1971, 'Growth and Structural Change', *Finance and Development*, 18.

Chocano, E. Molina, 1971, *Integración Centroamericana y Dominación Internacional*, San Jose: Editorial Universitora Centroamericana.

deLeeuw, F., 1962, 'The Demand for Capital Goods by Manufacturers: A Study of Quarterly Time Series', *Econometrica*, 30, July.

Dos Santos, T., 1970, 'The Structure of Dependence', *American Economic Review*, LX, May.

Eisner, R., 1960, 'A Distributed Lag Function', *Econometrica*, 28, January.

Eisner, R., 1967, 'A Permanent Income Theory for Investment: Some Empirical Explorations', *American Economic Review*, LVII, June.

Eshag, E., 1971, 'The Relative Efficacy of Monetary Policy in Selected Industrial and Less-developed Countries', *Economic Journal*, 81, June.

Evans, M. K., 1969, *Macroeconomic Activity*, New York: Harper and Row.

Guttentag, J., 1961, 'The Short Cycle in Residential Construction', *American Economic Review*, LI, June.

Hansen, R. D., 1967, *Central America: Regional Integration and Economic Development*, Washington, D.C.: National Planning Association.

Hart, A., 1970, 'Fiscal Policy in Latin America', *Journal of Political Economy*, 78, July/August.

Hayami, Y. and V. W. Ruttan, 1970, 'Agricultural Productivity Differences Among Countries', *American Economic Review*, LX, December.

Higgins, B., 1968, *Economic Development*, New York: W. W. Norton and Company.

Houthakker, H., 1957, 'An International Comparison of Household Expenditure Patterns Commemorating the Centenary of Engel's Law', *Econometrica*, 25, October.

Joel, C., 1971, 'Tax Incentives in Central America Development', *Economic Development and Cultural Change*, 18, January.

Klein, L. R., and A. S. Goldberger, 1955, *An Econometric Model of the United States, 1921–41*, Amsterdam: North-Holland Publishing Company.

Koyck, L. M., 1954, *Distributed Lags and Investment Analysis*, Amsterdam: North-Holland Publishing Company.

Kuh, E., 1953, *Capital Stock and Growth: A Microeconomic Approach*, Amsterdam: North-Holland Publishing Company.

Kuh, E., and R. Schmalensee, 1973, *Applied Econometrics*, Amsterdam: North-Holland Publishing Company.

Lee, M., 1962, 'An Analysis of Instalment Borrowing by Durable Goods Buyers', *Econometrica*, 30, October.

Lent, G., 1967, 'Tax Incentives for Investment in Developing Countries', *International Monetary Fund Staff Papers*, 14, July.

Lotz, J. and E. Morss, 1967, 'Measuring Tax Effort in Developing Countries', *International Monetary Fund Staff Papers*, 14, November.

MacBean, A., 1966, *Export Instability and Economic Development*, Cambridge: Harvard University Press.

McClelland, D. H., 1972, *The Central American Common Market*, New York: Praeger Publishers.

Odell, P. R. and D. A. Preston, 1973, *Economies and Societies in Latin America: A Geographical Interpretation*, New York: John Wiley & Sons.

Psacharopoulous, G., 1971, 'Measuring the Marginal Contributions of

Education to Economic Growth', *Economic Development and Cultural Change*, 20, October.

Schotta, C., Jr., 1966, 'The Money Supply, Exports and Income in an Open Economy: Mexico, 1939–63', *Economic Development and Cultural Change*, 14, July.

Selowsky, M., 1969, 'On the Measurement of Education's Contribution to Growth', *Quarterly Journal of Economics*, 83, August.

Singh, S., 1971, 'The Determinants of Aggregate Savings', Washington, D.C. International Bank for Reconstruction and Development (mimeo) April.

Siri, G., 1975, 'Indice de la Capacidad no Utilizada del Sector Industrial en Los Paises Centroamericanos', Guatemala: SIECA/Brookings Project (mimeo).

Thorbecke, E. and A. Condos, 1966, 'Macroeconomic Growth and Development Models of the Peruvian Economy', in *The Theory and Design of Economic Development*, ed. I. Adelman and E. Thorsbecke, Baltimore: The Johns Hopkins Press.

Weisskopf, R., 1971, 'Demand Elasticities for a Developing Economy: An International Comparison of Consumption Patterns', in *Studies in Development Planning*, ed. H. Chenery, Cambridge: Harvard University Press.

Wilmore, L. N., 1973, 'Direct Foreign Investment and Industrial Entrepreneurship in Central America', in *Latin American Prospects for the 1970's*, ed. D. H. Pollack and A. R. M. Ritter, New York: Praeger Publishers.

Wynia, G. W., 1972, *Politics and Planners: Economic Development Policy in Central America*, Madison: University of Wisconsin Press.

Chapter 6

The Fiscal Crisis of the Latin American State

E. V. K. FITZGERALD*

I INTRODUCTION

In this paper we shall explore the fiscal implications of the expansion of the economic activity of the state in Latin America during the post-war period. Such an analysis may also throw some light upon the role of the state in the process of industrialisation on the periphery of the world economy, and in particular on the part played by the public sector in mobilising resources for capital accumulation.

As the title of this paper may already have indicated the analysis of the 'fiscal crisis of the state' in metropolitan capitalist economies by O'Connor[1] provides our initial working hypothesis, although it clearly requires radical modification if it is to be applied to the periphery of the world market economy. O'Connor argues that in the later stages of monopoly capitalism the large corporations that dominate the US economy demand (and receive) ever-increasing public expenditure on physical infrastructure (e.g. roads), subsidies (e.g. investment incentives) and labour cost reduction (e.g. public health) while at the same time refusing to contribute the necessary profit taxes to pay for them. In consequence, the state is forced to raise taxes from workers (e.g. consumption

*Assistant Director of Development Studies, Faculty of Economics and Politics, University of Cambridge.

taxes) but these are inadequate to cover its increased financial requirements, so that borrowing and monetary creation become a chronic feature of public finance, resulting in another destabilising contradiction within monopoly capitalism: this is the 'fiscal crisis of the state'. O'Connor's view of the mature capitalist state is certainly open to considerable objections, above all his neglect of the 'relative autonomy' of the capitalist state[2] in general, and the real redistributive gains made by the working classes in particular.[3] Nonetheless, there is an important insight here, which in the case of Latin America—with elitist government, weak labour movements and powerful multinationals dominating key production branches—may well be more apposite than in the pluralist structure of mature capitalism.

In this paper, then, we shall explore the way in which the fiscal structure of the major Latin American economies[4] has developed since the Second World War in response to the expansion of state activities during the industrialisation process. We shall examine four sub-hypotheses derived from O'Connor: that with industrialisation state expenditure inevitably increases; that tax increases to finance this are borne by labour rather than by capital; that these increases are inadequate to finance the expansion; and that the means of covering the fiscal deficit tend to destabilise the economy. Specifically, we shall suggest that there is a substantive 'fiscal crisis of the state' in Latin America which seriously limits the viability of dependent capitalist development in the area.

II THE ECONOMIC EXPANSION OF THE LATIN AMERICAN STATE

The process of industrialisation is usually held to have been initiated in Latin America during the comparative isolation from the metropolitan economies brought about by the Great Depression and the Second World War, and to have been sustained by rapid import-substitution in the subsequent two decades—some countries such as Argentina and Brazil making earlier and more extensive progress than others such as Colombia and Peru. The state became an integral part of this process, not just by guaranteeing the property rights and labour control necessary for capitalist organisation, but also by participating directly in the economy. This participation has taken the form of intervention in the process of *exchange*, by controlling food prices, raising import tariffs and manipulating exchange rates, for example, and in the process of *production* by training the work-force, providing cheap industrial inputs and investment finance, and building transport networks. This intervention has been openly in support of capitalist industrialisation,[5] with extensive participation by multinational corporations, and is a response to control of the state by the bourgeoisie—although which fraction (or combination of fractions) thereof depends upon the economic and social structure of the country concerned. Generally, however, it was to be expected that the process of industrialisation would have led to two significant changes in the balance of class forces and thus of the nature of state intervention: first, the strengthening of a separate 'industrialist' fraction of the bourgeoisie, and second, the emergence of an organised proletariat. In practice, the penetration of foreign capital prevented either of these occurring: it permitted an alliance between the multinationals and the traditional agrarian or financial oligarchies on the one hand, and through the use of imported labour-saving technology it prevented proportionate growth of the industrial labour force, on the other.[6]

The 'current' activities of the Latin American state (reflected in current expenditure) have traditionally been considerable due to the colonial origins of the central administration and its subsequent continuance of a wide range of labour-intensive but ineffective regulatory functions.[7] Since the Second World War, there has been a considerable expansion in three directions. First, the new 'developmental' role for the state involved the establishment of ministries of industry and commerce, the strengthening of the ministries of finance, and to some extent the growth of the ministries of agriculture with the 'technification' of that sector. All these activities were designed to support private enterprise and make it more profitable, and accounted for about a quarter of current expenditure on average in the nineteen-sixties, general administration accounting for another quarter.[8] Second, the needs of an increased industrial workforce are reflected in the expansion of health and education services, although it should be noted that these are generally extended only to the 'modern sector' workforce and not to rural labour or slum dwellers. To a considerable extent, these expenditures also contribute to private profitability by improving labour productivity, but they are also the tangible result of class struggles in the past, and represent about a quarter of current expenditure on average. The last quarter is spent on defence and security, much of which contributes to the repression of popular movements and thus to profitability, as well as guaranteeing capitalism as a social formation. In terms of economic categories, the pattern for Latin America in the nineteen-sixties is quite stable too: 'about three-quarters of current expenditure goes on consumption (principally wages and salaries) and the other quarter goes to subsidise public services and enterprises, to the private sector, and to debt interest'[9]. In addition, unit costs of both these categories have tended to rise disproportionately over time because of the difficulty of increasing labour productivity while salaries rise in line with those in industry on the one hand, and rising interest rates on the other.

The pattern of fixed investment by the state altered as industrialisation got under way. Of the 'traditional' fields of transport infrastructure and irrigation, the latter has generally decreased and the former increased while shifting from rural roads and mineral ports towards urban and industrial infrastructure. Further, the state has either set up (or taken over and expanded) enterprises providing heavy industrial inputs such as electric power, steel and chemicals at low prices to the manufacturing sector. These are all sectors where large 'lumpy' investments are required which the private sector is unable or unwilling to undertake. In addition, the Latin American governments have traditionally established or nationalised oil companies which (with the state electricity and steel enterprises) are the largest corporations in Latin America. In consequence, there has been a shift in the pattern of state capital formation away from central government towards the public enterprises, as the latter category has expanded more rapidly than the former.[10] Moreover, the financial and technological links between these enterprises and foreign capital on the one hand, and the weakening of central budgetary control over their accumulation on the other, have tended to integrate the state into capitalist production relations. Finally, the rapid expansion of the *banca de desarrollo* (state development banks) has meant that the state provides the greater part of capital funds to the private sector, often borrowing on metropolitan financial markets for this purpose. By the mid-'sixties, these banks controlled three-quarters of development finance in Mexico and Chile, and two-thirds by the mid-'seventies in Brazil and Peru.[11]

Table 1 shows the extent of the resulting expenditure pattern. We have taken general government current expenditure plus total public sector gross fixed capital formation as an indicator of the extent of the total fiscal resources required by the state (which is the central theme of the paper) and overall, when expressed as a proportion of GDP, this indicator has more or less doubled between 1950 and 1975. Nevertheless, it still remains well below the level in (say) the OECD countries,[12] and also contrasts with the metropolis in terms of the very low levels of welfare expenditure as opposed to those on directly productive activities on the one hand, and the proportionately higher growth of capital as opposed to current expenditure on the other. In O'Connor's terminology,[13] the former contrast corresponds to the importance of 'social capital' (the state expenditure required for profitable private accumulation) as opposed to 'social expenses of production' (expenditure necessary to maintain social harmony)—due no doubt to the relative weakness of the working class in Latin America—and the latter contrast to the importance within 'social capital' of 'social investment' as opposed to 'social consumption', possibly arising from the relatively small size of the industrial labour force and the greater importance of 'bottlenecks' in the growth process to be overcome by public investment. With industrialisation, then, the resource requirements of the Latin American state have clearly increased enormously: this supports the first of our hypotheses.

III TAXATION AS A SOURCE OF SURPLUS FOR THE STATE

The prime source of surplus[14] available to the state in a capitalist economy must inevitably be taxation, which apart from covering current government expenditure may reasonably be expected to contribute towards government

TABLE 1

STATE EXPENDITURE AS A PERCENTAGE OF GROSS DOMESTIC PRODUCT

	General Government Current Expenditure				*Public Sector Gross Fixed Capital Formation*				*Total State Economic Expenditure*			
	1950	*1960*	*1970*	*1975*	*1950*	*1960*	*1970*	*1975*	*1950*	*1960*	*1970*	*1975*
Argentina	14·7	16·1	17·3	28·7	7·8	5·3	7·9	7·0	22·5	21·4	25·2	35·7
Brazil	13·3	18·6	24·3	23·0	4·2	6·7	9·0	9·5	17·5	25·3	33·3	32·5
Chile	13·7	22·5	25·6	24·8	3·3	6·8	9·0	5·0	17·0	29·3	34·6	29·8
Colombia	11·5	7·8	10·6	11·0	1·9	3·4	6·7	7·0	13·4	11·2	17·3	18·0
Mexico	6·5	5·1	6·0	9·5	6·1	5·6	7·5	10·5	12·6	10·7	13·5	20·0
Peru	12·1	12·3	17·0	17·4	1·8	2·3	4·5	8·5	13·9	14·6	21·5	25·9
Latin America	. .	15·1	18·4	. .	. .	5·6	7·3	. .	. .	20·7	25·7	. .

Note: TSEE = GGCE + PSGFCF

Sources: 1950—ECLA *Economic Survey of Latin America 1953* (Santiago, 1954): 1960 and 1970—ECLA *Evaluacion Regional de la Estrategia Internacional de Desarrollo* (Santiago, 1973); 1975—Argentina, Brazil and Chile updated from IMF *International Financial Statistics* (Washington, April 1977) estimate of total government expenditure. Mexico and Peru from FitzGerald [*1977a, 1976* respectively]. ECLA sources have been used to ensure consistency, but they do not define precisely what items are included. 'Latin America' in this and the following tables is the mean for the eighteen republics weighted by their GDP in 1960.

capital formation and even that of the rest of the public sector. To the extent that this does not occur, other sources of finance must be used which have a 'cost to the state' (such as interest charges) greater than that of taxation—although the political cost may well, of course, be less. From the discussion of the previous section, it should be clear that expenditure patterns are determined more or less independently of tax revenue (except in cases of severe crisis) and thus the problem is one of raising sufficient funds to cover them—rather than the fiscal revenue in any one year determining the extent of such expenditure.[15]

It is immediately clear from Table 2 that the level of tax pressure varies widely from one country to another in our 'sample' and the same is true for Latin America as a whole.[16] The reasons for this variance have more to do with the role of the state in the economy than any particular ease or difficulty of raising taxes arising from the level of income per head or 'tax handles' in the form of mineral exports or a large industrial sector. For instance, neither Brazil nor Mexico are mineral exporters, while both Chile and Peru are. Again, a rough division between Argentina, Brazil and Mexico on the one hand and Chile, Colombia and Peru on the other in terms of the degree of industrialisation does not produce a clear result either. Both these observations appear to hold true for the Latin American economies as a whole.[17]

Clearly tax pressure has increased during our period,

TABLE 2
TAX PRESSURE IN LATIN AMERICA

	Tax Income as per cent of GDP			
	1950	*1960*	*1970*	*1975*
Argentina	17·0	14·2	15·0	12·8
Brazil	16·0	20·1	27·0	30·7
Chile	16·7	16·5	21·8	22·7
Colombia	12·0	10·4	13·4	13·4
Mexico	7·5	7·1	7·9	10·5
Peru	14·0	14·9	18·9	17·6
Latin America	. .	14·4	17·2	. .

Sources: 1950—ECLA *Economic Survey of Latin America 1956* (Santiago, 1957); 1960, 1970, 1975 as Table 1.

indicating that tax revenues have been 'buoyant'. This buoyancy, however, was not the result of any inherent high income elasticity of the taxes that have been raised. That would imply tax systems that are generally progressive in their incidence, which is not characteristic of Latin America—as we shall see. Rather, the observed revenue buoyancy results from better tax enforcement, introduction of new taxes and the upward revision of rates for existing taxes—all often under the guise of the rationalisation and consolidation of a multiplicity of minor imposts frequently dating back to Independence or even before. However, this increase has not, in most cases, been nearly sufficient to cover increased expenditure, particularly public investment outlays. Indeed, for Latin America as a whole, although tax pressure rose by three percentage points between 1960 and 1970, current expenditure (as we have seen) also rose by three per cent of national product between those dates, and public investment by two points. This raised the overall resource deficit from six to eight per cent of GDP, and there is every sign that this represents a long-run trend.

TABLE 3

THE STRUCTURE OF TAXATION IN LATIN AMERICA

(per cent of total tax revenue)

		Argentina	*Brazil*	*Chile*	*Colombia*	*Mexico*	*Peru*
1950:	Income Property	37	26	40	28	46	41
	Consumption	57	63	15	47	36	30
	Import Export	6	11	45	25	28	29
1960:	Income	24	32	17	34	38	22
	Property	6	—	6	3	—	—
	Consumption	41	57	43	39	34	43
	Import Export	29	11 —	21 14	24	24 4	32 3
1970:	Income	19	28	30	33	51	25
	Property	13	—	4	2	—	2
	Consumption	32	65	46	47	36	42
	Import Export	16	7 —	11 19	18	11 2	28 3

Note: 'Income tax' includes both personal and profits taxes.
Source: ECLA [*1956, 1973*].

Turning to the structure of taxation, shown in Table 3, there are a number of outstanding features. Taking the period as a whole, there seems to be a rough balance between the three main sources of tax—direct, indirect and external trade. These represented, for our sample of six countries in the nineteen-sixties, roughly 5 per cent, 7 per cent and 4 per cent of GDP respectively. In very approximate terms, they are equivalent to: about a tenth of profits and salaries in direct taxes; about one fifth of external trade flows in import and export duties; and about a tenth of private consumption in the case of indirect tax. In more detail, we have no standardised data for the division between personal and corporate taxation, and although it is true that for the upper reaches of domestic management in the private sector the two may be almost equivalent, there is clearly a considerable difference between (say) civil servants and multinational corporations as sources of taxation. However, professional groups such as doctors and lawyers have always been lightly taxed in Latin America, ostensibly because of the difficulty of collection.[18] Civil servants pay similarly low rates, possibly because these only represent an accounting transaction. The two categories of corporation tax of most interest are those on major export enterprises (particularly multinationals operating in mining) which pay comparatively high rates of about fifty per cent on the one hand, and industrial corporations, which commonly pay very low rates as the result of investment incentives.[19] There is some argument for defining export taxes as direct taxation, because generally they cannot be passed on to the purchaser as prices are determined on international markets. Finally, taxes on property are an insignificant item[20]—land tax of any form being notably absent. In the case of both urban and rural land, this arises from the power of large landlords and (although this is often forgotten) the absence of a recent heritage of a prosperous peasantry taxed by a colonial power.

Indirect taxation is the main single tax category in Latin America, and this is distributed over the usual range of sales taxes on major retail outlets and excise duties on goods such as alcohol and tobacco which are often categorised as 'luxuries' but which are in fact an essential component of wage-goods. To these should be added import duty, which is passed on to the consumer in the case of consumer goods and usually low in the case of industrial inputs. Unfortunately, the published statistics do not distinguish between tax on capital and tax on labour as sources of surplus for the state: but if we take corporation and export taxes plus those on wealth (e.g. inheritance and estate duties, although wealth taxes are comparatively unimportant in Latin America) as making up more or less unshiftable taxes on capital, then it accounted for only about a fifth of total tax income in the nineteen-sixties, and thus only about three per cent of GDP.

As we have stated before, the main determinant of tax income in societies where capitalism is so developed as to provide a substantial proletariat, petty bourgeoisie and profit income (i.e. surplus mobilised through the market) is the 'willingness' of particular classes to give up their income to the state. Thus we cannot argue that there is a lack of taxable *capacity* in Latin America.[21] However, there are structural characteristics of the different economies in our sample that affect the tax structure, possibly because of their influence on the class structure itself, and particularly upon the balance of power between different fractions of capital on the one hand, and between capital and labour on the other. Broadly, we would expect that during the industrialisation process, a number of changes in the tax structure might well take place. First, the shift away from the dominance of the primary sector would not have much effect if this had been agriculture,[22] but the presence of large mining operations (even when controlled by foreign capital) does provide large export tax income[23] which would presumably diminish in importance as industrialisation proceeds. Second, the imposition of high tariff walls in order to protect 'domestic' industry as the first stage in import-substitution[24] has always meant barriers against consumer goods rather than industrial inputs, and although this would yield considerable tax income initially it would rapidly fall off as import-substitution took place. Third, the yield from industrial corporations would be low because of the numerous tax incentives granted to potential investors which usually extend to reinvestment in existing concerns as well. Fourth, the industrialisation process would bring into existence both a white-collar salariat and a blue-collar proletariat from which income tax and social security contributions could be levied, while the increasing per capita consumption of excisable goods after import-substitution would expand indirect tax income too.

Although we can discern some general statistical evidence to support these expectations in Table 3, particularly the declining importance of direct and external taxation, we must consider the six countries separately in order to get a clearer picture. In Argentina, there are no significant export taxes (given the political importance of large landowners exporting meat and wheat), and property taxes are similarly insubstantial, so that given the usual low corporation tax rates, direct tax comes mostly from salaries. Moreover, import duty is also a relatively small source of tax revenue, as the high tariff levels are applied to substituted imports after a long period of industrialisation. Indirect tax as a share of the total declined and rose again in consequence, consisting mainly in excise on tobacco and alcohol.[25] Brazil we shall consider separately below. The tax structure in Chile was traditionally dominated by export and profit tax on the large copper corporations—accounting for nearly half the total in the nineteen-fifties. With the progress of import-substituting industrialisation, both external and direct tax lost ground and indirect tax was expanded to make up the ground—particularly in the form of value-added taxes introduced in the mid-nineteen-sixties. Again, the rising industrial bourgeoisie could avoid taking on the burden of fiscal supply and shift it to others, but in this case to the proletariat in the form of taxes on consumption.

Colombia has a far less industrialised economy than these three, and although in the absence of mining activity large-scale agricultural enterprise is central to exports and output, corporation and property taxes are relatively unimportant and the increase in direct tax share has been met from income tax on white-collar workers. Import duties have remained relatively important, but retail sales taxes remain as the centrepiece of fiscal income. The central position of the farming oligarchy which has penetrated industry in alliance with foreign capital accounts for much of this pattern.[26] Mexico has a large agrarian sector too, but the absence of rural property tax arises from revolution rather than reaction. Despite the relative importance of income tax, it contains a declining profit element. Taxes on corporate profits, dividends and other property income declined from 70 to 58 per cent of income tax between 1960 and 1978. Import duties declined in importance with effective import substitution but in contrast with other cases the main tax source became the higher salary brackets, rather than mass consumption duties. The balance between capital and organised labour in Mexico within the *Partido Revolucionario Institucional* is clearly reflected, then, in the resulting tax structure. Finally, Peru has a direct tax structure dominated by receipts from mining companies, with virtually no property tax and low personal and industrial company taxation—due to the small size of the salariat and the large fiscal incentives to industrialists. Import duties remained important as the process of import-substitution was not far advanced by 1970. Overall, then, we can confirm that there are low capital taxes in Latin America and that the bulk of existing and increased fiscal income has been met from taxes on wages or wage-expenditure.

Tax reform has been an insistent theme of Latin American tax studies and was particularly stressed by the Organisation of American States,[27] in order to raise enough current revenue to balance the central government budget, to introduce an element of progressivity in the tax structure and rationalise the chaotic patterns of consumption taxes. By the end of the nineteen-sixties, most countries had raised the indirect tax burden by just this kind of 'rationalisation', but the OAS' insistence on not discouraging investment by taxing capital was more than welcome to Latin American tax authorities. Attempts by the Echeverria administration to tax Mexican real estate profits, for instance, met with resistance extending to capital flight, while efforts by the Belaunde administration in Peru to raise corporation tax were blocked by Congress. In general, in no case has tax reform involving either higher taxes on capital or sufficient funds to cover state expenditure been carried out in Latin America since the Second World War.

As we have seen, Brazil is a case of an economy enjoying rapid capitalist expansion with considerable state involvement where the tax burden has increased considerably.[28] We have already noted the substantial expansion of the economic activity of the Brazilian state in the nineteen-fifties and sixties, mainly due to an increased rate of support for private capital occurring *before* 1964. Fiscal pressure was also increased substantially under the Kubischeck administration (1956–60), but mainly by large increases in consumption taxes: export taxes broadly equivalent to a tax on agrarian profits were eliminated, while excise duties were raised from two to three tenths of total tax income and sales taxes by a similar proportion—these latter two rising from about six to twelve per cent of GDP from the mid-fifties to the mid-sixties. The second step in increased tax revenue was somewhat different: in 1964 the income tax system was reorganised but tightened only on personal income, while the effective rate of corporate tax actually fell after 1964—in 1970 it was only three per cent of gross profits in the manufacturing sector. In 1967, sales taxes were reorganised in the form of a value-added tax collected by the states, but without greatly affecting the resources so mobilised.[29] In sum, a substantial increase in tax income was obtained but it was achieved by shifting the greater burden of resource acquisition for the state away from capital and towards labour. The resources necessary for the state to support capital in the long run (or at least for the decade subsequent to 1964) were mobilised without increased cost to capital in the short term (indeed tax paid by capital has *fallen* from seven per cent of GDP in 1950–54 to four per cent in 1974–75 while the share of profits in national income was rising)[30]—but with a concomitant social repression of labour that was not politically viable in our other cases.[31] Thus the second of our hypotheses can be said to have been supported: the tendency for tax increases to take the form of indirect taxation— and to be borne by labour rather than by capital.

IV FISCAL INCIDENCE

Apart from its primary function of mobilising enough of the surplus to finance state expenditure, a fiscal system has the potential to generate a significant incentive or redistributive effect.

We have already noted the very low level of effective taxation on capital in Latin America: on a conservative estimate the average yield of profit and rent taxes would be about three per cent of GDP on a property share of total product of thirty per cent—a rate of only one-tenth. This does not arise from a lack of tax bases or suitable instruments, but rather from the extensive array of rebates granted as incentives for investment—sometimes for investment in any sector, and at others for particular branches considered as productive (e.g. agribusiness) or as foreign exchange earners (e.g. tourism) as well as strategic branches such as heavy industry. There has been comparatively little study of the effect of these incentives, but what there is[32] indicates that these concessions tend to be seen as 'windfall' gains *after* an investment decision has been made, and are often assigned to *existing* branches—particularly since only after an industry has been established can it lobby effectively for such arrangements. The 'fiscal loss' of these incentives (assuming that the high nominal rates could be applied and are not just tolerated because of the rebates) can be of the order of five per cent of GDP—a third of tax income in the form of profits already and no evidence of savings *ex ante* being a constraint upon investment,[33] the overall incentive effect can hardly be significant. Much more attention has been paid to the impact of tariffs upon investment patterns, where it is clear[34] that the simultaneous protection of domestic output and low duties on imported inputs has stimulated the establishment of domestic manufacturing plant. Although the rationality or efficiency of the resulting industrial pattern is open to debate, the concurrent control of key branches by multinational corporations is not, and it would seem that these have been the major beneficiaries of both protection and investment incentives.[35]

Turning now to fiscal incidence, we find that surprisingly enough, Latin America is the area where most studies of this type have been carried out.[36] One of the studies quoted by Bird and de Wulf with approval is that for Peru carried out by Webb.[37] The progression of the Peruvian tax system observed between quartiles arises from the reliance on indirect taxes (two-thirds of the total), especially on luxuries, and the large size of the quasi-subsistence rural sector. However, the incidence declined from 40 per cent in the top decile to only 25 per cent in the top percentile in 1969, due to the effect of investment incentives. Although the bulk of tax revenue comes from the richest quartile, it is upon the third quartile (corresponding to the urban proletariat and the richer peasantry) that taxes have risen fastest within the rising overall level of tributary pressure.

TABLE 4

TAX INCIDENCE IN PERU

	1961			*1969*		
Population Quartile	*% of income*	*% incidence*	*% of Total Tax Revenue*	*% of income*	*% incidence*	*% of Total Tax Revenue*
I (poorest)	4	4	1	3	5	1
II	9	6	4	9	9	4
III	17	8	9	17	16	13
IV (richest)	70	18	86	71	23	82
Total	100	15	100	100	20	100

Source: Webb [*1977:47*].

An interesting attempt to estimate *net* fiscal incidence (so as to include the distributional impact of not only tax but the resultant public expenditure) for Colombia is given in Urrutia and de Sandoval [*1976*]. Although they find the Colombian direct tax system to be progressive (except in the top percentiles) indirect taxes are broadly regressive and counteract them, making for an overall impact roughly proportional to personal income. The authors proceed to allocate public expenditure to the various income groups, finding that although education and health have a strong redistributive impact, this only accounts for a quarter of total state outlays, and the other assignable items mainly benefit capitalists (such as public works) or organised urban labour (such as social security) and thus have a *progressive* bias in the sense of increasing the dispersion of personal income distribution. Even the allocation of the remainder (two-fifths of Colombian public expenditure goes on central administration and security) on an equal per capita basis leaves the personal income distribution much as it was before the fiscal process, while their alternative (and more realistic) allocation to the top two deciles on the assumption that this includes all those that benefit from the maintenance of the existing social system, makes for a net fiscal impact that is redistributive *upwards*.

But perhaps the most wide-ranging estimate of fiscal incidence is given by Furtado in his discussion[38] of state intervention in the Latin American economies. On the basis of ECLA estimates for the region as a whole in the mid-nineteen-sixties,[39] he divides the population into four groups, corresponding broadly to the mass of rural workers ('Group I'), the mass of urban workers ('Group II'), higher salary earners and small entrepreneurs ('Group III'), and finally the large landowners and entrepreneurs ('Group IV'). Looking first at the tax burden (including social security payments), he finds that the system as a whole is not very progressive, bearing fairly heavily on the working classes, and rising only slightly from the petty to the grand bourgeoisie. This arises from the reliance on indirect taxation (which as we have already seen is progressive as between rural and urban workers) while the relative inefficacy of professional income taxes reduces the burden on professional groups and the low rates on profits do not raise it much even on capital. As far as resource mobilisation is concerned, the main source is 'Group II'—the urban proletariat who consume the bulk of taxed goods (e.g. cigarettes and televisions) and contribute to the social security system. Turning to expenditure, the ECLA could only identify education and health expenditure, a third of the total, with particular income groups. If we allow this as a relevant measure (leaving aside the fact that the value of health and education to the recipient presumably exceeds the cost of supplying them on the one hand, and the undoubted benefits to employers of a trained and healthy work-force on the other) then the 'non-allocable excess' calculated by the ECLA is still generated by the urban proletariat, with rural workers' benefits balancing their tax contribution and the bourgeoisie (Groups III and IV) using these public services comparatively little.

The allocation of this 'excess' depends upon an interpretation of the Latin American political economy. Allocation on an equal per capita basis ('Hypothesis A' in Table 5) yields, not surprisingly, a heavy net transfer to the rural poor, but it is difficult to see how they benefit from expenditure on defence and motorways. Allocation *pro rata* to

TABLE 5

FISCAL INCIDENCE IN LATIN AMERICA

	Group I	*Group II*	*Group III*	*Group IV*	*Total*
1. Proportion of Population	50%	45%	3%	2%	100%
2. Average Income*	$120	$400	$1750	$3500	$365
Taxes & Social Security:					
3. as % of disposable income	13·0	20·0	16·5	21·0	18·4
4. as % of GDP	1·7	8·4	1·9	3·2	15·2
5. Identifiable expenditure	1·7	3·2	0·3	0·2	5·4
6. Non-allocated surplus	—	5·2	1·6	3·0	9·8
7. Allocation: Hypothesis A	4·9	4·4	0·3	0·2	9·8
Hypothesis B	1·7	4·7	1·5	1·9	9·8
Hypothesis C	—	—	—	9·8	9·8
8. Net Fiscal Incidence:					
Hypothesis A	+4·9	−0·8	−1·3	−2·8	—
Hypothesis B	+1·7	−0·5	−0·1	−1·1	—
Hypothesis C	—	−5·2	−1·6	+6·8	—

Source: Rows 1–6 from Furtado (1970, p.66); 7 as in text; 8 = 4 − 5 − 7.
* US dollars in 1960.

income per head ('Hypothesis B' in Table 5), on the grounds that this represents proportional socio-economic power, yields a more or less balanced result, with each group nearly paying for the benefits it receives, with a modest progressive bias. Furtado's view (upon which 'Hypothesis C' is based) is as follows:

> Since public investment[40] is largely intended to create external economies for private investment and since the latter is in the hands of the two per cent minority whose savings represent a significant proportion of its income, it may be deduced that both in the way it finances its expenditure and the way it allocates its resources, the action of the State serves not only to consolidate the existing pattern of wealth and income distribution but to foster an even more concentrated one [*op. cit.: 67*].

V FINANCING THE FISCAL DEFICIT

We can now put the two sides of the fiscal structure together—total expenditure as we have defined it above, and total tax income—in order to derive what we shall call the *fiscal deficit* of the state sector. This is equivalent to the extra economic resources that the state must acquire through enterprise surpluses, non-tax items such as rents and fees (which are comparatively unimportant in the Latin American case), borrowing or monetary creation so that *ex post* the public sector accounts can balance. This excludes the investment flows undertaken by the 'state as banker', which increases both the outlays and borrowing requirements substantially in all cases. This measure of 'fiscal deficit' is of more analytical and practical use to us than that of the government budget deficit, which includes transactions such as amortisation of the national debt and excludes public enterprise investment except in so far as this requires capital transfers from the treasury. Estimates for *total* public sector savings would not yield this problem, but these are not usually presented in a national accounting framework if at all, in Latin America. Moreover, we are interested in separating taxation from all other forms of income to the state as being one of two essential characteristics of the state itself—its *legal* claim on resources from the private sector—as opposed to borrowing and enterprise surpluses, while the monetary creation necessary to balance the books at the end of the day is the other. Table 6 shows our estimates of the fiscal deficit for our six countries and the Latin American average. Overall, there is a clear tendency for this gap to widen as a proportion of GDP—broadly confirming our third hypothesis.

TABLE 6

FISCAL DEFICIT AS A PERCENTAGE OF GDP

	General Government 'saving[a]				*State Sector 'saving*[b]			
	1950	*1960*	*1970*	*1975*	*1950*	*1960*	*1970*	*1975*
Argentina	−2·3	−1·9	−2·3	−15·9	−5·5	−7·2	−10·2	−22·9
Brazil	+2·7	+1·5	+2·7	+7·7	−1·5	−5·2	−6·3	−1·8
Chile	+3·0	−6·0	−3·8	−2·1	−0·3	−12·8	−12·8	−7·1
Colombia	+0·5	+2·6	+2·8	+2·4	−1·4	−0·8	−4·3	−4·7
Mexico	+1·0	+2·0	+1·9	+0·2	+0·1	+0·3	−2·6	−8·3
Latin America	—	−0·7	−1·2	—	—	−6·3	−8·5	

Notes: (a) defined as tax income *less* general government current expenditure; (b) defined as (a) less public sector gross fixed capital formation.

Source: Tables 1 and 2.

We can distinguish then three main ways in which the extra resources required are obtained: the operating surpluses of public enterprises and social security funds; borrowing on domestic or foreign financial markets; and monetary creation by fiduciary issue. There are other sources—such as sales of publicly-owned assets and grants from foreign governments—but these are not of great quantitative significance in the Latin American case.

Given the extent of public enterprise activities in Latin America, a reasonable profit margin as a contribution to ongoing accumulation might be expected. However, it should be remembered that the underlying function of state activity in Latin America is to support the profitability and accumulation of private capital, so that low prices for public enterprise outputs such as industrial power, steel and port facilities are only to be expected. Indeed low profitability is one of the key reasons for their being in the state sector in the first place. An IMF survey[41] of public enterprise accounts in the mid-'sixties indicated that Latin American enterprises were even less profitable than the average for underdeveloped economies as a whole, their average surplus on current operations being two per cent (as opposed to eight per cent for the whole sample), and *minus* 22 per cent after depreciation. It has been calculated[42] that it would be necessary to raise public enterprise prices by about one-half in order to attain an 'equivalent exchange of value' (i.e. to cover depreciation and investment requirements), and if we apply this to the ECLA estimate[43] that public enterprise turnover in Latin America is equivalent to about ten per cent of GDP—the implicit resource transfer is of the order of five per cent of national income. Even in cases[44] such as Peru and Mexico, where the state has taken a determinedly interventionist role in the economy, the profitability of state enterprise remains well below market rates, let alone those required to finance their own capital accumulation.

It has frequently been suggested[45] that social security funds should provide an important means of financing state investment, both in the form of operating surpluses accumulated during the expansion of the system, and in that of acquisition of financial assets so as to yield future income flows. This has evidently not been so in the past. Except in two cases

(Argentina and Chile) social security does not extend to even half the workforce, and under conditions of chronic inflation internal financing from securities is naturally difficult, so that in real terms these schemes tend to end up as a drain on the resources of the state—mainly to the benefit of white-collar workers.

We have already noted how Brazil, in response to higher expenditure commitments, significantly raised tax revenue between the mid-'fifties and mid-'sixties, but this did not cover the expanded requirements even though the rate of central government savings was slightly increased. However, the rate of public sector savings was increased substantially between the beginning and the end of the nineteen-sixties, partly by raising public enterprise prices but mostly by tapping social security funds, so as to increase the public sector share of domestic savings from about one-fifth to nearly one-half.[46] In terms of Table 6, this means that in addition to general government savings, the surplus acquired from the rest of the public sector must have risen from 1·5 per cent in 1960 to 5·0 per cent of GDP in 1970. This then reduced the net 'economic' borrowing requirement by two-thirds, although the financial activities of state banks, the import requirements of state enterprises, and balance of payments support loans did lead to a massive increase in external indebtedness as well over the period, as we shall see.

In the event, public enterprise profits have not been very large in Brazil, as any signs of profitability tend to lead to demands for reversion to the private sector.[47] However, when depreciation provisions are included (because we are considering the financing of *gross* fixed capital formation), by 1969 the state enterprises were able to fund nearly a half of their own fixed investment—a sum equivalent to over two per cent of GDP. In addition the social security system has become a major source of surplus for the state: both the INPS (National Health and Social Security Institute) and the FGTS (Redundancy Payments Fund) run substantial surpluses, which have been used to fund state investment in the former case and to finance middle-class housing in the latter. This contrasts strongly with the net losses made by the social security system at the beginning of the nineteen-sixties.

However, in neither case has this new income been a great burden on private sector profits: in the case of enterprise pricing the burden was mostly borne by households; and in that of social security, half the charges fall on employees and the other half are passed on as indirect taxation in the form of higher industrial prices.

The second recourse open to the state to achieve the required finance is borrowing. Domestic borrowing can take several forms, including the direct sale of treasury bonds and public enterprise stock to the public, the purchase of government paper by the commercial banking system, and credits from state banks to other public-sector entities. All these usually involve rates of interest at or below the current rate of inflation, and in the first instance certainly involve a relatively cheap form of resource acquisition. However, the scope for bond sales to the public in Latin America is limited by the narrowness of capital markets and their unattractiveness in comparison with, say, urban real estate as a vehicle of private financial investment. Commercial banks will take up treasury stocks because they are a vehicle for further credit creation: given the reserve ratio, loans to the public several times greater than this are made in the normal way, and the profit on these more than counterbalances the loss on holding the treasury stock. If reserve requirements are raised at the same time, of course, then such purchases are equivalent to a direct tax on bank profits—but this procedure has obvious limitations. Finally, the extension of credit by state banks to the government or state enterprises is almost equivalent to monetary creation. It is extremely difficult to piece together the exact scale of all this borrowing without detailed analysis of a particular country and there are certainly no comparable figures published for different countries.

A point of concern in the analysis of public sector borrowing in metropolitan economies is the 'crowding out'[48] of private investment by the shortage of investment funds for firms if the capital market is overladen with government paper. This rests on the supposition of a constraint on total private saving and thus the more that is taken by the state means less for the private sector and thus a decline in private investment. However, the very high share of post-tax profits in national income and the tendency for constraints on private investment to be of a 'structural' nature[49] would tend to indicate that this does not hold true for private enterprise in Latin America. Given the high degree of self-financing still customary, where viable private projects exist then capitalist consumption out of profits—which takes roughly two-thirds of the total after all—can easily be curtailed, and it is difficult to imagine that government borrowing affects the investment decisions of the multinationals! The undeniable fact that the purpose of most public investment is to *increase* private profitability and stimulate further private investment, would tend to reinforce this suggestion that domestic borrowing by the state does not reduce private investment. We shall return to the problem of the inflationary impact shortly.

The post-war economic development of Mexico is often cited as a case of successful capitalist industrialisation, the role of the public sector in general and its use of the capital market in particular are seen as central to that success.[50] An authority on this period writes:

> The programmes and policies of the Mexican government since 1940 have been designed to stimulate private-sector activities in the development process... [but]... Mexican monetary and fiscal policy represent a second-best solution to the problem posed by public sector deficit financing of infrastructure investment.[51]

In the absence of tax reform, the extra financial needs of the public sector (of the order of three per cent of GDP in the 1960s) were met mainly through manipulation of the Mexican capital market—itself dominated by state banks—by imposing high marginal reserve requirements and quasi-obligatory purchases of state enterprise bonds on private banks. As they maintained a low rate of interest relative to private rates, state banks were faced by an excess demand for their own funds, so that between these two instruments, the correct volume of private savings could be absorbed to balance the fiscal deficit without allowing an inflationary or deflationary situation to develop. In addition, by limiting available funds on the Mexican capital market in times of external deficit, the monetary authorities obliged the private sector to borrow abroad, thus avoiding external public debt increases. Thus, this mechanism allowed steady and rapid economic growth despite the deficits on both fiscal and trade accounts arising from that growth. However, in the past decade, as the 'Mexican miracle' began to show serious signs of strain, state expenditure was expanded to increase welfare outlays and break severe production bottlenecks (by investing in oil and heavy industry) but tax pressure was not increased commensurately, as we have seen. The delicate mechanism for financing the deficit was placed under increasing pressure until in 1973–6 about five per cent of GDP was being drained off the private capital market in addition to the borrowing of state banks for re-lending to private borrowers (three times greater in relation to GDP than a decade previously), while the state banks raised foreign loans at a net rate equivalent to four per cent of GDP in that year. The resulting strain placed upon the capital market contributed substantially to the instability because the authorities were forced to release more liquidity to sustain the domestic banking system, thus contributing to inflationary pressures sparked off by higher import prices. More importantly, the serious limitations of a nascent capital market as a major source of *net* state finance (as opposed to borrowing for on-lending) were underlined—and Mexico has the most developed financial market in Latin America.

Borrowing abroad is a traditional source of finance for fiscal deficits. Although historically loans made to Latin American governments have not been always very secure, there have been no significant defaults since the Second World War, mainly because of the monitoring role of the US government in the continent which is exercised either directly or indirectly through multilateral institutions. Whether borrowed from a government, multinational 'aid' institutions or private banks, such funds are relatively cheap when international inflation is taken into account, and although they are often nominally linked to a specific investment project, they effectively form an addition to the foreign exchange reserves under state control. The scale of foreign borrowing to cover the fiscal deficit as we have defined it (in real resource terms) is obscured by the raising of loans abroad by state banks for on-lending to the private sector (primarily to finance equipment imports) on the

TABLE 7
OUTSTANDING PUBLIC SECTOR DEBT (US $ BILLIONS)

	1955	*1963*	*1970*	*1975*
Argentina	0·6	2·1	1·9	3·0
Brazil	1·4	2·3	3·5	11·5
Chile	0·4	0·9	2·1	3·6
Colombia	0·3	0·7	1·3	2·4
Mexico	0·5	1·6	3·2	11·3
Peru	0·1	0·2	0·9	2·7
All Latin America	—	—	15·8	41·3

Source: IBRD *Debt Tables* [*1977*] and *Annual Report* [*1965*].

one hand, and by the governments for general balance of payments support on the other; either of which can increase without the fiscal deficit having altered. Nonetheless, as Table 7 indicates, there has been a massive increase in external public debt in recent years, and a corresponding increase in the balance-of-payments cost of debt servicing, which for many Latin American countries approaches a quarter of export income.[52] The burden of external debt cannot be measured in these terms alone, however. The existence of large external obligations, requiring constant renegotiations, places government policy at the disposition of foreign creditors or their joint representative such as the IBRD or IMF.[53] Such policy directives frequently involve commitments to balance the budget, but by curtailing expenditure rather than by tax reform.

The Peruvian case illustrates[54] this problem clearly. After the coup in 1968, the military government initiated radical economic strategy aimed at the roots of underdevelopment: ambitious social reforms (including sweeping land reform and worker participation in industry); the nationalisation of foreign firms in exports, heavy industry and finance; and the rapid recapitalisation of mining and industry through state enterprise. In the absence of radical tax reform (which would have alienated middle-class and industrialist support for the regime) or an adequate domestic capital market, although tax pressure was raised and a considerable volume of treasury bonds were floated, considerable reliance was placed on foreign borrowing to cover the rising deficit, which arose not from current expenditure (which was severely restrained) but from massive investment in oil, mining, energy fertilisers and heavy industry. These required not only budgetary funds but also foriegn exchange. Despite the 'freeze' of official inter-governmental and multilateral loans as the reforms got under way, the US banks (faced with excess funds in the early nineteen-seventies) were willing to lend to Peru, and the public debt rose from some US $0·7 billions in 1968 to US $3·0 billions in 1975, this latter figure being equivalent to 24 per cent of Peruvian GDP in that year. The shift from official to private sources raised interest rates and lowered repayment periods, and the cost of debt servicing rose from 15 to 27 per cent of exports between the two years. However, the most serious effects were the 'leverage' on domestic policy afforded to foreign capital: in 1975 a debt consortium under the chairmanship of the IBRD was able to prevent further nationalisation and curtail plans for worker participation; in 1976 the IMF attempted to impose massive public expenditure cuts as a condition for support, and the Peruvian authorities only avoided this by negotiating new loans with a private US bank consortium; and by 1977 the multinationals were being openly encouraged once more and labour organisations supressed. It was undoubtedly a strategic error to rely so heavily on foreign finance, but not because of the cost of debt service.

Finally, the last resort is the printing press.[55] As Table 8 shows, monetary emission is a not inconsiderable source of finance for the Latin American state: it allows the books to be balanced at the end of the day, and has been traditionally defended by Latin American economists as a reasonably efficient form of resource acquisition. Much of the controversy arises, however, from the inflationary impact associated with it. The 'monetarist' position is that budget deficits generate inflation, while the 'structuralist' position would be that it is brought about by constraints on domestic supply and social struggles over the distribution of national income, and that it is therefore the differential effect of inflation upon fiscal income and expenditure which brings about the budget deficits. Unfortunately, although inflation is undeniably associated with monetary creation, there is no theoretical or empirical basis for settling the dispute unambiguously.[56] Our own analysis so far would tend to indicate that the deficit is brought about by structural factors rather than inflation, and as it could hardly be argued that there is a Keynesian lack of effective demand in Latin America,[57] it would seem to follow that monetary creation is a structural phenomenon but undoubtedly inflationary in effect—a suitably heterodox answer! Although the effects of inflation on private savings and investment are not at all clear,[58] it would be reasonable to conclude that the traditional analysis in terms of the effect on cash balances is not so relevant here, rather that the impact of rising prices on real wages ensures that the resource transfer to the state comes from labour rather than capital, acting as it does as a general turnover tax to which firms can react more flexibly than workers, and by the same token from unorganised workers rather than unionised workers. Nonetheless, excessive inflation clearly has deletorious effects on capitalist expansion, and is generally resisted by private enterprise, so its use as a mechanism of resource acquisition by the state has definite limits, if not definable ones, particularly since the resource gains are presumably counteracted by the differential impact on state income and expenditure at relatively low levels of inflation.

TABLE 8

INCREASE IN MONEY SUPPLY AS A PERCENTAGE OF GDP

	1950	*1960*	*1970*	*1975*
Argentina	..	..	1·8	8·7
Brazil	..	4·5	1·4	2·8
Chile	0·6	0·6	2·9	7·3
Colombia	..	0·4	1·5	1·9
Mexico	3·9	0·4	0·5	3·6
Peru	1·0	0·4	0·7	2·7

Note: 'Money Supply' defined as 'reserve money' (M_0) by the IMF.
Source: IMF *International Financial Statistics* (various years).

VI CONCLUDING REMARKS

In sum, we have seen how, in response to the needs of both foreign and domestic private capital in the industrialisation process, the economic activities of the state in Latin America have been substantially expanded since the Second World War. The level of taxation, however, has not risen fast enough to keep up with this growth in current and capital expenditure, leading to a widening 'fiscal deficit' to be covered by other means of resource acquisition for the state. Moreover, the increased tax pressure that has taken place has come from heavier taxes on labour rather than on capital. Although we have not entered into the empirical detail required for reasonable proof, we can suggest that these trends confirm the hypotheses put forward at the opening of this paper and consist in a substantive 'fiscal crisis of the state'.

The finance of the fiscal deficit involves a number of different mechanisms: given the role of public enterprise in supporting the private sector, profitability is low, and social security funds are also a limited source of funds; domestic borrowing can be secured through state banks and manipulation of the capital market, but too much reliance on this source can destabilise the private accumulation mechanism; foreign borrowing is relatively simple and cheap (although it can place considerable strain on the balance of payments) but it does subject government policy to a degree of external control; finally, monetary emission is the traditional means of balancing the books in Latin American, but this too has destabilising inflationary consequences.

The chronic nature of this problem is our final puzzle, and it may well have some bearing upon our opening reference to the 'relative autonomy of that state'. The puzzle is this: as the fiscal crisis is structural (in the sense of being part of the pattern of underdevelopment in Latin America as such and not just a 'conjunctural' phenomenon) and generates a contradiction in the capitalist expansion that the state serves to support, why is an adequate fiscal reform not instituted? Clearly the level of tax pressure is a central concern of political economy: it is not, on the one hand, just a matter of one more form of capitalist exploitation of labour (as a traditional Marxist might argue) as the resistance to, and the payment by, all classes indicates; nor is it, on the other, a question of the post-tax income distribution being determined by class-conflict and the pre-tax distribution, and thus fiscal incidence, being essentially irrelevant (as a neo-Ricardian might argue) for much the same reason. In general, the alternative forms of finance involve resource transfer from various social groups to the state by some means or other, and thus formally at least could be substituted by an equivalent tax pattern, with less destabilising effects and presumably no more *real* social impact. In particular, capital as a whole clearly benefits from state activities in Latin America (with temporary exceptions such as Allende's Chile) it should not logically object to our addition to those few taxes it does pay, while the working classes are usually without great legislative representation and are regularly subjected to real wage depression in any case. An argument is frequently expressed to the effect that methods of financing the state other than from taxation, even if destabilising, do have the advantage of having less 'political visibility'. But this does not seem very convincing under these circumstances. In two particular respects the argument is very weak indeed: in countries without effective democratic institutions (i.e. the whole of Latin America at present and for much of the post-war period) the administrative distinction between tax changes as requiring legislation and borrowing or monetary emission by executive fiat is an empty one; second, the bourgeois press throughout the continent constantly complains about budget deficits, brought to a crescendo by the recent revival of imported monetarism.

There *is* an alternative line of argument that seems to be of potentially greater help, however. One of the more important attributes of the capitalist state is its relative autonomy; that is, its capacity to take action against the interests of any one fraction of capital (or even of national capital as a whole at any one point in time) in order to promote the long-run survival and expansion of capitalism as a social formation. In periods of structural stagnation or economic crisis, this relative autonomy may be of crucial importance in order that the necessary returns can be undertaken. At the outset of the industrialisation process, such an autonomy was certainly crucial in forcing through the transition from an agrarian export economy—examples are Vargas in Brazil and Cardenas in Mexico—and will probably be as important in getting beyond import-substitution and establish self-sustained industrial growth. The fiscal crisis we have examined not only deprives the Latin American state of the resources required to restructure the respective economies through public investment but is also on the political plane a concrete manifestation of the refusal of private capital to grant relative autonomy to the state. Indeed, the drastic reactions of the Pinochet and Videla regimes in Chile and Argentina represent the refusal of an insecure domestic bourgeoisie to contemplate the modernisation of the economy and to prefer state expenditure on repression rather than welfare to contain the working class. To the extent that the next stage of industrialisation will require the state opposing foreign capital (rather than the joint ventures between multinationals and public enterprise that have become current practice) the relative autonomy from domestic capital the Latin American state has obtained may be of little avail precisely because it derives from a weakness of the domestic bourgeoisie in the face of penetration by foreign enterprise.

Hopefully, further research into the fiscal crisis of the Latin American state should lead to greater understanding of the role of the state in the continued expansion of dependent capitalism in the area. Indeed, it would seem, therefore, that fiscal studies—which for some strange reason have always been a neo-classical redoubt—would repay research in the classical tradition of political economy, in which taxation was such a central theme.

NOTES

1. O'Connor [*1973*].
2. Poulantzas [*1973*].
3. Gough [*1975*].
4. The economies to which we shall mainly refer (Argentina, Brazil, Chile, Colombia, Mexico and Peru) account for three-quarters of population and output in the continent. We exclude Venezuela, as having the peculiar fiscal fortunes of an oil-exporting nation.
5. A clear statement of this may be found in the 'Alliance for Progress' charter itself, upon which see Levinson and Onis [*1970*].
6. Cardoso [*1977*].
7. Kaplan [*1969*].
8. These shares are given in ECLA [*1973*], and refer to the Latin American mean in the nineteen-sixties.

9. ECLA [*1973: 195*].
10. Baer [*1974*], FitzGerald [*1974*].
11. FitzGerald [*1977*].
12. OECD [*1977*].
13. *Op. cit.*, especially Chapter 4, 5 and 6.
14. We use this word in the sense employed by Baran [*1957*]: the difference between total material product and the basic consumption requirements of the workforce. The quantitative measurement of the surplus is highly dependent on the definition of the latter term, but a reasonable estimate for Latin America might be based on the fact than on average (see ECLA [*1973*]) two-thirds of the population received only a third of the product in the nineteen-sixties. If we define this as the 'basic consumption requirement', then for the economy as a whole roughly half the product is surplus. This is then used for private investment, luxury consumption by capitalists and salary-earners, government consumption and public investment.
15. The recent experience of oil-exporting countries such as Venezuela and Ecuador is an exception, although only temporarily it appears.
16. See ECLA [*1973*].
17. ECLA (*op cit*).
18. Ironically, the corporate organisation of the economy in Spain provides an efficient method of collection from the *profesiones libres*: the *Colegio de Medicos*, for example, is assessed for a lump sum which it must then collect from its members. This is both cheap to administer and reasonably fair—after all the only people who know how much doctors earn are their colleagues!
19. OAS [*1977*].
20. Domike and Tokman [*1971*].
21. The limits of taxation in terms of reducing the incomes of those taxed (even labour) below subsistence level clearly has not been reached, while the limit of a major disincentive to investment (i.e. by capital taxes) is even more removed, as we shall see.
22. As agricultural taxation is so low—see Domike and Tokman [*1971*].
23. It should be noted that this is mainly a tax on *rent* rather than profit.
24. Hirschman [*1971*].
25. See Diaz Alejandro [*1971*] for a fuller discussion of the Argentine case.
26. See Berry [*1971*] for a further discussion of the Colombian case.
27. OAS [*1965*]. Consequently an ambitious 'Joint Tax Program' was launched of which many of the resulting reports are cited in Bird and de Wulf [*1973*].
28. This discussion is based on Souza and Afonso [*1975*] and Wells [*1977*].
29. Guerard [*1973*].
30. Souza and Afonso [*1975: 120–2*].
31. Until recently that is; but in the cases of the regimes of Pinochet in Chile and Videla in Argentina, repression has been accompanied by massive cuts in public expenditure.
32. See Thorp [*1977*] on Peru, King [*1970*] on Mexico: ECLA [*1972a,b*] sustains this view for Latin America in general, as does Mendive [*1964*].

33. Griffin [*1971*].
34. Hirschman [*1971*].
35. Ffrench-Davis [*1973*].
36. See Bird and de Wulf [*1973*] and de Wulf [*1975*]. They mostly consist in estimates of incidence by income class, an interesting exception being the sectoral analysis in Best [*1976*]—moreover, his main sector (agriculture) can be identified with the top-most income class in Central America.
37. Webb [*1977*].
38. Furtado [*1970: 65–7*].
39. This seems to be consistent with the Peru and Colombia data we have already seen and with other studies quoted in Bird and de Wulf [*1973*].
40. Celso Furtado has indicated to the author that he would include general administration (e.g. ministries of industry and agriculture) and security under this heading as 'overhead expenditure'.
41. Gandtt and Dutto [*1968*].
42. Whitehead [*1971*], working from Gandtt and Dutto (*op cit*).
43. ECLA [*1973*].
44. See FitzGerald [*1976*] and [*1978*], respectively.
45. Reviglio [*1967*], Whitehead [*1971*], Pinto [*1973*].
46. Baer [*1976*].
47. Wells [*1977*], upon which the rest of this paragraph is also based.
48. In other words, 'crowding out' as understood in orthodox theory for developed countries—Buiter [*1977*] is a recent survey—does not apply in Latin America as the private sector (and above all private capital) can maintain its own consumption and investment rates irrespective of the fiscal deficit. In consequence, the effect of this deficit is mainly reflected on *external* account and monetary phenomena—as DAE [*1976*] argues for the case of the British economy.
49. See Furtado [*1970*] and the introduction to Griffin [*1971*].
50. Indeed, it is included in Rostow's pantheon. The rest of the paragraph is based on data and references given in FitzGerald [*1978*].
51. Vernon [*1965: 55*].
52. Moreover, it is only held down to this level by continual re-scheduling of debt and even capitalisation of interest due—which just makes the problem worse later on.
53. Payer [*1975*].
54. This paragraph is based on FitzGerald [*1976*].
55. Known affectionately as the 'maquinita' in Spanish.
56. See Thorp [*1971*] for a perceptive but inconclusive discussion of the problem.
57. As opposed to the narrowness of domestic markets due to concentrated income distribution, a crucial aspect of the structuralist interpretation.
58. Thorp, *op. cit.*, detects no connection between inflation on the one hand, and investment or growth on the other, either.
59. An argument the bases of which are set out in FitzGerald [*1977a*].

REFERENCES

Baer, W., 1974, 'The Role of Government Enterprises in Latin America's Industrialisation', in D. T. Geithman, *Fiscal Policy for Industrialisation and Development in Latin America*, Gainsville: University of Florida Press.

Baran, P., 1957, *The Political Economy of Growth*, New York: Monthly Review Press.

Berry, R. A., 1971, 'Some Implications of Elitist Rule for Economic Development in Colombia' in Ranis [*1971*].

Best, M. H., 1976, 'Political Power and Tax Revenues in Central America', *Journal of Development Economies*, Vol. 3, No. 1.

Bird, R. M., and L. H. De Wulf, 1973, 'Taxation and Income Distribution in Latin America: A Critical Review of Empirical Studies', *IMF Staff Papers*, Vol. XX, No. 3.

Buiter, W. H., 1977, '"Crowding Out" and the Effectiveness of Fiscal Policy', *Journal of Public Economics*, Vol. 7, No. 3.

Cardoso, F. H., 1977, 'Capitalist Development and the State: Bases and Alternatives' in FitzGerald, Floto and Lehmann [*1977*].

DAE, 1976, *Economic Policy Review*, Cambridge: Department of Applied Economics.

De Wulf, L. H., 1975, 'Fiscal Incidence Studies in Developing Countries: Survey and Critique', *IMF Staff Papers*, Vol. 22.1, March.

Diaz Alejandro, C. F., 1971, 'The Argentine State and Economic Growth: A Historical Review' in Ranis [*1971*].

Domike, A. L., and V. E. Tokman, 1971, 'The Role of Agricultural Taxation in Financing Agricultural Development in Latin America' in Griffin [*1971*].

ECLA, 1956, 'Government Income and Expenditure 1947–1954' in *Economic Survey of Latin America 1955*, Santiago: Economic Commission for Latin America.

ECLA, 1972, 'Mobilisation of Domestic Resources', *Economic Bulletin for Latin America*, Vol. XV, No. 2.

ECLA, 1973, *Las Tareas de la Politica Fiscal y Tributaria a la Luz de los Problemas del Desarrollo*, Santiago: Economic Commission for Latin America.

Ffrench-Davis, R., 1973, 'Foreign Investment in Latin America: Recent Trends and Prospects' in V. Urquidi and R. Thorp, eds., *Latin America in the International Economy*, London: Macmillan.

FitzGerald, E. V. K., 1974, *The Public Sector in Latin America*, Cambridge: Working Paper No. 18, Centre of Latin American Studies.

FitzGerald, E. V. K., 1976, *The State and Economic Development: Peru since 1968*, Cambridge: Cambridge University Press.

FitzGerald, E. V. K., 1978, 'Patterns of Public Sector Income and Expenditure in Mexico, 1940–76' *Institute of Latin American Studies Technical Papers Series*, Austin: University of Texas.

FitzGerald, E. V. K., 1977, 'On State Accumulation in Latin America' in FitzGerald, Floto, and Lehmann [*1977*].

FitzGerald, E. V. K., E. Floto, and D. Lehmann, (eds), 1977, *Proceedings of the Cambridge Conference on the State and Economic Development of Latin America,* Cambridge: Centre of Latin American Studies.

Furtado, C., 1970, *Economic Development of Latin America,* Cambridge: Cambridge University Press.

Gandtt, A. and G. Dutto, 1968, 'Financial Performance of Government Owned Corporations in Less Developed Countries', *IMF Staff Papers,* March.

Gough, I., 1975, 'State Expenditure in Advanced Capitalism', *New Left Review,* August.

Griffin, K., 1971, *Financing Development in Latin America,* London: Macmillan.

Guerard, M., 1973, 'The Brazilian State Value-Added Tax'. *IMF Staff Papers,* Vol. 20.1.

Hirschman, A. O., 1971, 'The Political Economy of Import-substituting Industrialisation in Latin America' in *A Bias for Hope,* New Haven: Yale University Press.

Kaplan, M., 1969, *Formacion del Estado Nacional en America Latina,* Santiago: Editorial Universidad.

King, T., 1970, *Mexico: Industrialisation and Trade Policies since 1940.* Oxford: Oxford University Press for OECD.

Levinson, J. and J. Onis, 1970, *The Alliance that lost its way,* Chicago: Quadrangle Books.

Mendive, P., 1964, 'Tax Incentives in Latin America', *Economic Bulletin for Latin America,* Vol. IX.

O'Connor, J., 1973, *The Fiscal Crisis of the State,* New York: St Martin's Press.

OAS, 1965, *Fiscal Policy for Economic Growth in Latin America,* Baltimore: Johns Hopkins for the Organisation of American States.

OAS, 1977, 'La Imposicion a la Renta de las Empresas', *Comercio Exterior* Vol. 27.1.

OECD, 1977, *Statistical Yearbook of National Accounts,* Paris: Organisation for Economic Co-operation and Development.

Payer, C., 1975, *The Debt Trap* London: Penguin.

Pinto, A., 1973, 'Un Itinerario Realista para la Reforma Provisional' in H. Assael, *Ensayos de Politica Fiscal,* Mexico: Fondo de Cultura Economica.

Poulantzas, N., 1973, *Political Power and Social Classes,* London: New Left Books.

Ranis, G., 1971, *Government and Economic Development* New Haven: Yale University Press.

Reviglio, F., 1967, 'Social Security: A Means of Savings Mobilization for Economic Development', *IMF Staff Papers* Vol. 14.2.

Souza, H. and C. Afonso, 1975, *The Fiscal Crisis of the Brazilian State,* (mimeo) York University, Toronto.

Thorp, R., 1971, 'Inflation and the Financing of Economic Development' in Griffin [*1971*].

Thorp, R., 1977, 'The Post-Import Substitution Era: The Case of Peru', *World Development* Vol. 5.1.

Urrutia, M. and C. E. De Sandoval, 1976. 'Fiscal Policy and Income Distribution in Colombia' in A. Foxley, (ed) *Income Distribution in Latin America,* Cambridge University Press.

Vernon, R., 1965, *The Dilemma of Mexico's Development,* Cambridge, Mass.: Harvard University Press.

Webb, R. C., 1977, *Government Policy and the Distribution of Income in Peru, 1963–73,* Cambridge, Mass.: Harvard University Press.

Wells, J. R., 1977, 'State Expenditures and the Brazilian Economic Miracle' in FitzGerald, Floto and Lehmann [*1977*].

Whitehead, L., 1971, 'Public Sector Activities' in Griffin [*1971*].

PART THREE

EQUITY ASPECTS OF TAXATION

The author of Chapter 7 is grateful to the editor of this volume for helpful comments.

Chapter 8 is the outgrowth of a post-evaluation of the Penang Water Supply Project for the Asian Development Bank. The author thanks Kam U. Tee, managing director of the Authority, and Professor Donald Blake of the University Sains Malaysia, for making the necessary data available. Johannes Linn provided useful guidance at several crucial points.

Chapter 9 was written for the Fifth Inter-regional Seminar on Development Planning held in Bangkok in September 1969. The seminar was organised by the Centre for Development Planning, Projections and Policies, the Secretariat of E.C.A.F.E. and the Asian Institute for Economic Development and Planning in collaboration with the Office of Technical Co-operation. Although the paper was circulated as document ISDP 5/A/R.12 by the United Nations Department of Economic and Social Affairs, the views expressed in it are those of the author and not necessarily those of the United Nations.

Chapter 7

Income Tax Evasion and Income Distribution

NANAK C. KAKWANI*

I. INTRODUCTION

It is a fact that there is a considerable amount of income which is understated in individual income tax returns. This phenomenon, which appears to be widespread in developing and developed countries, has two serious consequencies. First, it leads to a loss in tax revenue for the Government which could otherwise be used for many constructive purposes. Secondly, it may reduce the progressivity of the tax system, thus altering the after-tax income distribution.

The problem of illegal income tax evasion has been recently considered by several authors. Allingham and Sandmo [*1972*] have presented a tax evasion model which analyses the individual taxpayer's decision on whether and to what extent to avoid taxes by deliberately understating his income. In their model, the taxpayer maximises his cardinal utility function, which is assumed to be a function of income only. Further, the marginal utility of the taxpayer is assumed to be everywhere positive and strictly decreasing, which implies that the taxpayer is risk averse. Their analysis is limited to the case of a proportional tax system.[1]

Srinivasan [*1973*] proposed an alternative model of tax evasion which is more general in the sense that it allows for a progressive tax system. In his model, the taxpayer is assumed

*Professor of Econometrics, University of New South Wales, Australia.

to maximise his after-tax expected income instead of his cardinal utility function. This amounts to the assumption that the taxpayer is risk neutral. In this respect, this model is less general than the one considered by Allingham and Sandmo.[2]

The purpose of this paper is to investigate the effect of tax evasion on income distribution. Although this problem is important from a policy point of view, it has not been theoretically explored. In the next section we confine ourselves to the framework of Srinivasan's model, but in the subsequent section, the analysis is extended to a model by Allingham and Sandmo [*1972*].

II SRINIVASAN'S MODEL OF TAX EVASION

Let x be the true income of a taxpayer which is assumed to be a random variable with probability distribution function F(x). This income is known to the taxpayer, but not to the income tax authorities. Suppose the taxpayer knows that π is the probability of his being detected if he understates his income, and let λ be the proportion by which he understates his income. Then his declared income will be

$$y = (1-\lambda)x \tag{2.1}$$

The tax is levied on the declared income provided that he is not detected. If, however, he is detected, he pays both tax on his true income and a penalty on the understated income. If $P(\lambda)$ is the penalty multiplier, then $P(\lambda)\lambda x$ is the penalty on the understated income λx. If T(x) is the tax function, then the expected income of a taxpayer with true income x, will be, after paying taxes and penalty

$$Z(x) = \pi[x - T(x) - \lambda P(\lambda)x] + (1-\pi)[x - T(y)] \tag{2.2}$$

He will now choose λ so as to maximise Z(x). The first order condition for a maximum of (2.2) will then be given by

$$\frac{\partial Z(x)}{\partial \lambda} = -\pi[P(\lambda) + \lambda P'(\lambda)]x + (1-\pi)T'(y)x = 0 \tag{2.3}$$

where use has been made of equation (2.1). The second order condition

$$D = -\pi[2P'(\lambda) + \lambda P''(\lambda)]x - (1-\pi)T''(y)x^2 \tag{2.4}$$

will always be satisfied if we assume that the tax system is progressive, i.e., $T''(x) > 0$ and for all $\lambda \geqslant 0$, $P(\lambda) \geqslant 0$, $P'(\lambda) \geqslant 0$. This means that the penalty multiplier is a positive, increasing and convex function of λ.

With additional assumptions that $P(0) = 0$, i.e., the penalty multiplier is zero when there is no understatement of income, and $T'(0) = 0$, i.e., the marginal tax rate is zero at zero income, it can be seen that

$$\left.\frac{\partial Z(x)}{\partial \lambda}\right|_{\lambda=0} = (1-\pi)T'(x)x > 0 \tag{2.5}$$

and

$$\left.\frac{\partial Z(x)}{\partial \lambda}\right|_{\lambda=1} = -\pi[P(1)+P'(1)]x < 0 \tag{2.6}$$

Together, these two equations imply that there exists a unique solution of λ in the interior of (0,1) which maximises the expected income after taxes and penalties.

If we denote $\epsilon = \frac{\partial \pi}{\partial \xi} \frac{x}{\pi}$ to be the elasticity of the probability of detection with respect to income, then differentiating (2.3) with respect to x, and solving for $\frac{\partial \lambda}{\partial x}$, we obtain

$$\frac{\partial \lambda}{\partial x} = -\frac{(1-\pi)(1-\lambda)\,T''(y)x - \varepsilon T'(y)}{D} \tag{2.7}$$

which is positive for a progressive tax system if $\varepsilon \leqslant 0$. $\varepsilon = 0$ implies that the probability of detection π is independent of income x. If $\varepsilon < 0$, it implies the probability of detection actually falls as income rises. This corresponds to a situation where the richer class of taxpayer succeeds in buying greater immunity from detection because of the greater resources for corrupt gratification which are at its disposal. Therefore, equation (2.7) leads to the conclusion that *given a progressive tax function, the richer a person, the larger the optimal proportion by which he will understate his income, provided the probability of detection π is either independent of x or a decreasing function of x.*

Differentiating (2.1) and using (2.7), we obtain the elasticity of the declared income y with respect to true income x as

$$\eta_y(x) = 1 + \frac{(1-\pi)T''(y)x^2}{D} - \frac{x^2\varepsilon T'(y)}{Dy} \tag{2.8}$$

The second term in (2.8) is negative and its magnitude is less than unity. If $\epsilon=0$, the elasticity $\eta_y(x)$ will be positive. Therefore, from Theorem 2 of Kakwani [*1975*] it follows that the concentration curve of the declared income coincides with its Lorenz curve.[3] Further, it can be seen that the elasticity $\eta_y(x)$ is strictly less than unity for a progressive tax system. Hence, from Corollary 2 of Kakwani [*1977*] it follows that the distribution of the declared income will be Lorenz superior to the distribution of true income. From this we can conclude that *the declared income is more equally distributed than the true income, provided the tax system is progressive and the probability of detection π is independent of x.*

Next, we consider the distribution of the expected after-tax income when there is tax evasion. Differentiating Z(x) in (2.2) with respect to x, and using (2.3) we obtain.

$$\frac{\partial Z}{\partial x} = \pi[1-T'(x)-\lambda P(\lambda)]+(1-\pi)[1-(1-\lambda)T'(y)] \tag{2.9}$$
$$- \frac{\pi\varepsilon}{x}[T(x)-T(y)+\lambda P(\lambda)x]$$

From this equation it is not clear whether the sign of $\frac{\partial Z}{\partial x}$ is unambiguously positive or negative. In order to determine the sign, we consider the value of this derivative at $\lambda=0$. Thus, we have

$$\left.\frac{\partial Z}{\partial x}\right|_{\lambda=0} = 1-T'(x) \tag{2.10}$$

which is positive if the marginal tax-rate is less than unity for all values of x. Differentiating the equation (2.9) with respect to λ gives

$$\frac{\partial}{\partial\lambda}\left(\frac{\partial Z}{\partial x}\right)=(1-\pi)T''(y)-\varepsilon T'(y) \qquad (2.11)$$

where use has been made of (2.3). The right hand side of (2.11) is always positive for $\varepsilon \leqslant 0$. Therefore, this equation implies that $\frac{\partial Z}{\partial x}$ is a monotonic increasing function of λ. Since $\frac{\partial Z}{\partial x}$ is a positive at $\lambda=0$, $\frac{\partial Z}{\partial x}$ will also be positive for all values of x. Thus, applying Theorem 2 of Kakwani [*1975*], we arrive at the conclusion that the concentration curve of the after-tax income distribution coincides with its Lorenz curve, provided the tax system is progressive and $\varepsilon \leqslant 0$.

Elasticity of Z(x) with respect to x is obtained from (2.9) as

$$\eta_z(x)=1-\frac{1}{Z}\,[\pi T(x)\{\eta_t(x)-1\}+(1-\pi)T(y)\{\eta_t(y)-1\}] \qquad (2.12)$$
$$\pi\varepsilon\{T(x)-T(y)+\lambda P(\lambda)x\}]$$

where $\eta_t(x)$ is the elasticity of the tax function T(x) with respect to x. For a progressive tax system, $\eta_t(x)$ is clearly greater than unity for all values of x. Therefore, if $\varepsilon=0$ the equation (2.12) implies that the elasticity $\eta_z(x)$ will always be less than unity for all values of x. Hence, from Corollary 2 of Kakwani [*1977*] it follows that the distribution of the after-tax income distribution will be Lorenz superior to the distribution of the true before-tax income. From this we can conclude that *if the tax system is progressive the after-tax distribution will be more equally distributed than the before-tax income distribution, even if there is tax evasion, and provided the probability of detection is independent of income x.*

If the tax system is proportional, the tax elasticity $\eta_t(x)$ will be unity for all values of x which from (2.12) implies that if $\varepsilon<0$, $\eta_z(x)$ will be greater than unity for all x. Again, from Corollary 2 of Kakwani [*1977*] it follows that the distribution of after tax income will be Lorenz inferior to the distribution of the true before tax income. From this we can conclude that *if the tax system is proportional, the after-tax distribution will be more unequally distributed than the before-tax income distribution provided the probability of detection is a decreasing function of income*. Further, it can be seen that if $\varepsilon=0$, $\eta_z(x)$ will be unity for all x. This result immediately leads to the conclusion that *if the tax system is proportional and the probability of detection is independent of income, the inequality of both before- and after-tax incomes will be identical even if there is tax evasion.*

Substituting $\lambda=0$ in (2.12), $\eta_z(x)$ becomes

$$\eta_d(x)=1-\frac{T(x)[\eta_t(x)-1]}{x-T(x)} \tag{2.13}$$

which is the elasticity of after-tax income when there is no tax evasion. Therefore, the difference between the two elasticities, viz.,

$$\eta_z(x)-\eta_d(x) \tag{2.14}$$

will be zero when $\lambda=0$. Differentiating (2.14) with respect to λ gives

$$\frac{\partial}{\partial\lambda}[\eta_z(x)-\eta_d(x)]=\frac{x(1-\pi)yT''(y)-\varepsilon xT'(y)}{Z} \tag{2.15}$$

where use has been made of (2.11). The right hand side of (2.15) is positive if the tax system is progressive and $\varepsilon\leqslant 0$. This shows that $\eta_z(x)-\eta_d(x)$ is a monotonic increasing function of λ, and at $\lambda=0$, this function is equal to zero. Hence, $\eta_z(x)\geqslant\eta_d(x)$ must be true for any λ in the interior of (0, 1). From Theorem 2 of Kakwani [*1977*] it implies that the distribution Z(x) will be Lorenz inferior to the distribution of d(x). Note that d(x) is the after-tax income when there was no tax evasion. From this we can conclude that *given a progressive tax system and probability of detection π either independent of income x or a decreasing function of x, the after-tax income will be more unequally distributed in the presence of understatement than in its absence.*

We shall now examine the way in which the distribution of the after-tax income depends on the probability of detection.

Differentiating (2.3) with respect to π, and solving for $\frac{\partial \lambda}{\partial \pi}$, we obtain

$$\frac{\partial \lambda}{\partial \pi} = \frac{xT'(y)}{\pi D} \tag{2.16}$$

which is always negative. This leads to Corollary 1 of Srinivasan which states that, *ceteris paribus*, the optimal proportion λ by which income is understated decreases as the probability of detection π increases.

Differentiating the elasticity $\eta_z(x)$ with respect to π gives

$$\begin{aligned}\frac{\partial \eta_z(x)}{\partial \pi} = -\frac{T(x)}{Z}\,[\eta_t(x) - \eta_z(x)] + \frac{T(y)}{Z}\,[\eta_t(y) - \eta_z(x)] \\ -\frac{x\lambda P(\lambda)}{Z}\,[1 - \eta_z(x)] + x(1-\pi)yT''(y)\frac{\partial \lambda}{\partial \pi}\end{aligned} \tag{2.17}$$

Now we have to examine the sign of the expression on the right hand side of (2.17). It has been shown earlier that $\eta_z(x) < 1$ for all x and if the tax system is progressive and $\varepsilon = 0$. Further for a progressive tax system the elasticities $\eta_t(x)$ and $\eta_t(y)$ will be always greater than unity for all values of x and y. Therefore, the first term on the right hand side of (2.17) will be negative, whereas the second term will be positive. Since the tax system is progressive and $x \geqslant y$, therefore, $T(x) \geqslant T(y)$ and $\eta_t(x) \geqslant \eta_t(y)$. These two conditions together imply that the first term in (2.17) will be of higher magnitude than the second term. The third and fourth terms on the right hand side of (2.17) are clearly negative because $\eta_z(x) < 1$, and $\frac{\partial \lambda}{\partial \pi}$ has already been shown to be negative in (2.16). Hence, we have proved that the elasticity $\eta(x)$ decreases as $\pi(x)$ increases. This result has an interesting implication. From Theorem 1 of Kakwani (1977) it would imply that as we increase π, the Lorenz curve of the after-tax income distribution will shift upward towards the egalitarian line. *Thus, we can conclude that the inequality of the expected income, after paying taxes and penalties, decreases as the probability of detection π increases.*

This result is important from a policy point of view. An increase in probability of detection not only increases the tax revenue for the Government but also makes the after tax income distribution more egalitarian. Srinivasan [*1973*] and Singh [*1973*] have considered the problem of allocation of resources for detection of income understatement. Srinivasan [*1973*] arrived at the conclusion that so long as the marginal increase in the expected revenue (net of cost) to the Government remains positive, resources should be allocated to the detection of tax evasion. Both Srinivasan [*1973*] and Singh [*1973*] have ignored the egalitarian implications of increasing the probability of detection. In their model the amount of expenditure on the detection is determined by maximising the difference between the cost of scrutiny and the expected revenue and penalties. To incorporate the egalitarian aspect of the probability of detection, Srinivasan's model needs to be extended so that the amount of expenditure on detection is determined by maximising the social welfare function instead of the expected tax revenue.

III TAX EVASION MODEL INCORPORATING RISK AVERSION BEHAVIOUR OF TAXPAYERS

In this section, we consider an alternative model of tax evasion outlined by Allingham and Sandmo in 1972, which incorporates the observed phenomenon of risk aversion in the behaviour of taxpayers. Using the framework of this model we shall investigate the effect of tax evasion on income inequality.

Following Allingham and Sandmo, we assume that the taxpayer's behaviour conforms to the Von Neumann-Morgenstern axioms on behaviour under uncertainty. His cardinal utility u(x) is a function of income x only. The marginal utility is assumed to be everywhere positive and strictly decreasing so that the taxpayer is risk averse.

Assume that tax is levied at the constant rate θ on the declared income y. λ is again the proportion by which he understates his income. α is the additional penalty on his undeclared income λx, if caught. Note that the penalty rate α is higher than θ. The taxpayer will choose λ so as to maximise

$$E[u(x)]=(1-\pi)u(X)+\pi u(Y) \tag{3.1}$$

where

$$X=x-\theta(1-\lambda)x \tag{3.2}$$

and

$$Y=x-\theta(1-\lambda)x-\alpha\lambda x \tag{3.3}$$

The first order condition for the maximum of (3.1) can be written as

$$\frac{\partial E[u(x)]}{\partial\lambda}=(1-\pi)u'(X)\theta x-\pi u'(Y)x(\alpha-\theta)=0 \tag{3.4}$$

The second order condition,

$$\frac{\partial^2 E[u(x)]}{\partial\lambda^2}=D=(1-\pi)u''(X)\theta^2x^2+\pi u''(Y)x^2(\alpha-\theta)^2 \tag{3.5}$$

will always be satisfied because of the assumption of concave utility function.

We can now consider the conditions under which the optimal solution of λ lies in the interior of (0, 1). If $\lambda>0$, then $\frac{\partial E[u(x)]}{\partial\lambda}$ must increase with λ in the neighbourhood of $\lambda=0$.

This gives $$\left.\frac{\partial E[u(x)]}{\partial\lambda}\right|_{\lambda=0}=x(\theta-\alpha\pi)u'((1-\theta)x)>0 \tag{3.6}$$

Similarly for $\lambda<1$, $\frac{\partial E[u(x)]}{\partial\lambda}$ must decrease with λ in the neighbourhood of $\lambda=1$. This gives

$$\left.\frac{\partial E[u(x)]}{\partial\lambda}\right|_{\lambda=1}=(1-\pi)u'(x)\theta x-\pi u'((1-\alpha)x)x(\alpha-\theta)<0 \tag{3.7}$$

The conditions (3.4) and (3.5) can be written as

$$\theta>\pi\alpha \tag{3.8}$$

$$\pi\alpha>\theta[\pi+(1-\pi)\frac{u'(x)}{u'((1-\alpha)x)}] \tag{3.9}$$

which if satisfied will guarantee a unique optimal solution of λ in the interior of (0, 1).

It will be useful to introduce here the measures of risk aversion in order to evaluate our results on income distribution. The well-known Pratt-Arrow measures of risk aversion are:

Absolute risk aversion:

$$R_A(x) = -\frac{u''(x)}{u'(x)} \tag{3.10}$$

Relative risk aversion:

$$R_R(x) = -\frac{u''(x).x}{u'(x)} \tag{3.11}$$

The following hypotheses on risk aversion have been advanced by Arrow [*1965*].

(a) *Decreasing absolute risk aversion* i.e. $R_A(x)$ is a decreasing function of x. This hypothesis implies that the absolute amount invested in the risky assets increases with the size of the portfolio.

(b) *Increasing relative risk aversion,* i.e. $R_R(x)$ is an increasing function of x. This hypothesis implies that the proportion of the amount invested in the risky assets decreases with the size of portfolio.

Using the above definitions of risk aversion, D defined in (3.5) can now be written as

$$D = -(1-\pi)\theta x^2 u'(X)[\theta R_A(X) + (\alpha-\theta)R_A(Y)] \tag{3.12}$$

Further, differentiating (3.4) with respect to x and solving for $\frac{\partial\lambda}{\partial x}$, we obtain

$$\frac{\partial\lambda}{\partial x} = \frac{(1-\pi)\theta u'(X)}{D} \quad [R_R(X) - R_R(Y)] \tag{3.13}$$

where use has been made of equation (3.11). D is unambiguously negative and, therefore, the sign of $\frac{\partial\lambda}{\partial x}$ depends on whether the relative risk aversion is an increasing or decreasing function of x. Since $X>Y$, $R_R(X)>R_R(Y)$ would imply the hypothesis of increasing relative risk aversion. From this we can conclude that *the richer a person, the larger (smaller) is the optimal proportion by which he will understate his income if the relative risk aversion is a decreasing (increasing) function of income.*

The declared income of a taxpayer is given by (2.1) which on differentiating with respect to x and using (3.13), becomes

$$\frac{\partial y}{\partial x} = (1-\lambda) - x\frac{\partial \lambda}{\partial x} \tag{3.14}$$

$\frac{\partial \lambda}{\partial x}$ is negative under the hypothesis of increasing relative risk aversion which makes the derivative $\frac{\partial y}{\partial x}$ unambiguously positive. From this we can conclude that *given the hypothesis of increasing relative risk aversion, the richer a person, the larger will be his declared income.* Allingham and Sandmo [*1972*] arrived at the same conclusion under the assumption that $\alpha \geqslant 1$, which is rather restrictive.

Using Theorem 2 of Kakwani [*1975*] it follows immediately that the concentration curve of the declared income will coincide with its Lorenz curve. To compare the inequality of declared income with that of true income we need to derive the elasticity of y with respect to x. This elasticity is derived from (3.14)

$$\eta_y(x) = 1 - \frac{x^2}{y}\frac{\partial \lambda}{\partial x} \tag{3.15}$$

where use has been made of equation (2.1). The elasticity will be greater than unity for all x if $\frac{\partial \lambda}{\partial x}$ is negative for all x. $\frac{\partial \lambda}{\partial x}$ is indeed negative under the assumption of increasing relative risk aversion. Therefore, from Corollary 2 of Kakwani [*1977*] it immediately follows that the distribution of y will be Lorenz inferior to the distribution of x. Thus, we can conclude that *the declared income will be more unequally distributed than the true income provided the relative risk aversion is an increasing function of income.*

Next, we consider the distribution of the after-tax expected income which is given by

$$Z(x) = (1-\pi)X + \pi Y \tag{3.16}$$

The first derivative of Z(x) with respect to x is derived from (3.14) and (3.3) as

$$\frac{\partial Z(z)}{\partial x}=-\frac{(1-\pi)\theta x^2 u'(X)[\theta Y+(\alpha-\theta)X][\pi R_A(X)+(1-\pi)R_A(Y)]}{Dx} \tag{3.17}$$

which is unambiguously positive. This implies that *the larger the true income before tax, the larger will be the expected income after tax.* From Theorem 2 of Kakwani [*1975*] it immediately follows that the concentration curve for Z(x) will coincide with its Lorenz curve.

The elasticity of Z(x) with respect to x is obtained from (3.15) as

$$\eta_Z(x)=\frac{[\theta Y+(\alpha-\theta)X][\pi R_A(X)+(1-\pi)R_A(Y)]}{Z[\theta R_A(X)+(\alpha-\theta)R_A(Y)]} \tag{3.18}$$

which simplifies to

$$\eta_Z(x)=1-\frac{(\theta-\alpha\pi)[R_R(X)-R_R(Y)]}{Z[\theta R_A(X)+(\alpha-\theta)R_A(Y)]} \tag{3.19}$$

This equation implies that the elasticity $\eta_Z(x)$ will be less (greater) than unity for all x, if the relative risk aversion is an increasing (decreasing) function of x. Applying Corollary 2 of Kakwani [*1977*] it follows that the distribution of Z(x) will be Lorenz superior (inferior) to the distribution of x if the elasticity of Z(x) is less (greater) than unity for all x. Thus, we can conclude that *expected income after paying taxes and penalties will be more (or less) equally distributed than the before-tax true income if relative risk aversion is increasing (or decreasing).*

NOTES

1. Also see Kolm [*1973*] for a further analysis of this model.
2. Singh [*1973*], has analysed the policy implications of Srinivasan's model in the context of the Indian situation.
3. The concentration curve of the declared income y is the relationship between $F_1(y)$ and F(x), where $F_1(y)$ is the proportion of the declared income of the taxpayers who have true income less than or equal to x. For details see Kakwani [*1975, 1977*].

REFERENCES

Allingham, M. G. and A. Sandmo, 1972, 'Income Tax Evasion; A theoretical Analysis', *Journal of Public Economics*, Vol. 1, September.

Arrow, K. J., 1965, *Aspects of the Theory of Risk Bearing*, Helsinki.

Kakwani, N. C., 1975, 'Applications of Lorenz curves in Economic Analysis', International Bank for Reconstruction and Development, Development Research Center, Discussion Paper No. 12, August.

Kakwani, N. C., 1977, 'Applications of Lorenz Curves in Economic Analysis', *Econometrica*, Vol. 45, April.

Kolm, S. C., 1973, 'A Note on Optimum Tax Evasion', *Journal of Public Economics*, Vol. 2, pp. 265–70.

Singh, B., 1973, 'Making Honesty the Best Policy', *Journal of Public Economics*, Vol. 2, pp. 257–63.

Srinivasan, T. N., 1973, 'Tax Evasion a Model' *Journal of Public Economics*, Vol. 2, pp. 339–46.

Chapter 8

Progressive Public Utility Rates as an Income Redistribution Device in Developing Countries: the case of Municipal Water

MARTIN T. KATZMAN*

I. INTRODUCTION

The use of progressive public utility rates is one method by which several developing countries are attempting to redistribute income. In several cities of Venezuela, Colombia and Malaysia, for example, domestic water is priced at increasing-block rates, rather than the decreasing-block rates which are so common in the United States.[1] Increasing-block or progressive rate structures are intended to charge according to the ability-to-pay principle, with little regard to cost of service.

The utilisation of progressive rate structures as an income redistribution device rests upon two apparently reasonable assumptions, which are examined here. First, there is a perceived positive income-elasticity of demand for water, electricity, and telephone service, which implies that the 'taxable base' increases with income. Second, the price-elasticity of demand for utilities is perceived as close to zero, especially at the high income levels. This assumption implies that the 'tax' on utility consumption is not easily shifted from consumer to producer. Granted these assumptions, progressive rates engender a cross-subsidisation of consumers, which permits the poor to receive such 'necessities' as water

*Professor and Head, Graduate Program in Political Economy, University of Texas at Dallas.

below cost without violating the financial autonomy of the public utility enterprise. These considerations are especially attractive when financing is sought from multilateral development banks, which invariably insist upon the establishment of a self-financing enterprise fund as a prerequisite for the loan and which are increasingly demanding that projects they finance address the problems of the poor.

In this paper, the efficiency of progressive utility rates as an income-redistribution mechanism is examined through the analysis of a unique survey of domestic water consumers in Penang, Malaysia. In Section II, the conceptual rationale for progressive utility rates is examined. In particular, evidence for income-elasticity and price-inelasticity is considered with particular emphasis on developing countries. Section III presents empirical evidence on income redistributed through the progressive water rate structure in Penang. In contrast to most previous research on utilities consumption, this section is based upon a cross-sectional survey that identifies other influences on consumption in addition to income. This survey demonstrates that the zero-order correlation between income and water consumption is quite low, because other major influences on consumption like family size are not highly correlated with income. Consequently, a substantial share of poor families consume more water than many rich families, which implies that progressive rates are an inefficient technique of income redistribution. Section IV suggests that a more efficient technique of income redistribution is charging flat rates and earmarking property taxes for the water authority.

II. THE CASE FOR PROGRESSIVE UTILITY RATES

(a) *The Setting*

The case for progressive utility rates in developing countries must be placed in the context of conventional patterns of service delivery and the techniques of financing these services. Unlike developed countries, where electricity, piped-in water, telephone service, and to a lesser extent piped-in gas, are ubiquitous, these services are generally available only in urban areas, particularly in high-income neighbourhoods. To the extent that these services are financed by users, this pattern of delivery does not result in any major transfers among income classes. While it is dangerous to generalise about all utilities in all developing countries, it has been typical for 'populist' governments to place ceilings on utility rates that have forced public utilities to run deficits, which are often compounded by severe inflation. Such deficits are invariably covered by governmental subsidy.[2] Since governmental revenues are usually drawn from the whole population, this pattern of financing results in an income redistribution from poor to rich.

For example, in a review of domestic water supply conditions, the Ford Foundation International Urban Survey notes that

> repeatedly authors have stated that even when modern supply systems exist, they only supply a small proportion of the population, the wealthiest sector. . . . Another common feature of urban water systems in under-developed areas is that they frequently run at a loss. . . . Too often water is provided for high income houses, thus subsidising the rich from general taxation.[3]

In a similar vein, the World Bank, which is playing an increasing role in the financing of municipal utilities in developing countries, states:

> Within a particular service category . . . the poor are most likely to be excluded. In Latin America, for example, only 59 per cent of the urban population is served by piped water and another 17 per cent by public standpipes. Studies in Bogota, Catagena, and Mexico City show that variations in neighbourhood income explain most of the variations between neighbourhoods in piped water supply. In Libreville, Gabon, only one-fourth of all households have piped water, but only 5 per cent of the total water supply is available to other, presumably the poor, households. Similar results were obtained for sewerage and electricity. Alternatively, the structure of prices can be in such a form so as to price the services out of the reach of lower income groups. Declining block rate tariffs and quantity discounts also discriminate against those with limited purchasing power. Poor households often pay higher unit charges for services under these arrangements.[4]

(b) *New Pressures for Rate Reform*

The inability of many developing countries to finance the

'needed' public utility investments internally has given increased leverage to multilateral lending agencies such as the World Bank and the several regional development banks. As a condition of lending, these financial intermediaries generally insist that revenue-generating projects be financed entirely out of user charges rather than general tax revenue. The purpose of this stricture is to enhance the managerial autonomy of the project managers, who do not have to rely upon 'political' appropriation decisions and who can therefore operate 'professionally'. This principle invariably results in increases in rates above those of the pricing rules conventionally employed in developing countries. While such an increase in user charges can potentially reduce the tax burden on that segment of the poor not served by the utilities, it increases the total financial burden at that segment of the lower-income population which is served. An increasingly important condition of lending that the development banks are attempting to impose, is that projects improve, or at least do not make worse, the income distribution. To the extent that total reliance on user charges results in an increase in burden on at least a portion of the poor, the goal of financial-managerial autonomy may conflict with the goal of income redistribution. The progressive rate structure provides one mechanism for reconciling the pressures for managerial autonomy and equity.

(c) *The Triple Trade-off*

The recent literature on the income redistribution effects of public utility pricing assumes the conventional two-parameter consumption function, with price and income as the arguments. From this follows that larger consumers are of higher income and that surcharges above marginal cost on 'luxuries' such as higher levels of water is redistributive. Since greater amounts of redistribution requires greater violations of the marginal cost pricing rule, the familiar trade-off between equity and allocative efficiency emerges.[5] To the extent that consumption depends upon other arguments, like family size and age composition, the additional consideration of redistributive efficiency is necessary.

(d) *The Mechanics of Progressive Rates*

The current rate structure of the Penang Water Authority in Malaysia is not atypical of the progressive structures which exist in some other developing countries (Table 1, Panel A). Almost a mirror image of the declining-block rate structure common in the United States, the rate structure in Penang divides consumers into domestic and 'trade'—i.e. commercial or industrial. Domestic consumers pay according to an increasing-block rate, while trade users pay according to a flat rate schedule, which is considerably above the maximum for domestic users.

TABLE 1

WATER RATE SCHEDULES, PENANG STATE*

	minimum	*thousands of gallons/month* <5	5–10	10–30	30–50	50+
A. Penang Water Authority						
residential	$2.00	·60	·95	·95	·95	·95
commercial	5.00	1·30	1·30	1·30	1·30	1·30
B. City Water Department						
urban	1.00	·50	·50	·55	·65	·80
rural	1.00	·60	·60	·60	·80	·90

* In January 1973, the Penang Water Authority assumed the functions of the City Water Department and state waterworks, which served the remainder of the state. In May 1973, the rate structure in Panel A superseded that in Panel B.

As indicated above, there are several attractive features of this rate structure. First, the income-elasticity of demand for water is significantly different from zero. In the American context, this elasticity is of the order of 0·5—1·0 for domestic water. While the data are sparse for developing countries, one study suggests an income elasticity of demand of 0·4.[6] Second, the price-elasticity of demand is perceived to be low. Engineers, who dominate domestic water resource planning throughout the world, tend to perceive the price elasticity of demand as zero. In fact, a plethora of American studies of water demand indicate a price-elasticity of demand of the order of —0·1 to −0·4, while a study of water demand across cities in developing countries obtains a price-elasticity of demand for electricity of the order of −0·5.[7] To the extent that both price- and income-elasticities of demand differ from zero, progressive rate structures result in an underconsumption on the part of the rich and overconsumption on the part of the poor, with respect to that generated by a cost-of-service pricing rule.

(e) *Critique*

The progressive rate structure can be criticised as violating the marginal cost pricing rules for efficient resource allocation. For domestic consumption, this critique is not so telling as it initially appears. While it is clear that the marginal cost of water will tend to exceed its marginal utility to the poor (the contrary being true for the rich), the total resources devoted to the production of water may not differ substantially from the optimum since these 'distortions' in consumption will more or less cancel. It is in the distribution of water that the inefficiencies exist: i.e. the marginal utility of water to the rich surpasses that of the poor. Since arbitrage in water is practically impossible, potentially Pareto optimal redistribution of consumption cannot be achieved.

Such inefficiencies in consumption suggest the nostrum of lump-sum cash transfers as a method of income redistribution rather than transfers in kind. This remedy is subject to two objections, one practical, the other conceptual. The practical objection, which may not apply so forcefully in advanced countries, is that the fiscal system in developing countries is administratively incapable of delivering cash subsidies to the poor. Direct delivery of services may be the only mechanism by which transfer to the poor can be operationalised. The conceptual objection is that the rich derive external economies from the consumption of the poor for only certain 'necessities' or 'merit goods', such as education, shelter, health care, or water. In other words, when the direct marginal utility the poor obtain from consuming water is added to the external marginal utility generated for the rich, distortions in consumption patterns may vanish. This is clearly apparent when the rich collectively vote to institute progressive rates for the benefit of the poor.[8]

The objection to placing the burden of subsidising the poor on commercial-industrial consumers is more persuasive. To the extent that capital markets and product markets are internationally competitive, the higher rates for industrial water will be passed on to the local workers in the form of lower wages, rather than being borne by capital.[9] To the extent that capital markets and product markets are localised, higher water rates will be partially borne by the consumer through increased prices and partially by owners of capital through decreased sales and hence profits. In fact, goods produced in Penang compete internationally (e.g. assembly of computer equipment), and include goods of low-income elasticity of demand (necessities) and that are unskilled-labour intensive, such as textiles. These factors suggest that the incidence of higher than average industrial rates may be regressive.

These theoretical arguments aside, the empirically interesting question is what difference a particular progressive rate structure makes in the utility bills paid by each income class, relative to a flat rate schedule. This depends upon two relationships: (1) between income and consumption, and (2) between the particular distribution of consumption and the particular block schedule. The former may be taken as exogenous; the latter, as subject to pricing policy.

The relationship between income and consumption not only refers to the income-elasticity of demand, which is an average relationship, but also the correlation between income and consumption. To the extent that consumption is influenced by other factors, such as family size and life cycle, which may be randomly distributed among income groups, the zero-order relationship between income and consumption becomes attenuated. The weaker this zero-order correlation, the less efficient is a progressive rate structure as an income redistribution device.

The relationship between the distribution of consumption and the block structure, i.e. the number of steps and their steepness, is a matter of policy. Conceivably, any degree of progressivity can be obtained by varying the steepness. This does not imply that any degree of income redistribution can be thus obtained. Only in the extreme case that income and consumption are perfectly correlated can any desired degree of redistribution be obtained by altering the steepness of the rate schedule, regardless of the numerical value of the income elasticity. In the more general case, the correlation between income and consumption takes some low, but positive, value. While any degree of income redistribution can be achieved *on the average*, fewer of the poor and more of the rich will be receiving subsidies, the lower the above correlation. The lower the correlation, the greater the inefficiency of income redistribution through manipulation of the steepness of the rate structure.

III. EMPIRICAL RESULTS

In the entire literature on the demand for services of public utilities, there are few household data which permit any measures of the efficiency of progressive rate structures. Nearly all of the previous studies of electricity and water utilise aggregate (municipal or state) time-series or cross-section data. The few studies that use individual data do not report the zero-order correlations between income and utility consumption. Given this tradition, the household water consumption survey for Penang stands out as a unique, although far from ideal, data source.[10]

(a) *The Survey*

At the instigation of the City Water Department, social scientists from Universiti Sains Malaysia undertook a survey of households in April 1972. A stratified random sample of domestic consumers was selected for closed-end interviews. Approximately 85 per cent of the target population eventually were interviewed about their patterns of water consumption and other family characteristics. At most only three to six per cent of the respondents refused to answer sensitive questions, such as the level of the family income. About 1400 usable questionnaires were generated, comprising five per cent of the users in most metering districts, and a 20–25 per cent sample in especially selected districts discussed below. Reported monthly water consumption was verified against actually recorded consumption for the months of February, March, and April of 1972.

(b) *The Rate Structure in 1972*

Before May 1973, the City Water Department had a progressive rate schedule which differentiated between different urban and rural areas, delineated by the city limits of the capital city (Table 1, Panel B). Because population was sparser in the rural areas, the cost of main extensions per household was higher. The cost differential was estimated as M$0·10 per thousand gallons, which separated urban and rural schedules at most levels of consumption. In both urban and rural areas, there was a minimum monthly fee of M$1. In the period 1968–72, revenues were sufficient to meet operating costs and debt service, as well as to provide internal financing for normal main extension. These three items averaged M$0·57–0·63 per thousand gallons in that period.[11]

While the rate structure of the City Water Department, unlike that of other parts of Penang, made no distinction between domestic and trade users, almost all consumers in the highest rate classes are from the latter group.

It is noteworthy that only two per cent of all consumers fall into the minimum rate category and another two per cent consume more than 30 thousand gallons per month. In other words, although the rate schedule gives an appearance of great progressivity, domestic consumers essentially fall into two blocks.

Average monthly consumption and average monthly water bills are regressed against family size, income (represented by dummy variables), and urban-rural residence. With families of monthly incomes below M$150 as the reference point, it is apparent that water consumption increases with income, especially above the M$500 level. Similarly water bills tend to rise with income (Table 2).

By inserting the mean value of family size (7·87) into the regressions in Table 2, an estimate of the water consumption-income relationship can be derived as in Table 3.

This regression, however, does not imply that progressive rates are an efficient form of income redistribution. It is

TABLE 2

DETERMINANTS OF MONTHLY WATER CONSUMPTION AND WATER BILLS, SPRING 1972

	average monthly consumption, thous. gal. b	(S_b)	*average monthly bill, M$* b	(S_b)
persons/household	·93*	(·03)	·57*	(·02)
income >M$800	4·72*	(·51)	3·55*	(·37)
income, M$500–800	2·53*	(·55)	2·35*	(·40)
income, M$150–500	·08	(·41)	·41*	(·30)
urban (1=yes/0=no)	2·01*	(·34)	·82*	(·25)
constant	·65		1·88	
r^2=	·45*		·37*	
s.e.	5·99		4·31	

Source: Universiti Sains Survey; n=1400.
*significant, 0·05

TABLE 3

ESTIMATES OF WATER CONSUMPTION BY DIFFERENT INCOME GROUPS

monthly income	*thous. gals* *urban*	*rural*
M$ 0–150	10·00	7·99
150–500	10·08	8·07
500–800	12·53	10·52
800 plus	14·72	12·71

noteworthy that the rank-order correlation between family size and water consumption (r=0·62) is considerably higher than income and water consumption (r=0·16). Since family size is essentially uncorrelated (r=0·09) with income, there would appear to be a substantial number of poor, but large families paying higher water bills than wealthy, but small families.

This can be verified by cross-tabulating income with water consumption and water bills. The distribution of each income group across consumption classes shows only forty per cent of the poorest families fall entirely into the lowest rate class, while fully 10 per cent of the wealthy families fall into that class (Table 4, Panel A). Similarly, about 22 per cent of the very poor are paying more than M$6 per month, while about 31 per cent of the rich are paying less than this amount (Table 4, Panel B).

TABLE 4

INCOME VS. WATER CONSUMPTION AND WATER BILL, 1972

Panel A. Income vs. monthly water consumption

income	*gals, thous.* *rates*	*< 10* *50¢/60¢*	*10+* *55¢/60¢*	*total*
M$ < 150		80·7	19·3	100.
150–500		68·5	31·5	100.
500–800		67·7	32·3	100.
800 plus		57·4	42·6	100.
total		68·6	31·4	100.

Chi-square significant < ·001
Cramer's V=0·188

Panel B. Income vs. monthly water bill

income	*M$ 1–3*	*4–5*	*6–8*	*9+*	*total*
M$ < 150	51·4	26·4	10·1	12·1	100.
150–500	27·2	32·5	24·3	16·3	100.
500–800	18·1	33·0	28·2	20·9	100.
800 plus	7·1	23·4	39·2	30·3	100.
total	26·8	29·7	25·0	18·6	100.

Chi-square significant < ·001
Cramer's V=0·221

(c) Effect of Alternative Rate Structures

Two assumptions are critical in comparing the water bills of income groups under alternative rate structures: first, that the price-elasticity of demand is zero;[12] second, that the alternative rate structures all raise the same average revenue per thousand gallons. In addition, we assume that the mean incomes of the four groups are M$100, 325, 650, and 800, respectively.

As a baseline, the water bills of the four income groups are computed on the actual 1972 rates, consumption by income and by residence category having been estimated above (see Table 3). Water bills in Malaysian dollars and as a percentage of income are listed in Table 5.

TABLE 5

WATER BILLS M$ AND AS PERCENTAGE OF INCOME, 1972 RATES, PENANG

	mean income	*Malaysian dollars*		*% of income*	
		urban	*rural*	*urban*	*rural*
very poor	100	5·00	4·80	5·0%	4·8%
poor	325	5·04	4·84	1·6	1·5
medium	650	6·39	6·31	1·0	1·0
rich	800	7·60	7·63	1·0	1·0

The change in water bills from the baseline above, as a percentage of income, is examined under alternative rate structures, e.g. elimination of cross-subsidies among domestic consumers, and elimination of cross-subsidies from commercial-industrial to domestic consumers (Table 6).

TABLE 6

CHANGES IN URBAN WATER BILLS IN M$ AND AS A PERCENTAGE OF INCOME UNDER ALTERNATIVE RATE STRUCTURES

Case 1. *Elimination of cross-subsidy among domestic consumers.*

	M$	% of income
very poor	+0·06	+0·06
poor	+0·06	+0·01
medium	−0·05	−0·01
rich	−0·15	−0·02

Case 2. *Elimination of cross-subsidy from trade to domestic consumers.*

	M$	% of income
very poor	+1·43	+1·43
poor	+1·44	+0·44
medium	+1·67	+0·26
rich	+1·86	+0·23

Case 1. *Elimination of cross-subsidies among domestic consumers* is equivalent to retaining the distinction between domestic and trade consumers, but charging at two different flat rates. To test the effects of this change, it is assumed that the revenues raised from domestic consumers remain the same, but that all urban consumers are charged at a constant rate regardless of level of consumption.

The weighted averages of domestic consumption and domestic water bills are 11·25 thousand gallons and M$5·69, respectively (Table 7, cols. a-c). The average charge per thousand gallons, then is M$0·506.

Applying this flat rate to average consumption levels of each income group, one finds that water bills for the very poor and poor rise by about M$0·06, which is less than one-tenth of one per cent of income. Cross-subsidies among consumers, then, can hardly contribute to a major income redistribution in Penang.

Case 2. *Elimination of cross-subsidies from trade to domestic users* is equivalent to applying a flat rate to all consumers regardless of purpose or level of consumption. In 1972, average revenue of M$0·643 was raised from the sale of water.[13] Applying this rate to the average consumption level of each income group, one finds that water bills increase for all. While the absolute increase is greater for the higher-income groups, the percentage increase is greater for the lower-income groups. For example, in the absence of cross-subsidisation, the very poor would be spending 1·43 per cent more of their income on water; the rich, only 0·23 per cent more.

This gain by the very poor from the progressive rate structure may be overstated. As suggested above, to the extent that commercial-industrial consumers pass their increased cost on to consumers, in the form of higher prices, or to workers, in the form of lower wages, the gain by the very poor may be more imaginary than real. In the absence of an empirical general equilibrium model of the Penang economy, however, it is impossible to quantify these effects.

IV. EARMARKED PROPERTY TAXATION AS AN ALTERNATIVE

An alternative technique for redistributing income through public utilities is suggested by the technique of earmarking property taxes, which is used in some cities of Colombia[14] as well as in areas of Malaysia. In parts of Penang state outside of the jurisdiction of the City Water Department, a three per cent tax was levied on the annual (rental) value of real property and earmarked for the water department. As the tax was only administered in urban areas, only a small proportion of water revenues (10–15 per cent) were raised in this manner; the remainder, through a proportional water charge.

As an alternative to the progressive rate structure, we can consider a residential property tax-cum-proportional user charge that raises the same sum from domestic consumers as does the current progressive rate structure. This implies the retention of cross-subsidies from trade to domestic users. The method of estimation involves several steps:

1. *Calculating rental payments for each income group.* The Universiti Sains Water Survey reports rents by seven categories. Unfortunately, only 36 per cent of all respondents rented their dwellings, the remainder being owners. Since there is no significant difference in income distribution between renters and the population as a whole on Penang Island, the pattern of observed rental payments can be assumed to correspond to the pattern of imputed rentals for which an owner can be assessed. From this rental distribution, the mean rent of each income group is computed.

2. *Calculating the property tax bills.* The monthly property tax bills that a three per cent levy implies is computed for each income group. As can be seen in Table 7 (col. d), property taxes would be only M$1·35 for the very poor and fully M$8·10 for the rich. Given the income distribution, the average property tax bill per household is M$3·06.

3. *Calculating the necessary user fees.* Since the average urban water bill is M$5.69, only M$2.63 must be raised from the average household from user fees. With the average household consuming 11·25 thousand gallons per month (col. 2), the average charge need be only M$2·23 per thousand gallons.

4. *Recalculating the household user charges.* Charging a flat rate of 23 cents per thousand, the user charges for each income group are recalculated (col. e).

5. *Summing taxes and user charges.* The total water charges for each income group is now obtained by summing property

TABLE 7

EFFECTS OF RETURNING TO A THREE PER CENT PROPERTY TAX PLUS PROPORTIONAL USER CHARGES

	a	b	c	d	e	f	g	h
				hypothetical				
income group	*monthly consumption thous. gal*	*% of all consumers*	*actual bills*	*3% property tax bill*	*user charges*	*total d+e*	*c-f/income*	*bill under efficient pricing*
very poor	10·00	18·8	M$5·00	M$1·35	M$2·30	M$3·65	−1·35%	4·27
poor	10·08	48·5	5·04	1·74	2·32	4·06	−0·30%	4·52
medium	12·53	14·3	6·39	3·36	2·88	6·24	+0·02%	6·31
rich	14·72	18·3	7·60	8·10	3·39	11·49	+0·49%	9·77
weighted ave.	11·25	100.00	5·69	3·06	2·68	5·69		5·69

tax payments and user charges (col f). These can be compared to actual water bills (col. c).

A comparison of actual and hypothetical water bills by income group indicates that the shift from progressive water rates to property taxation would have pro-poor consequences on the average.

The most interesting aspect of the use of property taxes is their efficiency. On the basis of the Universiti Sains Survey, it is clear that the correlation between rents and water consumption (r=0·04) is even lower than that between income and water consumption (r=0·16). What is more striking is the very high correlation between rents and income (r=0·68; Cramer V=0·46). These latter correlations imply that a proportional tax on rentals can be a more efficient method of income distribution, even if the burden of the tax is completely shifted from the owner to the renter. To the extent that the burden of the tax is borne by the owner, as the new view of property taxation implies,[15] and that owners are generally more wealthy, the progressivity of this mode of financing the water system is enhanced. Since water consumption has a lower correlation with income than does rental expenditures, the move towards earmarked property taxation and away from progressive rates is in the direction of a more efficient redistributive mechanism.

The use of property taxes to finance water systems points up an interesting trade-off between efficiency in redistribution and efficiency in production. The user charge implicit in the three per cent property tax package (M$0.23) is substantially below the short-run marginal costs of the Water Department, as approximated by variable costs (M$0.35 in 1972). Given a price-elasticity of demand in the range −0·1 to −0·4 for Penang,[16] a charge of 33 per cent below marginal cost implies excess consumption and production of 3–13 per cent.

An alternative property tax-user charge package would set the latter at variable costs (M$0·35) and set the property tax rate as a residual.[17] Elementary calculations suggest that M$3.94 would have to be raised from the average household through user charges, leaving M$1.75 to be raised from property taxes, rather than M$2.63 and M$3.06 respectively, as in the bottom line of Table 7. In this new package, property taxes can drop to less than 2 per cent. The total bills under efficient pricing (Table 7, col. h) are less favorable for the poor than under the three per cent property tax package (Table 7, col. f), but more so than the existing system based entirely on progressive user charges (Table 7, col. c). The conclusion from this exercise is that the more efficient the pricing rule from the point of view of production, the less efficient is the income redistribution obtained and the less benefited are the poor on the average.

V. IMPLICATIONS

The analysis above does not suggest that progressive rate structures are invariably inappropriate tools for income redistribution. What it does suggest is that a government contemplating the use of such a tool ought to have at least two pieces of information at its disposal: 1) the distribution of consumption levels of individual households within each income class; and 2) the zero-order correlation between consumption and income.

Despite the obvious pro-poor intentions of the City Water Department, which reflects the redistributive propensities of the Malaysian fisc as a whole,[18] the progressive rate structure places a heavier burden on the very poor and poor than would a flat rate plus a property tax.

No restructuring of the rates could have improved the efficiency of the subsidy. This depends upon the correlation between consumption and income, which happens to be low for the case of water. For this reason, taking a base with a higher correlation with income, such as housing, would increase the efficiency of the subsidy.

NOTES

1. See for example, Azpurua *et al.* [*1968*] on Venezuela water rates and Linn [*1975*] on Colombian water and electricity rates. A description of rate structures in the United States can be found in Hirshleifer *et al.* [*1960*] and Taylor [*1975*] for water and electricity, respectively. Progressive electricity rates are currently being considered in Massachusetts under the 'Lifeline' proposal.
2. See Tendler [*1968*], which is the best microeconomic study of public utility in the developing country context.

3. Rees [*1972: 20*].
4. Quoted from IBRD [*1975*], drawn from Hubbell [*1974*].
5. On the theory of income redistribution through pricing see Feldstein [*1972*] and LeGrand [*1975*].
6. Reviews of the literature on income-elasticity of demand for water and for electricity are found in Hanke [*1972*] and Taylor [*1975*], respectively. See Meroz [*1968*] for a cross-sectional analysis of water demand in developing countries.
7. *Ibid.*
8. See Thurow [*1974*]. The importance of externalities in consumption as a justification of progressive water rates is suggested by a survey undertaken in Penang in January 1976 by the author with John D. Montgomery, chief of the post-evaluation team for the Penang Water Supply Project. This survey was administered to all 31 members attending a luncheon of the Rotary Club, which comprises the professional and business elites of Penang. When asked to choose a preferred water rate structure, about two-thirds opted for a subsidised or self-supporting system in which the poor would pay the lowest rates; about one-quarter, for a self-supporting system where all consumers would pay equal rates; and the remainder, for a system where industrial rates would be subsidised. While hardly definitive, such a survey suggests that at least some members of the elite perceive benefits from water consumption on the part of the poor.
9. This argument is similar to McClure's [*1974*].
10. See the reviews by Taylor [*1975*] and Hanke [*1972*].
11. The Malaysian dollar (M$) fluctuated in the range of M$2.50–M$3.00 per U.S. dollar during the 1970s.
12. The short-run price elasticity of demand has been estimated in the course of the post-evaluation of −0·1 to −0·2.
13. This figure is drawn from City Council of Georgetown, Penang, Malaysia, *City Treasurer's Annual Report and Audited Accounts*, Year ending 31 Dec. 1972, pp. 136–62. Since the late 1960s, revenues per thousand gallons have been on the order of M$0.635–0.658.
14. See Linn [*1975*].
15. Mieszkowski [*1967*] and [*1972*].
16. The lower estimate is from Katzman [*1976*]; the higher from Meroz [*1968*].
17. Derived from the *City Treasurer's Annual Report* cited above.
18. Snodgrass [*1974*].

REFERENCES

Azpurua, Pedro P., Andres Sucre Eduardo, and Pedro F. M. Ruiz, 1968, 'New Water Rates for Caracas', *Journal of the American Water Works Association*, 60, July, pp. 774–80.

Feldstein, Martin, 1972, 'Equity and Efficiency in Public Sector Pricing: The Optimal Two-Part Tariff', *Quarterly Journal of Economics*, 86, May, pp. 175–87.

Hanke, Steve, 1972, 'Pricing urban water', in Selma Mushkin (ed.), *Public Prices for Public Products,* Washington: Urban Institute, pp. 283–306.

Hirschleifer, Jack, James, C. De Haven, Jerome W. Milliman, 1960, *Water Supply: Economics, Technology, and Policy* (Chicago: University of Chicago).

Houthhaker, Hendrik and Lester Taylor, 1966, *Consumer Demand in the United States, 1929–1970,* Cambridge: Harvard University, pp. 88–93.

Hubbell, Kenneth, 1974, 'The Provision and Pricing of Public Utilities for the Poor in Less Developed Countries', International Bank for Reconstruction and Development, The Urban Poverty Task Force, November.

International Bank for Reconstruction and Development (IBRD), 1975, 'The Task Ahead for the Cities of the Developing Countries', Staff Working Paper No. 209, July, pp. 57–66.

Katsman, Martin, forthcoming, 'The income and Price Elasticity of Demand for Water in Developing Countries', *Water Resources Bulletin.*

LeGrand, Julian, 1975 'Public Price Discrimination and Aid to Low-Income Groups', *Economica,* 42, pp. 32–42.

Linn, Johannes F., 1976, 'The distributive effects of local government finance in Colombia: A review of the evidence', World Bank Staff Working Paper No. 235.

McClure, Jr., Charles E., 1974, 'A Diagrammatic Exposition of the Harberger Model with One Immobile Factor', *Journal of Political Economy,* 82 Jan./Feb., pp. 56–82.

Meroz, Avigdor, 1968, 'A quantitative analysis of urban water demand in developing countries', International Bank for Reconstruction and Development, Economics Department, Working Paper No. 17, 17 July.

Mieszkowski, Peter, 1967, 'on the Theory of Tax Incidence', *Journal of Political Economy,* 75, June pp. 250–62.

Mieszkowski, Peter, 1972, 'The Property Tax: an Excise Tax or a Profits Tax?' *Journal of Public Economy,* 1, April, pp. 73–96.

Rees, Judith, 1972, 'Studies of Infrastructure Elements'. in Otto Koeningsberger (ed.), *Infrastructure Problems of Cities in Developing Countries,* Ford Foundation International Urban Survey.

Snodgrass, Donald, 1974, 'The fiscal system as an income redistributor in West Malaysia', *Public Finance/Finances Publiques,* 29, pp. 56–76.

Taylor, Lester D., 1975, 'The Demand for Electricity: A Survey', *Bell Journal of Economics,* 6, Spring, pp. 74–110.

Tendler, Judith, 1968, *Electric Power in Brazil: Entrepreneurship in the Public Sector,* Cambridge: Harvard University.

Thurow, Lester, 1974, 'Cash versus In-Kind Transfers', *American Economic Review,* 64, May, pp. 190–95.

Chapter 9

Transfer of Resources from Agriculture to Non-agricultural Activities: the Case of India

MICHAEL LIPTON*

I. SURPLUSES: DOCTRINE AND FACT

Of India's 540 million people, about 70 per cent depend on farming for their livelihood. They are supported by only 20–25 per cent of India's capital stock. Largely as a result, they produce only 40–45 per cent of India's gross output. Despite the substantial growth in Indian living levels, these relationships have not been substantially disturbed by twenty years of development planning; if anything, the inequality between farmers and townsmen, both in capital endowment and in levels of living, has increased somewhat. Yet the average productivity of labour is much lower in agriculture than in industry; of capital, much higher; and in this case what is true of the average products is almost certainly also true of the marginal products.[1] The *a priori* implication is that general labour should leave agriculture for industry, while capital should be transferred from industry to agriculture.

It is, however, the conventional wisdom that efficient development requires, in the early stages, the rapid transfer from village to town of almost all types of resources:[2] both resources generating output (investment finance, general labour, skilled or highly educable persons) and income corresponding to

*Professorial Fellow, Institute of Development Studies at the University of Sussex.

output already generated (cheap food, a surplus of rural taxes over rural current outlays). It is widely believed[3] that such transfers have not happened in India. In fact, there has been a substantial and undesirable net transfer of many resources out of agriculture, as compared to what *would* have taken place in the absence of government intervention. It will be shown that the Government of India *has* succeeded in transferring agricultural families' saving and skills for investment into non-agricultural fixed and human capital respectively, and also (contrary to the general opinion, and largely by trade policy) in manipulating relative tax rates and prices to the advantage of the non-agricultural sector, most clearly before 1965; but that, owing to demographic and technological factors, there has been no similar success in transferring unskilled workers and their families. There has thus been an *unbalanced surplus transfer*, progressively increasing inequality between village and town, because the village (initially poorer and worse-endowed) has retained a decreasing share of the capital and skill resources needed to generate growth, but an almost constant share of the people who might benefit from growth. Apart from the effects on income distribution, the transference of agricultural capital surpluses—agriculturists' saving in excess of investment in agriculture—to non-agricultural uses has damaged the rate of growth of Indian total output. Furthermore, the structuring of farm output to cater for urban needs has militated against the efficient use of rural inputs.

II. NO POPULATION TRANSFER

The first thing to show, and the least controversial, is that there has been no substantial fall in the proportion of Indian workers employed in agriculture, or of Indians dependent upon agriculture for survival. The proportion of the Indian workforce engaged in agriculture was much the same in the 1951 and 1961 Censuses—around 70 per cent.[4] This plainly surprised the planners, who expected the inflow of new entrants to the workforce to grow much faster outside agriculture than inside, and who weighted the provision of jobs in favour of the towns even more than in proportion to this expected trend, with the presumed intention of encouraging it.[5]

The main reason why the rural share of India's population (and hence the associated workforce) has not fallen is demographic. For a very long time, migrants to towns have been largely men, aged fifteen to thirty, formerly agricultural labourers or smallholders. Such migrants form a significant proportion of India's urban population. They have enormously swollen the male/female ratio in the cities, especially in the marriageable age-groups, and hence reduced the urban birth-*rate* (per 1,000 *persons*) substantially. Since the number of migrants is much less significant compared to the huge rural population, the village birth-*rate* is hardly affected at all, especially as the young married migrant men return home frequently. Hence the selective urban-rural movement of young men, while instantaneously raising the urban (and hence the non-agricultural) population share, sets up countervailing demographic forces lowering the share again.[6] The urban birth-rate has been lower than the rural rate for long enough to affect workforces. In the Indian case, this factor has sufficed to prevent a decline in the share of workers employed in agriculture, or, indeed, much of a decline in the share of rural residents. Much the same, by the way, applies to Pakistan, for the same demographic reason. In both countries, of course, the capital-intensive nature of planned industrial development has also played its part in preventing any substantial transfer of workers from agriculture to industry.

III. THE RURAL SKILL DRAIN

While there has been little movement in the agricultural share of workers as a whole, there has been a substantial movement of the skilled, the literate, the intelligent, the progressive and the young from villages to towns. Some part of this is inevitable in development, and it is not easy to delay the process, without impinging on free choice of workplace, or else denying the villager his schooling lest he leave the land.

In a way, the rural skill drain reflects the Indian Government's success in extending primary schooling to the villages, and its refusal to restrict the free movement of labour. But this is not the whole story. The education of the Indian villager—the pictures in his very first textbooks, the preferences of his teachers, the subjects he learns—is geared towards town life. The faster growth of urban income-per-head, in part a result of government policy, attracts into the cities that large majority of highly intelligent men who provide scarce services in income-elastic demand. The idealistic public servant, too, is sucked inexorably into the centres of discussion and action, which are urban; and it is public policy that fails to reverse this trend. As a result, very many young men, their education supported by rural adult workers, are going to the cities, thus further improving the cities' income levels relative to the villages, and hence recruiting even more potential engineers, doctors and accountants from the villages. The (usually well-off) village family that pays for its bright son's education is proud of his Delhi job and pleased with his remissions of income; but rural growth, leadership and modernisation suffer.

The rural skill drain is the equivalent, between the 'two nations' that comprise a single dualistic economy, of the brain drain from poorer to richer countries. It is far harder to quantify, as a rural contribution to urban growth, than tax or savings transfers; but it may well be more important as a drag on agricultural development. I strongly suspect (though in the existing state of the art one cannot prove) that the marginal hydraulic engineer, doctor or good teacher raises output *more* in agriculture than in industry.

In the matter of sheer numbers. though not of marginal production foregone, a few indicators of rural skill drain do exist. A survey of Delhi University students by Khusro in 1957–58 showed that 22·2 per cent came from rural areas (though only 3·8 per cent from farming families); yet only 1·1 per cent wished to return to agricultural work.[7] Rao's study of the employment patterns, in 1958–59, of Delhi University graduates of 1950 and 1954 does not analyse them by urban-rural residence, but the occupational breakdown makes it clear that very few can have returned to the villages—a generous estimate would be 7½ per cent.[8]

Delhi University students are much abler, and almost certainly from much wealthier backgrounds, than Indian university students generally. Hence many of those of rural origin would probably have been 'urbanised' even without university education, so that the 'removal' of at least 15 per cent (22 less 7) of the total student intake from village to town might give an exaggerated picture of the rural brain drain caused by Delhi University. Can one find data for India as a whole? In 1967–68, 69·7 per cent of primary and pre-primary schoolchildren were from rural areas; but the 1961 proportion of Indian literates who lived in rural areas was only 65·3 per cent, and of those who had carried their education at least to Primary or Junior Basic Level only 53·0 per cent (as against 82 per cent of India's total population in rural areas). It is recorded (incredibly) that the proportion of secondary and middle school attenders who came from rural areas was 75·9 per cent; but of matriculates and above in 1961, only 30 to 32 per cent lived in rural areas. In 1957–58, 34·1 per cent of university and college students came from rural areas, but only 26·9 per cent of graduates lived in rural areas in 1961. Though no data are available for the origin of students by father's occupation, the skill drain of bright children out of agriculture must have been even larger than from rural areas; in 1961 the 70 per cent Indian workers in agriculture included 9·6 per cent of India's matriculates and above, and a negligible 5·9 per cent of Indian graduates were employed in agriculture.[9]

We thus see that, at each educational level, the proportion of rural children declines; yet, at the same time, a much smaller share of children *return* to rural life *from* any given level training than *leave* rural life to *obtain* that level of training. These two tendencies apply even more strongly to farm families' children; and both tendencies grow more powerful as the educational level rises.

It is thus consistent, and indeed correct, to say *both*

(a) that the rural sector gets too small a share of *educational* resources,[10] since the share of rural children receiving any given level of education is so *low* compared to the share of urban children; *and*

(b) that the rural sector gets too small a share of *educated* resources, since the share of rural children receiving any given level of education is so *high* compared to the share of rural children returning to use that level of education in the villages.

Both propositions are even truer for agricultural than for rural children, and get more true as the level of education rises.

To (b) above corresponds the rural skill drain, which, because it is skilled labour and enterprise that organises and controls all other resources, is surely the biggest 'transfer of resources from agriculture to non-agriculture activities' of all. To (a) corresponds a part of the public sector's resource transfer out of agriculture by taxation and government spending to be considered below. The policy significance of (a) and (b), taken together, is that efforts to correct (a) by training more rural children at each level are likely to worsen (b) by increasing the share of rural people's effort used to support educands who are going to work in towns, to raise urban incomes. This can be avoided if there is a simultaneous effort to make rural work attractive and lucrative for educated persons, or to get them to the villages by other means, including short-term bonding as a condition of training, as with Indian para-medical personnel for the family planning programme. It is not my purpose to oppose rural education, but to point out that at present it is a vast funnel of bright young men[11] out of rural life. More and better rural education, unless supported by more and better rural job opportunities, means merely a wider funnel.

IV. PRIVATE SAVING AND PRIVATE INVESTMENT

The data do not allow us to be sure whether the rural sector (or the agricultural sector) contributes more or less to private savings than it draws from them for private investment. The All-India Rural Household Survey concludes that rural saving in 1962, including currency increases but excluding consumer durables, was 697 Crore rupees, as against gross physical investment, also excluding consumer durables, of 729 Crore rupees. The corresponding net figures are 469 Crore rupees (saving), 494 Crore rupees (investment). Unfortunately, the apparent 'transfer *into* the rural sector' of some six per cent of the value of its private investment—i.e. the estimated excess of rural investment over rural savings—is so small that we can place no confidence in it, because (for the sample used in this survey) the statistical probability of *either* a savings under-estimate *or* a physical-investment overestimate, sufficient to wipe out the estimated excess, is at least 1 in 15.[12] Doubts are increased by the widely different Reserve Bank estimate of rural household net saving—236·6 Crore rupees in 1961–62 and 237·0 Crore rupees in 1962–63.[13] There is good reason to suspect major concealment of inventory-building by big food growers, and major underestimation of physical investment in the subsistence sector, in all these figures; but these would bias downwards the estimates for *both* rural saving *and* rural investment.[14]

On balance, however, I suspect that the rural sector is a substantial net contributor to non-rural savings funds. In the whole period 1950–51/1962–63, rural households contributed about 27 per cent of private saving, *excluding* that embodied in non-monetised investment. The rest of private monetised saving came from urban households and private corporations.[15] Even if all the latter are assigned to the urban sector, so that only 27 per cent of private monetised saving came from the rural sector, it is quite impossible to believe that this was not substantially larger than the rural share of private *monetised* investment.[16] A very crude estimate would be that the rural sector financed between five and ten per cent of urban investment: nearer the upper figure in 1951, nearer the lower figure in recent years. This is based on the Reserve Bank's aggregate figures, and the problem of confidence limits for sampling does not arise.

V. PUBLIC TAXATION AND PUBLIC EXPENDITURE

There is an almost universal view that Indian agriculture is 'undertaxed'. We have to separate out three possible meanings of this view.

(i) 'Undertaxation' may mean the existence of a substantial body of rich men, and/or of luxury consumption, in the rural sector. These imply the existence of incomes which could be diverted into the financing of productive investment, if this were politically possible. In this sense agriculture is certainly undertaxed (relative to its taxable capacity), but substantially less so than other sectors of the Indian economy.

(ii) 'Undertaxation' may mean that agriculture (or the rural sector) is paying less in contributions to government than it is receiving in benefits from government. This is demonstrably false, even before taking into account the private non-agricultural sector's hidden benefits from the underpricing of public-sector services like power and transport. Agriculture is overtaxed relative to non-agriculture, in the sense that farm families pay more in tax than they get in public benefits.

(iii) Most usually, the alleged 'undertaxation' of agriculture is based on a comparison of the sector's 'ability to pay' with that of other sectors. Income per head is calculated, net of subsistence needs, for agriculture and non-agriculture; allowance is made for equity considerations, so that higher income-per-head is regarded as taxable at a higher percentage rate; and it is alleged that, even after considering the greater poverty (and the greater, tax-inhibiting, equality) of the agricultural sector, it is paying a smaller share of taxation than would reflect its 'ability to pay' relative to the non-agricultural sector. This allegation is demonstrably incorrect. Indeed the agricultural sector, on the concept of equity usually used, has been slightly, but persistently—and until recently increasingly—overtaxed. This overtaxation may be seen as a measure of the resource transfer (desirable or otherwise) from agriculture to non-agriculture by public taxation activities: the tax burden on agriculture *in excess* of what it would have borne if the total burden were distributed according to ability to pay.

It is with this sense of 'undertaxation', the most usual and important, that I begin. Owing to the data available, the discussion of income *distribution* will proceed in terms of 'rural' and 'urban' rather than agricultural and non-agricultural sectors, but the errors involved are not likely to invalidate the results. It is first necessary to calculate the 'taxable capacity' of rural and urban persons—income *less* subsistence *plus* some allowance for wealth. The next step is to estimate, on some stated equity principle, the 'proper' share of total tax payable in each sector; to do this properly it is essential that the prior calculation of 'taxable capacity' allows for income distribution *within* each sector. Finally, we must compare the 'proper' share with the actual share of each sector. The non-agricultural sector does, of course, pay more tax per head than the agricultural sector. The gap comprises (i) a sum due to ability-to-pay considerations based on the latter sector's greater poverty and equality and the State's equity concepts, *minus* (ii) a sum due to resource transfer out of agriculture. We propose to identify the second component.

Table 1 indicates the approximate distribution of income in urban and rural India. This must be the start of any attempt to measure taxable capacity. The alternative—to summarise each sector's distribution in an overall indicator of equality such as a Lorenz coefficient, and take account of it separately from sectoral income-per-head as an independent determinant of taxable capacity—is doubly unsatisfactory. Firstly, the Lorenz coefficient tells us nothing about distribution at the really high (and really taxable) end of the income scale. Second, and more fundamentally, there is a serious weighting problem, which has trapped some estimators.[17] In India, income per head is smaller in the rural sector than in the urban sector. It is also more equally distributed. Both factors reduce the taxable capacity of villages. Yet a widely quoted estimate by Ved Gandhi, following a natural but fallacious procedure, assesses the relative urban/rural taxable capacity by weighting the two urban/rural ratios, of income-per-head and of Lorenz coefficients. Since the ratio of rural to urban Lorenz coefficients (whole less than unity) is greater than the ratio of rural to urban incomes-per-head, the effect of this treatment is to *increase* the apparent taxable capacity of the villages relative to the towns. Greater rural equality *than urban equality,* in logic, should reduce relative rural taxable capacity; in Gandhi's treatment, the ratio of the rural to urban Lorenz coeffients must fall short, not just of unity (as would make sense), but of the ratio of rural to urban income-per-head. This odd result could be avoided, e.g. by some non-linear weights, but this would be quite arbitrary. Moreover, the problem that a single coefficient conceals high (taxable) incomes would remain.

TABLE 1

RURAL AND URBAN INCOME DISTRIBUTION

Percentile group of households in declining order of income per household	Rural sector 1 Percentage of sectoral income RBI (1953–54/1956–57)	2 NCAER (1962)	3 Percentage of sectoral population	4 Income per head ÷ sectoral average income RBI	5 NCAER	Urban sector 6 Percentage of sectoral income RBI (1953–54/1956–57)	7 NCAER (1961)	8 Percentage of sectoral population	9 Income per head ÷ sectoral average income RBI	10 NCAER
Top 1%		8·87	1·71		5·19		16·0	1·60		10·00
Second 1%		4·27	1·67		2·56		6·1	1·54		3·96
Third 1%	17	3·39	1·54	2·15	2·20	26	3·5	1·48	3·43	2·36
Fourth 1%		2·97	1·49		1·99		2·9	1·48		1·96
Fifth 1%		2·69	1·49		1·81		2·5	1·48		1·69
Second 5%	8	10·65	7·40	1·08	1·44	11	11·4	6·70	1·64	1·70
Second 10%	14	15·31	13·27	1·06	1·15	12	15·2	13·01	0·92	1·17
Third 10%	13	11·65	11·64	1·12	1·00	10	10·3	11·53	0·87	0·89
Fourth 10%	9	9·49	10·82	0·95	0·88	8	8·1	10·32	0·78	0·78
Fifth 10%	9	8·23	10·25	0·88	0·80	8	6·5	10·32	0·78	0·63
Sixth 10%	8	6·28	9·97	0·80	0·63	6	5·4	9·87	0·61	0·55
Seventh 10%	7	5·62	8·79	0·80	0·64	6	4·5	8·49	0·71	0·53
Eighth 10%	6	4·70	7·94	0·76	0·59	6	3·6	8·49	0·71	0·42
Ninth 10%	5	3·76	6·97	0·72	0·54	4	2·7	7·63	0·52	0·35
Bottom 10%	4	2·12	5·06	0·80	0·42	3	1·3	6·07	0·49	0·21

Sources: Cols. 1 and 6 from P. D. Ojha and V. V. Bhatt, 'Pattern of Income Distribution in India: 1953–54 to 1956–57', *Reserve Bank of India Bulletin*, Sept. 1963, p. 1138. (This source is referred to as RBI); Other cols. from National Council of Applied Economic Research (NCAER), *Urban Income and Saving*, Delhi, 1962, pp. 42, 44, and *All India Rural Household Survey*, Vol. II, Delhi, 1965, pp. 11, 55.

Method: The percentages in cols. 1, 2, 6 and 7, for both 'Rural sector' and 'Urban sector' are taken directly from the sources cited. The top five percentiles for 'Urban sector' are added by linear interpolation (*Urban Income*, p. 42) into cols. 2 and 7.

Cols. 3 and 8 are calculated by linear interpolation of NCAER average household incomes (from *Urban Income*, p. 42, and *All India Rural*, p. 50) into the respective listings of average size of household by income classes (respectively p. 42 and p. 55). We then know, for each percentile/decile of households, the ratio of persons per household to the All-India sectoral average, which

Of the alternative sources in Table 1, Gandhi uses the Reserve Bank (RBI) source. This is unplausibly egalitarian by international standards, both for urban and for rural sectors; heavily rounded off, impeding precise calculations; and, most serious for the assessment of taxable capacity, highly aggregated for the upper income groups. We shall therefore use the NCAER data, which we have adjusted to show income *per head* in each income group, allowing for differing household sizes. It would be preferable to rank persons, not households, in decreasing order of income; bigger households have bigger incomes, which is why the figures in Cols. 4–5 and Cols. 9–10 of Table 1 do not always decrease, and why this table understates intrasectoral inequality and hence taxable capacity in both sectors. It would also be preferable to break down population, in each income group, into 'Lusk consumption units' to allow more precisely for *available* taxable resources per household group—adults consume more than children. But, even with the limited data of Table 1, quite firm conclusions about sectoral tax capacities can be reached. First of all, we need some estimates of subsistence requirements in each sector.

Quite astonishing estimates have been used in the course of attempts to demonstrate that, relative to its ability to pay, the rural sector pays too small a share of tax. Thus Gandhi[18] actually identifies urban and rural 'subsistence' requirements with the income per person of the lowest thirtieth percentile of households in urban and rural sectors respectively; so the urban sector is rewarded for its greater affluence by being assigned a greater subsistence 'requirement' and hence, *ceteris paribus*, a smaller taxable capacity. But Gandhi's conclusion, that in 1952 urban subsistence needs at 240 Rs. per head were almost double rural needs at 170 Rs. per head, scarcely commends itself.

Dwivedi[19] has estimated nutritional and other subsistence requirements per person in rural Uttar Pradesh at Rs. 151·23 in 1965–66, at prices of that year. An estimate for 1963–64 showed all-India urban prices 15·99 per cent above rural prices.[20] Thus the townsman would have had to pay Rs. 175·41 for these goods. In addition, the budgets include a variety of items not in the price index—12 per cent of the rural budget but 25 per cent of the urban budget, including in each case 'services' like house-rent, furniture and transport, as well as sports, education, footwear, etc. If (generously) we allow half these services as part of 'subsistence' in each sector, the townsman's excess subsistence needs rise by half of (25–12) per cent of that Rs. 175·41, or by 61·39 Rs., to 236·80 Rs. Being even more generous to the townsman, we shall reprice these 61·39 Rs. worth of commodities on the assumption that they all fall into the class of items which, in the Uttar Pradesh study, showed the largest excess of urban over rural prices—'non-food items', where urban prices were 128·85 per cent of rural prices as against 115·99 per cent for the whole consumer bundle priced. So we blow up the excess 61·39 Rs. by (128·85/115·99) to 68·20 Rs. Then we estimate, for U.P. in 1965–6,

Rural subsistence	Rs. 175·41 per person
Urban subsistence (max.)	Rs. 243·61 per person

We shall assume these figures to apply to all-India, and we shall deflate them (so as to evaluate rural and urban subsistence needs in different years) by all-India price indices, in Table 2. These are, of course, unsatisfactory procedures, but we cannot use statistics that do not exist.[21]

In Table 2, we estimate urban and rural subsistence for 1950–1 to 1965–6. The spurious accuracy is solely to facilitate further calculations. Improvements would be (a) separate rural and urban price indexes, (b) an all-India (instead of UP) estimate for subsistence needs.

To allow for wealth, we shall assume that wealth-per-person confers one-tenth as much spending power as income per person, the lowest of the inevitably arbitrary ratios usually proposed,[22] and hence the most likely to inflate the apparent affluence (and hence relative taxable capacity) of the rural sector, which has a lower wealth-to-income ratio than the urban sector. In the agricultural sector, wealth per person (assuming two-thirds of land values in that sector,[23] and allowing for consumer durables at three per cent of agricultural wealth outside land and livestock[24]) was 733 rupees in 1949–50 and 811 rupees in 1960–61.[25] Arbitrarily assuming that consumer durables are only four per cent of non-agricultural non-land wealth, and allocating the non-agricultural sector only one-third of Indian land values, we place non-agricultural

TABLE 2

URBAN AND RURAL SUBSISTENCE INCOMES

Financial year	*Price index (1965–6 = 100)*	*Rural subsistence (current Rs.)*	*Urban subsistence (current Rs.)*
1950–1	59·7	104·72	145·44
1951–2	61·2	107·35	149·09
1952–3	60·8	106·65	148·11
1953–4	61·3	107·53	149·33
1954–5	58·4	102·44	142·27
1955–6	57·5	100·86	140·08
1956–7	62·4	109·46	152·01
1957–8	65·7	115·24	160·05
1958–9	68·7	120·51	167·36
1959–60	71·3	125·07	173·69
1960–1	72·9	127·87	177·59
1961–2	74·4	130·51	181·25
1962–3	76·8	134·71	187·09
1963–4	81·1	142·26	197·57
1964–5	91·0	159·62	221·69
1965–6	100	175·41	243·61

Sources: Statistical Abstract of the Indian Union, 1953–4, p. 420; 1961, p. 233, 1963–4, p. 241; 1965, p. 233; U.N. *Statistical Yearbook 1968*, p. 543. Prices from these sources (obtaining price index for each financial year—say 1956–7—by adding 75% of the first year's index to 25% of the second year's) used to deflate 1965–6 urban and rural subsistence needs calculated as in text.

wealth-per-head at 1799 rupees in 1949–50 and 2217 rupees in 1960–61.[26] We assume smooth growth in both non-agricultural and agricultural wealth per head (0·92 per cent yearly in agriculture, 1·91 per cent in non-agriculture) and construct a table showing wealth-per-head and income-per-head in 1950–51/1962–63:

One more step is needed: to estimate the distribution of wealth. For agricultural wealth, we can make a rough approximation by using the known distribution of *rural* wealth, excluding land and livestock. We use NCAER data to regress wealth-per-household on income-per-household[27] ($w = -250{\cdot}81 + 0{\cdot}992y$) and to use this equation to estimate wealth-per-household in each of the rural-income percentile and decile groups for our Table 1, p. 202, from the income-per-household

TABLE 3
INDICATORS OF OVERALL TAXABLE CAPACITY (RUPEES)

	Agricultural sector		*Non-agricultural sector*	
	Income per head	*Wealth per head*	*Income per head*	*Wealth per head*
1950–51	212	733·0	411	1799·0
1951–52	210	739·7	440	1833·4
1952–53	199	746·5	422	1868·4
1953–54	215	753·4	428	1904·1
1954–55	175	760·3	427	1940·4
1955–56	177	767·3	434	1977·5
1956–57	210	774·4	431	2015·3
1957–58	198	781·5	478	2053·8
1958–59	228	788·7	578	2093·0
1959–60	221	796·0	489	2133·0
1960–61	239	803·3	529	2173·7
1961–62	227	810·7	567	2215·2

Sources: Income from Gandhi, *op. cit.*, p. 56; wealth per head calculated as described in text.

estimate given by NCAER.[28] We then work out the percentage of the rural sector's wealth in each income percentile/decile group of households.[29] Using Table 1, we can now use our knowledge about the size of households in each income-percentile, etc., group, to estimate the group's 'capital-per-head/rural-sector-capital-per-head' ratio, just as we did in Table 1 for income. For urban capital, unfortunately, we have no direct estimate of distribution. We have therefore assumed, in Table 4, that any given urban ratio, of (decile, etc.) income-per-head to overall urban income-per-head, is associated with the same ratio of capital-per-head to income-per-head that applies in the rural sector.[30] This assumption, once more, almost certainly understates the inequality of urban capital distribution, and hence urban affluence relative to rural affluence.

We can now combine Tables 1, 2, 3 and 4 to estimate taxable capacity in agricultural and non-agricultural sectors for 1950–1 to 1961–2. For each year, the figure for each group is (i) income per person, from Table 3 together with Cols. 5 and 10 of Table 1, *plus* (ii) one-tenth of wealth per person, from Table

TABLE 4
RELATIVE GROUP CAPITAL HOLDINGS

	Capital per head ÷ sectoral average	
Top 1%	Rural 6·28	Urban 11·83
Second 1%	2·96	4·55
Third 1%	2·58	2·67
Fourth 1%	2·32	2·21
Fifth 1%	2·07	2·05
Second 5%	1·62	1·85
Second 10%	1·25	1·24
Third 10%	1·03	0·89
Fourth 10%	0·87	0·72
Fifth 10%	0·72	0·58
Sixth 10%	0·59	0·46
Seventh 10%	0·52	0·42
Eighth 10%	0·43	0·27
Ninth 10%	0·33	0·13
Bottom 10%	0·05	0·02

Source: Note 30, divided by corresponding group figures from Table 1, Cols. 3 and 8.

3 together with Table 4, *minus* (iii) subsistence requirements per person, from Table 2. Of all the assumptions needed to obtain this estimate, the most doubtful is that rural and urban *distributions* of income and capital can be applied to agricultural and non-agricultural *totals* of income and capital. We prefer such an open assumption, however, to aprioristic attempts to reason our way from one distribution to another.

Tables 4a and 4b show the maximum total sum that could be taken from each income-group of households, urban and rural, and still leave members of each group enough to subsist (from income, services of consumer-capital like owner-occupied houses and cars, and realisable gains on capital and land). If the norm of inter-group equity were proportional taxation—that each group should pay as taxation the same share of taxable capacity—we should now simply find the weighted averages of taxable capacity, agricultural and non-agricultural, for each year, and see whether their ratios stood in the same proportions as the sectors' tax payments. For example, for 1950–1, we should use Table 4a, Col. 1, and Table

1, Col. 3, and calculate for agriculture [1·71 (1455·9)+1·67 (655·0)+. . .+6·97 (34·0)]÷100, the taxable capacity of the average member of the agricultural sector, assuming the bottom decile, with a negative entry in Table 4a, to have zero taxable capacity; perform a similar calculation from Table 4b, Col. 1, and Table 1, Col. 8, for non-agriculture; work out the ratio of the first result to the second; and compare it with the (known) ratios of tax paid by agriculture to tax paid by non-agriculture.

This procedure, however, would make the unwarranted assumption that *proportionate* taxation is equitable. Certainly in India, aiming at 'a socialist pattern of society' over and above considerations of diminishing marginal utility of income, and meaning by that 'pattern' chiefly the avoidance of great (or at least of increasing) inequalities of income and wealth, *progressive* taxation is the norm. But progressive at what rate? Proportionate taxation implies zero progression. It can be shown that a *constant* rate of regression is produced by taking each person, or group, in proportion to the *square* of its taxable capacity, i.e. of the entries in Table 4a and 4b. A generally acceptable compromise between constant progression, which is often regarded as equitable, is to tax each person, or group, in proportion to its taxable capacity *to the power of 1·5*—halfway between 1 (proportionality) and 2 (constant progression). To evaluate the implicit tax bases, we present in Tables 5a and 5b, for agricultural and non-agricultural sectors respectively, figures which, on this basis, would be the equitable ones for the *ratios* between any pair of percentile or decile groups, together with the weighted sums for each year. The proportion between the latter, for any given year, is the 'correct' proportion for the tax burden between the *sectors* for that year.

To complete the exercise, we need only compare the agricultural and non-agricultural ratios, year by year, between tax paid per head and 'equity-adjusted' weighted-average taxable capacity. If taxes were equitably split between the sectors in any particular year, the ratios for the two sectors would be the same in that year. We calculate the tax-per-head that would have been paid by the agricultural sector in the event of such an equitable split. The difference between this

TABLE 4a

TAXABLE CAPACITY: RURAL SECTOR (CURRENT PRICES)

Household Group by Household Income	*1950–1*	*1951–2*	*1952–3*	*1953–4*	*1954–5*	*1955–6*	*1956–7*	*1957–8*	*1958–9*	*1959–60*	*1960–61*	*1961–62*
Top 1%	1455·9	1447·1	1395·0	1481·4	1283·3	1299·6	1466·7	1403·2	1558·1	1521·8	1617·0	1552·1
Second 1%	655·0	649·3	623·8	665·9	570·6	579·4	657·3	620·9	696·7	676·3	721·7	690·6
Third 1%	550·8	545·5	523·8	559·9	478·8	486·5	552·3	522·0	584·6	566·5	605·2	578·1
Fourth 1%	487·3	482·2	462·6	495·1	422·2	429·3	488·1	460·1	516·2	499·4	534·1	509·3
Fifth 1%	430·7	425·9	408·1	437·6	371·7	378·3	430·9	405·0	455·5	439·7	471·0	448·2
Second 5%	319·3	314·9	300·9	324·2	272·8	278·3	318·4	296·5	335·6	322·1	346·4	327·7
Second 10%	230·7	226·7	215·5	233·9	193·8	198·5	228·8	210·2	240·3	228·5	247·3	231·8
Third 10%	182·8	179·1	169·3	185·1	150·9	155·1	180·3	163·3	188·7	177·9	193·8	180·0
Fourth 10%	145·7	141·9	133·4	147·2	117·7	121·7	142·7	127·0	148·7	138·7	152·3	139·8
Fifth 10%	117·7	114·7	106·3	118·9	92·3	95·9	114·3	99·5	118·7	109·0	121·1	109·5
Sixth 10%	72·1	68·6	62·8	72·4	52·7	55·9	68·5	55·6	69·6	61·1	70·1	60·3
Seventh 10%	69·1	65·6	59·6	69·3	49·5	52·3	65·2	52·1	66·4	57·7	66·9	57·0
Eighth 10%	51·9	48·4	42·9	51·7	33·5	36·5	47·7	35·2	47·6	39·5	47·6	38·3
Ninth 10%	34·0	30·5	25·5	33·5	17·2	20·0	29·5	17·5	28·6	20·5	27·7	18·9
Bottom 10%	(–12·0)	(–15·4)	(–19·3)	(–13·4)	(–25·1)	(–22·8)	(–17·5)	(–28·1)	(–20·1)	(–28·3)	(–23·5)	(–23·4)

Sources and Methods: Each entry is per head agricultural income for the year (from Table 3, Col. 1), *times* the ratio of rural group income per head to rural average income per head (Table 1, Col. 5); plus per-head agricultural wealth for the year (Table 3, Col. 2) *times* the ratio of rural group capital per head to rural average capital per head (Table 4, Col. 1); *minus* rural subsistence for the year (table 2, Col. 2).

TABLE 4b

TAXABLE CAPACITY: URBAN SECTOR (CURRENT PRICES)

Household Group by household income	*1950–1*	*1951–2*	*1952–3*	*1953–4*	*1954–5*	*1955–6*	*1956–7*	*1957–8*	*1958–9*	*1959–60*	*1960–61*	*1961–62*
Top 1%	6092·8	6459·3	6281·7	6383·10	6422·7	6538·7	6541·74	7049·83	8088·7	7239·6	7688·9	8109·10
Second 1%	2300·67	2427·33	2372·9	2411·8	2431·3	2470·2	2471·6	2667·4	3073·8	2733·2	2908·2	3071·90
Third 1%	1140·4	1378·7	1346·0	1369·12	1383·4	1412·02	1403·16	1516·45	1755·55	1549·9	1652·38	1748·28
Fourth 1%	1023·24	1118·40	1091·80	1110·35	1123·4	1147·48	1138·07	1230·8	1428·07	1256·14	1340·6	1419·14
Fifth 1%	917·95	970·28	948·0	964·31	977·1	998·67	989·46	1068·8	1238·53	1089·99	1162·91	1230·65
Second 5%	886·08	938·10	914·8	930·4	942·5	963·47	953·47	1032·5	1202·45	1052·2	1124·6	1192·43
Second 10%	558·5	593·00	577·2	587·50	597·8	613·2	602·2	653·9	768·43	662·93	711·41	756·8
Third 10%	380·46	405·6	393·72	401·05	410·4	422·1	410·92	448·2	533·43	451·36	487·06	517·85
Fourth 10%	304·67	326·09	315·5	321·59	330·76	340·78	329··3	360·68	434·26	358·3	391·85	420·5
Fifth 10%	217·8	234·42	226·08	230·74	239·3	248·0	236·4	260·22	318·17	267·09	282·0	304·4
Sixth 10%	163·3	177·2	169·92	173·65	181·0	189·6	177·7	197·33	246·82	193·38	213·55	232·5
Seventh 10%	147·95	161·10	154·01	154·48	165·5	172·98	161·1	179·56	226·89	175·07	194·26	212·3
Eighth 10%	75·75	85·2	79·57	81·84	89·5	95·6	83·1	96·17	131·91	59·3	103·4	116·70
Ninth 10%	21·80	28·74	23·87	25·22	32·4	37·52	25·04	33·95	62·15	25·49	35·87	45·99
Bottom 10%	55·53	53·01	55·75	55·64	48·7	44·99	57·5	55·56	41·81	66·73	62·14	57·8

Sources and method: Exactly as in Table 4a within appropriate changes.

and the tax-per-head in fact paid, as a percentage of agricultural *income*-per-head, shows the proportion of yearly agricultural income being transferred to non-agricultural activities *as compared with a system that taxed the two sectors equitably* (which would, of course, involve a large and possibly undesirable absolute resource transfer into the agricultural sector).

We can now conclude this arithmetically exhausting episode. Accepting the normal definition of inter-group equity (a compromise between proportional taxation and constant progression), and at every stage making assumptions tending to *overstate* the relative taxable capacity of agriculture, we have nevertheless found that there is a small but persistent (and, until recently, rising) resource transfer out of agriculture via the tax system. It comprises the difference between columns 1 and 7 of Table 6—in recent years, about 1½ per cent of average agricultural income. This represents the excess of agricultural tax payments, direct and indirect, over the payments that would reflect ability to pay.

What of resource transfer in sense (ii) of Para. 13, the excess of agricultural taxation over public outlay benefiting agriculture? The only investigation, that of Mathew, estimates that in 1958–9 tax per head in agriculture fell short of *current* spending benefiting agriculture by only 3·22 per cent of agricultural income.[31] His method of allocating education outlays—nearly half the current outlays allocated—among sectors, however, is faulty. Later official estimates put 37·5 per cent of this in the rural sector,[32] which on Mathew's estimates would imply 33·9 per cent benefiting agriculture, as against his own figure of 62·5 per cent.[33] Correction of this error cuts agriculturalists' 1958–9 government current outlay from Mathew's figure of 7·66 Rupees per head to 6·34 Rupees per head, and raises the net burden of agricultural taxation to 4·14 per cent of agricultural income. This is in excess of even the most optimistic possible estimate of public yearly capital-account spending to benefit agriculture.

VI SURPLUS TRANSFER VIA PRICING

There is a long and inconclusive discussion in the literature about whether the terms of trade have moved against Indian

TABLE 5a
RURAL 'EQUITY' TAX RATIOS

Household Group by Household Income	*1950–1*	*1951–2*	*1952–3*	*1953–4*	*1954–5*	*1955–6*	*1956–7*	*1957–8*	*1958–9*	*1959–60*	*1960–61*	*1961–2*	*Weights*
Top 1%	5555·3	5504·8	5305·8	5701·8	4598·1	4685·1	5617·1	5255·4	6150·3	5952·3	6502·4	6114·8	1·71
Second 1%	1676·3	1654·5	1558·0	1718·4	1362·9	1397·8	1684·9	1547·2	1838·9	1758·8	1938·8	1814·8	1·67
Third 1%	1292·7	1274·1	1197·7	1324·9	1047·7	1073·1	1298·3	1189·3	1413·6	1348·3	1488·8	1389·9	1·54
Fourth 1%	1075·8	1058·9	995·0	1101·6	867·4	889·5	1078·3	986·9	1172·9	1116·0	1234·3	1149·3	1·49
Fifth 1%	888·2	878·9	824·4	915·4	716·4	735·8	894·4	814·9	972·1	922·0	1018·9	948·9	1·49
Second 5%	570·5	558·8	522·0	583·7	450·6	464·3	568·1	510·5	614·8	578·1	644·7	591·9	7·40
Second 10%	349·4	341·3	316·4	357·6	269·8	279·8	346·1	304·7	372·5	345·4	388·9	352·9	13·27
Third 10%	247·2	241·8	220·3	251·8	185·4	193·2	242·1	208·7	259·2	237·3	269·8	241·5	11·64
Fourth 10%	175·8	169·0	154·1	178·6	127·7	134·2	170·5	143·1	181·3	163·4	187·9	165·3	10·82
Fifth 10%	127·7	122·8	109·6	129·6	88·7	93·9	122·2	99·3	129·3	114·1	133·3	144·6	10·25
Sixth 10%	61·2	56·8	49·7	61·6	38·3	41·8	56·7	41·5	58·1	47·8	58·7	46·9	9·97
Seventh 10%	57·4	53·1	46·0	57·7	34·8	37·8	52·6	37·6	54·1	43·8	54·7	43·0	8·79
Eighth 10%	37·4	33·7	28·1	37·2	19·4	27·1	32·9	20·9	32·8	24·8	32·8	23·7	7·94
Ninth 10%	19·8	16·8	12·9	19·4	7·1	8·9	16·0	7·3	15·3	9·3	14·6	8·2	6·97
Bottom 10%	—	—	—	.	—	—	—	—	—	—	—	—	5·06
Weighted Average	337·1	330·1	308·6	344·7	263·7	272·2	333·7	307·6	361·8	339·1	379·1	349·9	

Source: Entries under years are Table 4a entries to the power of 1·5, divided by 100. Only the ratios among entries are meaningful (signifying the equitable inter-group ratios of tax burden per head, if shared at a rate halfway between proportionality and constant progressiveness. Weights in the last column are percentages of rural persons in the row (see Table 1). The bottom decile, with negative entries in Table 4a, is assumed to have zero taxable capacity.

TABLE 5b
URBAN 'EQUITY' TAX RATIOS

Household Group by Household Income	*1950–1*	*1951–2*	*1952–3*	*1953–4*	*1954–5*	*1955–6*	*1956–7*	*1957–8*	*1958–9*	*1959–60*	*1960–61*	*1961–2*	*Weights*
Top 1%	47557·9	5193·8	49787·4	50997·4	51473·2	52873·5	52910·2	59192·7	72746·9	61599·4	67421·9	73022·8	1·60
Second 1%	11035·2	11958·1	11554·1	11844·9	11988·7	12277·0	12287·4	13776·3	17042·0	14289·7	15683·6	17025·9	1·54
Third 1%	4851·4	5199·3	4938·4	5065·9	5145·6	5305·9	5256·0	5905·3	7355·6	6101·5	6716·8	7309·9	1·48
Fourth 1%	3273·1	3740·2	3607·8	3699·8	3765·3	3887·0	3839·3	4317·8	5399·7	4452·0	4408·4	5346·1	1·48
Fifth 1%	2781·1	3022·3	2918·9	2994·5	3054·1	3155·9	3112·4	3474·4	4358·7	3598·6	3965·7	4317·2	1·48
Second 5%	2637·6	2873·2	2767·2	2838·3	2893·6	2990·6	2944·1	3317·9	4169·6	3413·1	3771·5	4117·6	6·70
Second 10%	1319·9	1444·1	1386·9	1424·0	1461·9	1518·4	1477·5	1672·1	2130·1	1706·9	1897·5	2082·0	13·01
Third 10%	742·1	817·0	781·2	803·1	831·5	867·3	833·0	948·8	1232·0	958·9	1074·9	1178·4	11·53
Fourth 10%	531·8	588·8	560·5	576·7	601·5	629·1	597·4	685·0	904·9	678·2	775·7	862·2	10·32
Fifth 10%	321·5	358·9	339·9	350·5	370·1	390·5	363·4	419·8	517·5	436·5	473·6	531·2	10·32
Sixth 10%	208·8	235·9	221·5	228·9	245·2	261·0	236·9	277·2	377·5	268·9	312·1	354·5	9·87
Seventh 10%	179·9	204·5	191·1	197·6	212·9	227·5	204·4	240·6	341·7	213·6	270·8	309·3	8·49
Eighth 10%	65·9	78·6	71·0	74·0	84·6	93·4	75·7	94·3	151·5	84·4	105·1	126·1	8·49
Ninth 10%	10·2	15·4	11·7	12·7	18·4	23·0	12·5	19·8	49·0	12·9	21·5	31·2	7·63
Bottom 10%	—	—	—	—	—	—	—		—	—	—	—	6·07
Weighted Average	1641·8	1811·5	1738·1	1782·8	1816·4	1875·7	1849·3	2082·8	2373·3	2144·3	2365·3	2582·6	

Source and Method: As in Table 5a.

TABLE 6

TAX, EQUITY TAX, AND IMPLICIT RESOURCE TRANSFER

	Agricultural			*Non-Agricultural*			
	1	2	3	4	5	6	7
	Tax per head (Rs.)	*Equity-adjusted taxable capacity per head*	*Ratio (per cent)*	*Tax per head (Rs.)*	*Equity-adjusted taxable capacity per head*	*Ratio (per cent)*	*Tax per head in agriculture if both sectors paid at the same ratio to 'equity' capacity (Rs.)*
1950–1	8·3	337·1	2·46	39·4	1641·8	2·40	8·2
1951–2	8·6	330·1	2·61	45·5	1811·5	2·51	8·4
1952–3	8·8	308·6	2·85	41·1	1738·1	2·37	7·7
1953–4	9·3	344·7	2·70	40·8	1782·8	2·29	8·3
1954–5	9·6	263·7	3·64	42·3	1816·4	2·34	7·0
1955–6	10·2	272·2	3·75	41·9	1875·7	2·23	7·1
1956–7	11·4	333·7	3·42	48·6	1849·3	2·63	9·5
1957–8	13·3	307·6	4·32	58·0	2082·8	2·78	9·8
1958–9	15·6	361·8	4·31	60·7	2373·3	2·56	10·8
1959–60	14·2	339·1	4·19	68·3	2144·3	3·19	11·5
1960–61	14·4	379·1	3·80	75·1	2365·3	3·18	12·7
1961–2	14·7	349·9	4·20	82·0	2582·5	3·18	12·0

Sources: Cols. 1, 4: Gandhi, *op. cit.*, p. 56, adjusted to include the very small element of local taxes (p. 65) on assumption that it grew at the same rate as central-plus-state tax in each sector. Cols. 2, 5: last rows of tables 5a, 5b; the entries are in rupees to the power of 1·5 and divided by 100, and have significance only relative to each other. Col. 3 is Col. 1 ÷ Col. 2. Col. 6 is Col. 4 ÷ Col. 5. Col. 7, for any given year, shows the tax-per-head that would be paid in agriculture to satisfy (i) intersectoral equity, (ii) the need to keep *all-India* tax (and hence tax-per-head) at the level actually attained in that year. Col. 7 is hence calculated as follows. To achieve (i), we require that the equitable tax-per-head in agriculture (A) and in non-agriculture (N) satisfy the equation

$$(1) \quad \frac{A}{\text{Col. 2}} = \frac{N}{\text{Col. 5}}$$

where 'Col. 2' and 'Col. 5' are the Table 6 values for that year. To achieve (ii), since 70 per cent of taxpayers are in agriculture and 30 per cent in non-agriculture, A and N must satisfy the equation

$$(2) \quad 0{\cdot}7A + 0{\cdot}3N = 0{\cdot}7\ (\text{Col. 1}) + 0{\cdot}3\ (\text{Col. 4})$$

where 'Col. 1' and 'Col. 4' are the actual Table 6 values for that year. Hence the entry in Col. 7 for each year, A, is obtained by solving (1) for N, substituting in (2), and then solving (2) for A. The solution is given by equation

$$(3) \quad A = [0{\cdot}7\ (\text{Col. 1}) + 0{\cdot}3\ (\text{Col. 4})] \div [0{\cdot}7 + 0{\cdot}3\ (\frac{\text{Col. 5}}{\text{Col. 2}})].$$

agriculture. This discussion is not relevant for our purposes. We need to know the effects of public policy on the terms of trade. The difference between prices received by farmers and those they *would* have received in the absence of public action affecting those prices, multiplied by the volume of commodities sold by farmers, is one part of the intersectoral surplus transfer brought about by price manipulation. The other part is the difference between prices paid by farmers and those they *would* have paid in the absence of public action affecting those prices, multiplied by the volume of commodities bought by farmers. The usual index-number problems arise in measuring 'volumes of commodities'—together with two special problems. First, the price manipulation causes both buyers and sellers to make substitutions, which in turn affect relative prices again; the impact of this distortion can be reduced by looking at broad groups of products (e.g. grains rather than wheat) where substitution is more difficult. Second, we know only the volumes of commodities *actually* bought and sold by farmers, so that these are the only things we can multiply by price differences to estimate resource transfers; but an equally valid procedure would be to multiply these differences by the (unfortunately unknown) volumes of commodities that *would have been* bought and sold, in the absence of public policy altering prices. Despite these methodological difficulties, we can reach four firm conclusions. First, PL 480 food aid transferred a substantial volume of resources from agriculture to non-agriculture—perhaps four per cent of total Indian farm income in 1960–66, far more than was transferred by the tax system. Second, high tariffs on processed industrial imports further increased the amount of agricultural product that the farmer needed to sell in order to buy his inputs and non-agricultural consumer goods. Third, the artificially low rate of exchange for the rupee, together with import licensing policy and the much higher role of foreign exchange in non-agricultural than in agricultural inputs, constituted a hidden resource transfer from agriculture to non-agriculture. Fourth, these three transfers have been substantially cut since 1976—by rupee devaluation, fertiliser subsidies, and Government stockbuilding policy in foodgrains and the consequent levels of *ex farm* food prices.

What affects *ex farm* food prices is not the quantum of PL 480 food aid made available to the Government of India, but the net market releases of foodgrains by the GOI (PL 480 sold *less* stock bought). Suppose, in a particular year, these releases raise marketed foodgrains from T tons (domestic marketings) to T (1+x) tons. Suppose E is the (assumed constant) price-elasticity of demand for cereals at points on the demand curve between T and T (1+x). The proportionate fall in foodgrain prices is then $\frac{x}{E}$, and the loss in revenue to the farmers as a result of the releases is $T(\frac{x}{E})$, which is transferred as benefit to non-agriculture. This is not the end of the matter, because the farmers will somewhat reduce T in future years in response to the price fall, which in turn causes some price recovery;[34] this further cuts farm income, and there is a shift to non-cereal crop production and sale with mixed effects on farm income. The only unambiguous 'transfer from agriculture to non-agriculture' (as opposed to this subsequent loss by agriculture) is the instantaneous PL 480 effect on prices, $T(\frac{x}{E})$. A fair estimate of E for foodgrains in India is 0·7.[35] It is estimated that about 5 per cent of Indian cereal availability in 1957–63 was from PL 480 sources;[36] in 1964–67 the proportion was probably nearer 10 per cent and in 1968–69 perhaps 3 per cent. Cereals are about 95 per cent of Indian foodgrain needs (the rest being pulses), so that PL 480 comprised perhaps 4·8 per cent, 9·5 per cent and 2·9 per cent of total foodgrains in these three periods. With E = 0·7 this implies falls in farm revenue from foodgrain sales, representing direct transfers to non-agricultural income, of respectively 6·9 per cent, 13·4 per cent, and 4·2 per cent in the three periods. There is no separate estimate for total farm foodgrain sales to non-agriculture, but total *food* sales seem to have made up about one-fifth of total consumer spending,[37] so that *foodgrain* sales might reasonably be estimated at one-sixth of total consumer spending. The latter is about 80 per cent of GNP and agricultural income is about 48 per cent. Thus income from food grain sales is between 25 and 30 per cent of agricultural income. The above estimate of proportionate PL-480-induced falls in farm revenue from these sales, therefore, implies transfers from agriculture to non-agriculture of about 1·9 per cent of farm income in 1957–63, about 7·7 per cent in 1964–7, and about 1·2 per cent in 1968–9.

This is very crude and approximate, but the scale of these transfers is clearly bigger than that attributable to direct public tax action. If we could make some estimate of the effect of other aspects of Indian foreign-exchange and tariff policy, a further substantial net transfer out of agriculture would be revealed.

VII CONCLUSIONS

Private agriculturalists' saving has been very slightly in excess of private agricultural investment. This is a pity, since the marginal capital/output ratio in agriculture is almost half the level in industry.[38] The excess, however, is probably barely one per cent of agricultural income. Public current outlay benefiting agriculturists (directly and indirectly) has fallen short of public taxation by rather more than public investment in agriculture.

Taxation of agriculture has exceeded the 'fair' amount (relative to ability to pay) by about 1½ per cent to 2½ per cent of agriculturists' incomes.

The main resource transfers out of agriculture, however, have not taken the conventional forms—extraction of a saving or tax surplus. They have been achieved by foreign trade and exchange-rate policies tending to worsen the agriculturists' terms of trade (although it is not apparent that these have deteriorated absolutely), and by rural skill drain. In the 1960s, PL 480 policy alone devoted about 2 to 4 per cent of yearly total farm income to the non-farm sector. The rural skill drain, while very hard to quantify, is probably the most important transfer of all. Since highly productive resources are transferred out of agriculture successfully, while demographic factors keep the share of people dependent on agriculture fairly steady, income distribution gradually moves against the already poorer agricultural sector. Moreover, there is a 'cumulative causation' by which the articulate, better-off towns attract more resources, become more articulate and better-off, attract more resources, and so on. This is obviously not conducive to rapid development.

NOTES AND REFERENCES

1. *Cf.* M. Lipton, 'Strategy for Agriculture: Urban Bias and Rural Planning', in P. Streeten and M. Lipton (eds.), *The Crisis of Indian Planning*, Oxford, 1968, pp. 88–95.
2. Among recent work, see, *inter alia*, G. Papanek, *Pakistan's Development*, Harvard, 1967, p. 207; H. M. Southworth and B. C. Johnston (eds.), *Agricultural Development and Economic Growth*, Cornell, 1966, p. 561; R. B. Bangs, *Financing Economic Development*, Chicago, 1968, p. 22.
3. V. Gandhi, *Tax Burden on Indian Agriculture*, Harvard Law School, 1966, has been widely cited in this regard. See also J. Cutt, *Taxation and Economic Development in India*, Praeger, 1969.
4. 69·7 per cent of India's 1951 working population were cultivators and agricultural labourers; in 1961 the percentage was exactly the same. There have been small changes in definitions, however. The result is supported by National Sample Surveys and other data. Institute of Applied Manpower Research, *Fact Book on Manpower*, New Delhi, 1962, esp. p. 18.
5. Streeten and Lipton, *loc. cit.*, pp. 142–4; and almost any Plan document, but notably *Second Five Year Plan*, Delhi, 1956, pp. 111–9.
6. Among people aged 15 to 44, there were 127 men for every 100 women in urban India in 1961. In the villages, the loss of migrant men was not even sufficient to outweigh the normal excess of male births, and men actually predominated in these age-groups (101 per 100 women). *U.N., Demographic Yearbook 1967*, pp. 172–3.
7. A. M. Khusro, *A Survey of Living and Working Conditions of Students of the University of Delhi*, Asia (London), 1967, pp. 31, 72, 77.
8. V.K.R.V. Rao, *University Education and Employment*, Institute of Economic Growth (Delhi), pp. 10–11.
9. Institute of Applied Manpower Research, *Fact Book on Manpower*, Delhi, 1963, pp. 6, 85; E. T. Mathew, *Agricultural Taxation and Economic Development in India*, Asia (London), 1968, p. 47; T. Burgess, R. Layard and P. Plant, *Manpower and Educational Development in India 1961–1968*, p. 3. The first and last source give slightly different results for the 1961 proportion of matriculates in rural areas—respectively 30·3 per cent and 32·1 per cent.
10. Not only on obvious equity grounds; it is inefficient too. Unless village children have systematically lower learning power than town children, to draw only 34 per cent of university students from the 82 per cent of children in rural areas is, at the margin, to use scarce teachers on dull town students instead of bright country students. Of course, the rural skill drain does ultimately deplete the rural genetic pool, as the more *educable* drift to the towns, stay there, and produce brighter children; but this cannot mean that the marginal return to the Indian university teacher's time, from training urban and rural children, is equated when the former's chance of getting to college is 8½ times as great as the latter's, as at present.

11. Much less of women. In my eight months in a Maharashtrian village I noticed more and more women replacing migrant brothers as farm operators. But the Indian educational system's bias against women is getting less and less, and the really able women will soon be drained townwards too.
12. *All-India Rural Household Survey*, N.C.A.E.R. (Delhi), 1965, 1966, vol. 3, pp. 59, 77, 111; for confidence limits, cf. vol. 2, pp. 57, 85.
13. Reserve Bank of India Bulletin, Bombay, March 1965, p. 322. The Bank estimates exclude non-monetised investment from both saving and investment data, but include inventory investment. However, non-monetised investment could account for, at very most, 90 Cr. rupees of the Household Survey's 1962 estimate (*loc. cit.*, pp. 58–9, estimate. (10) of net rural saving—half the value of extra 'buildings and business premises, means of irrigation, separate farm structures and land improvement'. That leaves a Household Survey estimate of *at least* 360 Cr.Rs. and an RBI estimate of Rs. 237 Cr.Rs. for rural net savings in 1962—both excluding non-monetised investment and purchases of consumers' durables, both including currency acquisitions and inventory investment!
14. An estimate by P. G. K. Panikar of *total* Indian rural savings in 1951 puts the rural saving/income ratio as high as 12 per cent, as against the Reserve Bank estimate (excluding non-monetised investment and consumers' durables but including inventories) for 1950–51/1952–53 of only 2·2 per cent! Reserve Bank, *Loc. cit.*, p. 327; P. G. K. Parikar, 'An Essay on Rural Savings in India', Ph.D. Thesis (unpub.) Vanderbilt University, 1959, p. 182; Mathew, *Loc. cit.*, p. 59.
15. Reserve Bank, *loc. cit.*, p. 330.
16. The Planning Commission's most recent sectoral estimate of Indian private investment, for 1956–7/1960–1, showed agriculture, community development, irrigation, and village and small industries (by no means all rural) getting exactly 27 per cent of total private investment (R. Hill, in Streeten and Lipton, *op. cit.*, p. 390). Since the overwhelming bulk of non-monetised investment is in the rural sector, the proportion of *monetised* investment there can hardly have exceeded 20 per cent.
17. Gandhi, *op. cit.*, p. 105–6.
18. *Ibid*, p. 58.
19. D. N. Dwivedi, 'Taxable Capacity of Agricultural Sector', *Economic and Political Weekly*, 14 Dec. 1968, p. 1911.
20. G. S. Chatterjee and N. Bhattacharya, 'Rural–Urban Differences in Consumer Prices', *Economic and Political Weekly*, 17 May 1969, p. 852. We use the index showing the price of the rural consumer bundle in urban areas (termed by the authors the 'Laspeyres' index!) because this index most inflates urban prices and hence differential subsistence requirements, and is hence the least likely to support the thesis of this paper, that the urban sector is *undertaxed* relative to the rural sector, taking account of ability to pay.
21. Some slight evidence does exist that Uttar Pradesh prices are not too far from All-India prices. A ranking of the 45 Indian cities, in decreasing

order of middle-class costliness in 1958–9, placed the four Uttar Pradesh cities twelfth, sixteenth, twenty-seventh and twenty-ninth—average 21 out of 45, almost exactly halfway down the list. C. G. Gopal Krishna, 'Ranking of Cities according to Costliness', *Economic and Political Weekly,* 30 Nov. 1968, p. 1851.

22. Gandhi, *op. cit.,* pp. 112–3.
23. Gandhi, *op. cit.,* pp. 107–8, actually allocates half the value of land to agriculture and *none* to non-agriculture 'because of [the] non-productive and hence non-taxable character' of urban land values! (n.12, p. 120). This, of course, enormously inflates agricultural wealth *relative to other wealth,* and further biases Gandhi's much-quoted estimates of taxable capacity. A comparison of Gandhi, pp. 107, 108, with 'Estimates of Tangible Wealth in India', *RBI Bulletin,* Jan. 1963, p. 18, shows that Gandhi has proceeded as described above in sectoral allocation of land values.
24. It is 3·48 per cent of such *rural* wealth. *All India Rural Survey,* Vol. 11, p. 18.
25. Gandhi, p. 108, (a) increasing his (RBI) data for non-land, non-livestock wealth by 3 per cent for consumer durables—see note 24, (b), increasing his (RBI) land values from half to two-thirds of the RBI all-India total.
26. Non-agricultural non-land wealth from Gandhi, p. 107; consumer durables are surely at least 4 per cent of this, if they are 3 per cent for agriculturists; non-agricultural land wealth from *RBI Bulletin,* Jan. 1963, p. 18.
27. Col. 3 on Col. 2 of Table 15, *All India Rural,* vol. 11, p. 55. I am grateful to Mr. S. Biggs for the regression; as stated (*ibid.,* p. 54) $r^2 = 0{\cdot}99$.
28. *Ibid.,* p. 50, table 11.
29. By calculating the ratio of capital-per-household for the group, as predicted by the regression, to capital-per-household (excluding land and livestock) for the whole rural sector in 1962 (1013 Rs: *ibid,* p. 55). Since the regression predicts only *average* capital in each group from *average* income we do not expect the groups' percentages of total group capital to total exactly 100 per cent, as indeed they do not (105·13 per cent). Hence each group's share of capital is scaled down by 100/105·13.
30. The shares of total sectoral capital in the rural (urban) sector for groups of households by *incomes per household* are: top percentile group 10·74% (18·93%); second, 4·95% (7·00%); third, 3·97% (3·95%); fourth, 3·45% (3·27%); fifth, 3·09% (3·03%); second 5 per cent 11·99% (12·42%); second decile, 16·57% (16·17%); third, 12·04% (10·30%); fourth, 9·39% (7·38%); fifth, 7·38% (6·00%); sixth, 5·85% (4·51%); seventh, 4·59% (3·56%); eighth, 3·43% (2·31%); ninth, 2·29% (1·02%); bottom decile, 0·26% (0·15%). Rural shares calculated as in Para. 21; urban shares by assuming that the association between income-share and capital-share is the same in rural and urban sectors. For example, from Table 1, col. 7, the top urban percentiles (by income) of households has 16·0 per cent of income; from Table 1, col. 2, 16 per cent of *rural* income goes to the top two rural household percentiles, *plus* about 82 per cent of the third

percentile; therefore, we assign the top urban percentile the same proportion of *urban* capital these groups get of *rural* capital, i.e., 10·74%+4·95%+(82 per cent of 73·95%) or 18·93%.

31. Mathew, *op. cit.*, p. 49.
32. *Statistical Abstract, India 1965*, pp. 589, 582. Figures for 1958–9.
33. Mathew, *op. cit.*, p. 48 for the ratio of rural to agricultural outlay.
34. J. S. Mann, 'The Impact of Public Law 480 Imports on Prices and Domestic Supply of Cereals in India', *Journal of Farm Economics*, Feb. 1967, pp. 131–146.
35. J. W. Mellor, *The Economics of Agricultural Development*, Cornell, 1966, pp. 66–72.
36. Mann, *loc. cit.*, p. 131.
37. R. Thamarajakshi, 'Intersectoral Terms of Trade and Marketed Surplus of Agricultural Produce, 1951–2 to 1965–6', *Economic and Political Weekly*, 28 June 1969, p. A-95, Table 5, Cols, 2, 6.
38. M. Lipton, 'Urban Bias and Rural Planning', in P. Streeten and M. Lipton (ed.), *The Crisis of Indian Planning*, Oxford, 1968.

Chapter 10

Equity *versus* Ease in Indian Land Tax Policy

J. F. J. TOYE

I. THE EQUITY/EASE TRADE-OFF

One of the central choices that confronts designers of direct taxes is that of the precise combination of equity and administrative ease. Both equity and administrative ease are normally accepted as desirable objectives in the design of taxes. But the objectives conflict with each other. Equity requires a tax sufficiently flexible to adjust the size of the tax payment to the individual taxpayer's ability to pay. Administrative simplicity, by contrast, requires a tax where the due payment can be quickly and simply calculated, and promptly and conveniently collected. Thus tax designers face the painful dilemma of being able to achieve improvements in equity only by increasing the difficulty of tax administration, or, alternatively, of being able to reduce these difficulties only by accepting additional inequities.

The general form of this dilemma, with reference to agricultural land taxation, is neatly illustrated by the difference of opinion between Haskell P. Wald, author of *Taxation of Agricultural Land in Underdeveloped Economies*, and Richard M. Bird, who has recently revised and greatly expanded Wald's classic 1959 study. Wald argued for an 'ideal land tax', levied progressively on a tax base of presumptive net income, despite the high information requirements and administrative costs that this would involve. Bird regards such a tax as a solution which assumes away the basic problem—the underdevelopment of administrative capacity in poor countries. He argues that, to the extent that a land tax is desirable at all, it should be designed exclusively for the purpose of producing revenue. It should be as simple as possible, and, by implication, as crude from the equity viewpoint as is politically tolerable. Attempts to personalise the land tax are to be discouraged because they 'generally succeed only in making it more complex, which in turn both makes the administrative task more difficult and also affords more opportunity for opponents to block and weaken its [revenue] impact'.[1]

This paper re-examines the proposal of an Agricultural Holding Tax (AHT) for India in the light of these opposing resolutions of the equity *versus* ease dilemma. The AHT, a tax on the value of normal net output of a family's agricultural landholding, was the centre piece recommendation of the Committee on Taxation of Agricultural Wealth and Income, which reported to the Government of India in October, 1972.[2] Although some of the Committee's minor supporting recommendations were implemented in the Central Government budget of 1973, hardly any state government has moved in the direction of introducing an AHT–like tax, and current indications are that such moves are not likely in the immediate future. The question naturally arises whether this poor political response to the AHT proposal should be interpreted as a vindication of Bird's view that 'attempts to achieve [improved resource allocation and income distribution through land taxation] are likely to confuse the main issue [the revenue objective] and make its attainment substantially more difficult'.[3] Assuming the need for some reform of existing direct taxes on Indian agriculture, should it take the form of a uniform, impersonal and proportional land tax?

The AHT proposal can be said to be in the broad tradition of Wald's 'ideal land tax', as reformulated in the Indian context by T. M. Joshi and his collaborators.[4] This is so in the sense that it involves an attempt to relate tax payments to ability to pay, a progressive rate structure and an alleged incentive to improve agricultural productivity. On the other hand, it also departs in some respects from that tradition. The rationale of the AHT proposal is not presented primarily in terms of the need for revenue. The fragmentation of landholding in India is so severe that the revenue prospect from almost any form of land taxation cannot be other than small in relation to total tax revenue and to total income originating in agriculture. Little's estimate of extra revenue from a reformed progressive land tax was 120–150 crores of rupees, an amount equal to 8–10 per cent of total tax revenue and 2 per cent of agricultural income in 1960–61.[5] In these circumstances, it is difficult to rest the case for agricultural tax reform on its contribution to the fisc, except on the principle that every little helps. The other difficulty in starting with a revenue objective is the absence of a sound criterion to determine how large the fiscal contribution of agriculture ought to be. The Committee on the Taxation of Agricultural Wealth and Income explicitly rejected the proposition that the magnitude of agriculture's fiscal contribution could be set in the light of a target rate of saving from the agricultural sector.[6]

The foundation on which the AHT proposal is said to rest is that 'equity has to be the major consideration'.[7] But its notion of equity was not that of equity between the tax/income ratios of the agricultural and non-agricultural *sectors*, on the grounds that the ability to pay of a sector cannot be defined independently of the abilities to pay of the individual taxpaying units of which each sector is composed.[8] The Committee's definition of equity was that 'the incidence of direct taxation should be broadly the same on comparable income and wealth groups irrespective of the sources of such income and the forms in which wealth is held'.

'To be broadly the same' is an insufficient guide to policy without an explicit paradigm. It is clear that for the Committee, the paradigm adopted was, with two exceptions, the existing Central income tax on non-agricultural incomes. (The two exceptions were (a) that the assessment unit for non-agricultural income tax should become the nuclear family, not the individual and the Hindu Undivided Family and (b) that the tax base should take in livestock breeding and poultry and dairy farming.) Although, within its terms of reference, the Committee could have recommended further changes, none apart from those mentioned were in fact recommended. Since silence in these circumstances must be interpreted as consent, it is manifest that the internal equity of the non-agricultural income tax was (with the two ammendments) endorsed.

Thus when we come to categorise the AHT proposal in the spectrum between Wald's ideal land tax and Bird's uniform, impersonal and proportional land tax, we find that it is very close to the former in terms of its rationale. The major difference is that, in the absence of really significant unexploited revenue potential, one of the secondary objectives of the ideal land tax (equity) is elevated to be its primary objective. Once this is done, however, the only thoroughly logical solution is to design an agricultural income tax, and not a land tax at all. This point is well understood by the Committee's chairman, Professor K. N. Raj. Since the Report's publication, he has written that 'in principle the best way of making direct taxes equitable and logical is to have a progressive tax on agricultural income'.[9] On this point, his position agrees with that of Bird, who correctly states that 'if we judge the land tax on how closely it resembles an income tax, it is virtually certain to look inferior [since] nothing resembles an income tax as much as an income tax'.[10] Professors Raj and Bird further agree that an effective and equitable tax on agricultural income is simply not administratively feasible. Put generally, infeasibility arises from the absence of six crucial favourable factors—high monetisation, mass literacy, the keeping of honest and reliable accounts, voluntary compliance, a favourable political context, and administrative competence. More specifically, it is said that assessment of actual income will, in the absence of these favourable influences, involve the tax authorities either in excessive harassment of assessees, or in the toleration of excessive evasion.[11]

This conflict between the claims of equity and the claims of administrative ease is susceptible of four possible resolutions. These may be mentioned, with brief comments.

(a) The initial premise that 'equity must be the major consideration' may be denied. That equity *need* not be the major consideration is well enough attested by its absence from most existing systems of agricultural taxation. But to endorse the existing state of affairs in this regard is to go against one of the fundamental elements in both the liberal and the socialist conceptions of political justice. Since development as a goal involves, among other things, precisely the realisation of one or other of these concepts of political justice, a denial of the importance of tax equity shifts the discussion to a plane that development theorists have little interest in inhabiting.

(b) If tax equity is retained as a major objective of tax design, a crude, but easily administered, land tax can be given a certain justification in terms of equity as a tax on an important category of wealth, ownership of which may be broadly related to ability to pay taxes. But even its advocates recognise that this is a relatively weak justification, which is at its weakest for a land tax levied in the *absence* of a tax on agricultural income. A land tax becomes more equitable when used as a supplement to an agricultural income tax, when it can tap taxable capacity that is not fully reflected in an household's flow of money income from agricultural operations.[12] If, by common consent, an agricultural income tax is administratively impossible, then the equity of a crude land tax, standing on its own, must be highly suspect.

(c) The view that taxing agricultural income is administratively impossible is widely held. But it seems to rest only on ritual incantations of the desiderata for effective income taxation. One tactic is, therefore, to deny the administrative impossibility of taxing agricultural income. Are all of the conventional desiderata necessary conditions? Are many of them sufficient conditions? Since the 'requirements' span both the technical and the political, can one identify the nature of the binding constraint?[13] If the binding constraint is indeed one of administrative technique (lack of administrative skills, rather than lack of funds or political authority to employ existing skills), what would be the cost of relaxing the constraint, and would the cost be justified by the consequent social benefits? There are examples of research in the Indian context aimed at defining the overall scale of the problem.[14] But it clearly needs to be reinforced by research on such questions as the percentage of potential assessees who do, or could easily, keep accounts, and who file financial statements with state lending institutions in the process of securing credit. One would also want to know the cost of tax assessment for non-agricultural income tax of petty urban traders or rural moneylenders, where assessment already proceeds with a similar level of information as is likely to be available for agricultural income tax assessment. This paper does not purport to answer any of these questions: it merely suggests that answers are needed, and that future research may show that the administrative costs of taxing agricultural income in an equitable manner have, through ignorance, been overstated.

(d) Since we are not prepared to deny outright, on the basis of existing evidence, the doctrine that an agricultural income tax is administratively impossible; and since we are neither prepared to abandon the tax equity objective or to be content with the equity of a crude land tax standing on its own; the only remaining approach is to search for an acceptable compromise between equity and administrative ease. The interest of the Indian AHT proposal is that it essays just such a compromise. As long as it is thought, notwithstanding the fiscal *realpolitik* of Professor Bird, that such compromises are desirable, the question of the precise form of the 'ideal land tax' will continue to merit re-examination. Does the AHT proposal constitute, in fact, a truly 'ideal' land tax?

II. EQUITY ASPECTS OF THE AHT PROPOSAL

The argument of this paper is that, even granting the administrative impossibility of an agricultural income tax, the AHT proposal is a compromise which unnecessarily departs from the equity objective, which is said to be the major consideration underlying its design. In sub-section (a) below, the problem of vertical inequity is presented. In the following sub-sections, three possible types of justification for vertical inequity are examined, (b)–(d). In sub-section (e), horizontal inequity is examined, along with the alleged production incentive effects of the AHT proposal. A summary of conclusions is given in Section III.

(a) *The Vertical Inequity of AHT*

Since the Committee on the Taxation of Agricultural Wealth and Income took equity as its major consideration, defined as similarity in incidence to the existing non-agricultural income tax, it is odd how poorly the rate structure of AHT resembles that of non-agricultural income tax. This oddity was briefly remarked by one of the Committee's early critics.[15] The point is elaborated in Table 1, which compares the amount of tax that would be payable at certain AHT rateable values with tax payable if the same sum were income assessed to tax.

TABLE 1

COMPARISON OF TAX LIABILITY UNDER AHT AND NON-AGRICULTURAL INCOME TAX

(1) *AHT Rateable Value or Taxable Income (Rs)*	(2) *AHT Payment (Rs)*	(3) *Non-agric Income tax payable (1972 rates) (Rs)*	(4) *Non-agric Income tax payable (1976 rates) (Rs)*
5,000	80	0	0
10,000	405	500	330
15,000	980	1350	1155
20,000	1805	2500	2145
25,000	2880	400	3520
30,000	4205	6000	5170
35,000	5780	8500	7370

Source: Col. (2), calculated from the formula in *Report*, pp. 41–42. Col. (3) and (4), calculated from old and new income tax rates given in *Times of India* (16 March 1976).

The figures in this table make it clear that, in the rateable value/taxable income range up to Rs. 35,000 (where the great bulk of agriculturists will fall), the proposed AHT is much less progressive than the non-agricultural income tax. This is so using 1972 or the lower 1976 tax rates for the latter. The 1976 Budget has not reduced to a significant extent the progressivity of the non-agricultural income tax because reductions have affected high and low rates almost proportionately. The inequitable treatment of agricultural and non-agricultural income that would have continued even if AHT had been imposed has thus not been righted *ex post facto*. All that has happened is that the 'income of equivalent burden' has risen from 6,500 Rs (with 150 Rs tax payment) to 11,000 Rs (with 500 Rs tax payment).

The above comparison of tax liability under the two types of tax assumes that a rateable value of X rupees for AHT purposes is equivalent to a taxable income of X rupees for the purposes of non-agricultural income tax. But is this assumption of equivalence valid? As has been mentioned, the tax base for AHT (the rateable value) is intended as measure of the normal net output of a landholding, derived from average output figures (related to crop-mix and soil type) valued at average prices, minus a percentage deduction for costs of cultivation. Since the output and price averages use historic data, when the trend of output and prices is upwards, the net income of the landholder will exceed the normal value of net output as indicated by rateable value. From this it follows that equity requires a threshold rateable value for AHT below the threshold for non-agricultural income tax. Therefore the discrepancy which appears in the first row of Table 1 does not necessarily involve any inequity. During an upward trend in output and prices, this is correct. But the implication of accepting this argument is that the AHT rate schedule produces a less progressive AHT incidence by income class than appears from Table 1. If (for illustration only) AHT rateable value must be multiplied by a factor of 2 to equate it with taxable income, the incidence of AHT as compared with non-agricultural income tax would be as shown in Table 2. The degree of AHT progression, which was already mild by comparison with that of non-agricultural income tax, becomes milder as a multiplication factor greater than unity is used to equate rateable value with taxable income.

One can try to escape from this conclusion by arguing that the multiplication should be less than unity. This might be done on the argument, for example, that the purchasing power of a rupee in the non-agricultural sector is greater than that of a rupee earned in agriculture (because of relative transport costs, differential impact of indirect taxes, etc.). But obviously, though this would lessen the difference between tax liabilities at the upper end of the income scale, it would widen the difference at the lower end, and would require, for equity, an AHT threshold *above* the threshold for non-agricultural income tax. One would simply have shifted one's position to the other horn of the same basic dilemma.

TABLE 2

COMPARISON OF TAX LIABILITY UNDER AHT AND NON-AGRICULTURAL INCOME TAX, IF R.V.=T.1/2

(1) *Taxable Income (Rs)*	(2) *Equivalent Rateable Value (Rs) =(1)÷2*	(3) *Income Tax Payment at 1976 rates (Rs)*	(4) *Equivalent AHT Payment (Rs)*
5,000	2,500	0	20
10,000	5,000	330	80
15,000	7,500	1155	211
20,000	10,000	2145	405
25,000	12,500	3520	661
30,000	15,000	5170	980
35,000	17,500	7370	1361

Source: Col. (3), as in Table 1.
Col. (4), calculated from the formula used in *Report*, pp. 41–42.

Table 3 shows that with a switch to a two-year period for the

(b) *Justification in Terms of a Minimum Revenue Constraint?*

It is as well to remind ourselves that that Committee's Report says only that equity has to be the *major* consideration. Is it possible that there are minor considerations which can justify the departure for complete equity (as defined by the Committee) which has been exhibited in sub-section (a)? Before discussing possible justifications in terms of the need for administrative simplicity, two other possibilities have to be examined. They are, first, that, without acknowledging it, the Committee was influenced, in choosing the form of AHT, by a minimum revenue target; and, second, that it was influenced by a view of the tactics most likely to win political acceptance for the AHT.

Although it may be suspected that, in fact, the Committee recommended the imposition of AHT below 5000 rupees out of consideration for the size of the revenue to be realised, the mildness of the AHT's progression cannot be justified by the need to meet a minimum revenue constraint. In the first place, the Report itself rejects a revenue target as something for which no satisfactory analytical basis can be found. Its logical standpoint therefore must be that if, after an equitable tax on agriculture is devised, the revenue estimate is very small, this merely disproves the popular contention that agriculture is under-taxed. If this logic was later regarded as unacceptable in all its starkness, and a minimum revenue constraint observed notwithstanding, it does not follow that the constraint had to be satisfied in the way chosen. If the AHT, as designed, would bring in 150 crores of rupees when imposed on rateable values above 500 rupees, and if in addition a minimum revenue constraint of 200 crores was implicitly accepted, there are at least two ways in which the extra 50 crores could have been brought in besides the extension of AHT to RVs between 600 and 5000 rupees.

One way of making AHT yield extra revenue would be to shorten the averaging period in calculating output norms for the determination of rateable value. The Chairman of the Committee indicated, after the Report was published, that he did not regard the 10-year averaging period as sacrosanct, and that it could be well shortened, if so desired.[16] In times of rising productivity and prices, an output norm based on current yields in areas of assured irrigation or on an average of a few recent years in areas of variable water availability will raise the revenue yield of the AHT. Some estimates have been made for two states, Andhra Pradesh and Punjab, to compare the revenue effects of a 10-year averaging period with those of a 2-year averaging period, using data for 1964–74.[17]

Table 3 shows that with a switch to a two year period for the averaging of output, the yield of AHT would increase by 37 per cent in Andhra Pradesh, and by an extraordinary 94 per cent in the Punjab. Of course, the Punjab figures reflects the 'green revolution' in wheat yield and thus is quite atypical of what is likely to be true of all-India. But it is noteworthy that even in Andhra, where the main crop is the dominant all-India crop of

TABLE 3

ESTIMATED REVENUE YIELD OF AHT ON ALTERNATIVE ASSUMPTIONS REGARDING LIABILITY AND OUTPUT AVERAGING

		(Rupees crores)
	Andhra Pradesh	*Punjab*
I. *AHT on all landholdings*		
(a) 10-year average	24·06	12·04
(b) 2-year average	33·14	23·42
II *AHT on landholdings of R.V. 5000 and above*		
(a) 10-year average	20·19	10·10
(b) 2-year average	27·84	21·27

Source: see reference number 17 at end of text.

paddy, use of a two-year average only for landholdings *above* 5000 rupees in rateable value would produce 15 per cent more revenue than use of a ten-year average in respect of all landholdings. In other words, if Andhra is at all typical of the all-India situation, the need for a minimum revenue from AHT cannot justify imposing AHT on landholdings below 500 rupees in R.V. unless both the rate structure formula and the ten-year output average are regarded as sacrosanct.

One can question the basis of the revenue estimates quoted above. They have certain crudities. In the absence of the demarcation of agro-climatically homogenous tracts in the two states (as required by the full procedure for determining rateable values), each state has been treated as a single tract. In addition, in computing the costs to be deducted from average gross output, a straight 40 per cent deduction was made for all costs of cultivation, without making a detailed study of actual costs of different types of irrigation as the method really requires. However, one can be morally certain that these crudities must also have affected the revenue estimates made by the Committee itself. This view is strengthened by the Report's reluctance to state any revenue estimates at all, and by the absence of any indication of the method used to arrive at the estimates that were reluctantly published. Thus the estimates in

Table 3 cannot be brushed aside on the grounds that the estimating method is defective, since the Committee, if it was trying to satisfy a minimum revenue constraint, must have been taking decisions using estimates that were just as defective, if not more so.

(c) *Justification as a Political Tactic?*

Apart from an implicit revenue target, one of the Committee's other unacknowledged minor considerations may have been the broad political acceptability of the AHT proposal. It may have taken the view that the progression of the AHT must be kept mild to mute the opposition that could be expected to confront a proposal with a more radical appearance. As the Report notes, the radical appearance of the non-agricultural income tax is, in fact, deceptive anyway: for a number of reasons, 'the actual progression is much less steep than the nominal rate structure suggests'.[18] Was it then necessary to design the AHT to approximate the actual progression of non-agricultural income tax and thereby avoid frightening off potential political support in advance? Although plausible, this line of reasoning does not really carry conviction. Why is it that the actual progression of the income tax is more moderate than the nominal rate structure? The causes are threefold: numerous exemptions and rebates, the scope left for splitting income between individuals within a family and evasion of tax on an extensive scale. The Report itself suggests a change to the nuclear family as the unit of tax assessment, which, if implemented, would remove the second factor. The Committee does not endorse the popular view that tax evasion is generated by 'unrealistic' nominal rates: since it neither recommends reduced rates nor condones tax evasion, its preference must be for more vigorous enforcement of existing rates—which would remove the third factor listed above. The Report says nothing on the questions of the first factor—exemptions and rebates—but presumably it thinks that they are justifiable, and presumably it has built those exemptions and rebates it considers appropriate into its design of the AHT. It follows therefore one cannot justify the milder rate structure formula for AHT on the ground that this brings the AHT into line with the effective progression of non-agricultural income tax.

So is the AHT's mild progression acceptable purely as a political tactic to ensure a positive political response? There is a school of thought, perhaps now a rather old-fashioned one, which holds that the function of a committee of experts is to formulate and advocate that solution which in their collective opinion is the most rational method of attaining the objectives in their terms of reference. Experts may have ideas on whether their solution in whole or in part will win political support, but, according to this school, the responsibility for adjusting the most rational solution to maximise its political support ought to rest with politicians, whose expertise is supposed to lie precisely in calculating what compromises are necessary. If the tax experts doctor their advice in advance on political calculations (e.g. mild progression will avert the wrath of the rich farmer lobby), they may anticipate correctly and gain the satisfaction of seeing their compromise plan accepted *in toto*. But they may anticipate incorrectly and fail, simultaneously, to influence events and to leave on the proverbial dusty shelf a plan whose internal rationality will preserve it until political circumstances alter. If the latter is considered a serious departure from the tax adviser's responsibilities, 'tactical' inequity cannot be justifiable.

(d) *Justification in Terms of Administrative Ease*

The progressiveness of the AHT is a reflection of its rate structure formula which was chosen in the interests of administrative simplicity. As the Report says, 'in the interests of AHT's uniform application all over the country and ease of application at the village level, it will be desirable to have the rate structure of the AHT as simple as possible'.[19] It is true that, as originally conceived, the rate structure formula was a very simple one, viz.

$$\text{AHT payment in rupees} = \text{RV}\left(\frac{\text{RV}}{2000} \times \frac{1}{100}\right) \qquad (1)$$

where RV is the rateable value in rupees. However, that is not the formula as finally recommended in the Report. Instead a 'development allowance' was introduced, calculated as 20 per cent of the rateable value for RVs between 600 and 500 rupees, or as a flat 1000 rupees for RVs of 500 and above. Thus formula (1) becomes

For 600 Rs < RV < 5000 Rs,

AHT payment in rupees =

$$(\text{RV} \times 0{\cdot}8)\ \left(\frac{[\text{RV} \times 0{\cdot}8]}{2000} \times \frac{1}{100}\right) \tag{2}$$

For RV > 5000 Rs,

AHT payment in rupees =

$$(\text{RV} - 1000)\ \frac{[\text{RV} - 1000]}{2000} \times \frac{1}{100} \tag{3}$$

The broad alternative to formulae like these would be to divide rateable values into, say, half-a-dozen assessment brackets, to apply to each bracket the appropriate tax percentage from an upward graduated set and sum the tax payment due on each packet. The arithmetical skills required by this alternative are actually fewer (involving multiplication and addition, instead of subtraction, multiplication and division) but the number of operational stages may be greater and therefore the opportunity for error may be a little greater. It is difficult to see that the administrative advantages of the formulae are anything other than marginal. Yet to gain this slight advantage, one has to give up an alternative which is far more flexible for the purpose of achieving equity between AHT and non-agricultural income tax payers.

The rigidity of the formulae is most evident in relation to very high rateable values, where it leads to not merely confiscatory, but 'over-confiscatory' taxation. No doubt the Committee operated on the assumption that there are no potential assessees with rateable values high enough to enter the range where the formula makes AHT confiscatory. This may well be true. Using the Report's own estimate, 18 acres of best quality land might earn an income not exceeding 25,000–30,000 Rs annually. To earn more than this while observing the new agricultural land ownership ceiling, a cultivator would have to be leasing an additional 50–60 acres of best quality land before he would be in the range where his average tax rate would exceed 50 per cent.[20] It may well be that the number of farmers who farm on such a scale is, at present, negligible. However, designing a new, permanent tax should mean planning for its adjustment to the anticipated circumstantial changes of at least the next decade. Between 1963–64 and 1973–74, price and productivity changes tripled the value added by agriculture at current prices.[21] Should a similar tripling occur in the decade after AHT's introduction, as well it may, the problem of assessees liable to an average tax rate of 50 per cent or more would cease to be negligible—unless the existing formulae are modified. How could it be? Little can be done by manipulating the 'development allowance' unless it is to be made monstrously large and lose its existing tenuous rationale. So either the 2000 R divisor must be increased, or a maximum average tax rate set *ab initio*. Since, for simplicity's sake, increase of the 2000 R divisor would have to be made in round thousands of rupees, this adjustment would lead to undesirable, and otherwise unnecessary, fluctuations in the revenue yield of AHT. To avoid this, it would be preferable to set a maximum average tax rate right from the start. Yet to do this is to add a third formula to the two which are at present proposed, and, once this is done, the claim that the three formulae are greatly preferable, on grounds of administrative simplicity, to the sum of percentages of slabs method begins to look quite indefensible.

It is still possible to stick at two formulae even with a maximum average tax rate—by exempting all land with RVs of less than 5000 Rs from AHT. This move would improve the vertical equity of the AHT while preserving such administrative advantages as it possesses. However, the Report firmly sets its face against such a solution. It is true that extension of AHT to holdings with an RV below 5000 Rs is regarded as a second stage of implementation, but it also definitely states that such a second stage is desirable. Why is this opportunity to improve equity at virtually no cost in administrative ease passed up?

The professed reasons are very curious ones, and, in the last resort, have no force. The Report says that 'payment of land revenue or some tax on holdings is itself widely regarded by landholders as necessary evidence of rights in their holdings'.[22] This may be true, but it is irrelevant. Small landholders may be willing to pay AHT, but that does not make it desirable to levy AHT from them. In any case, their willingness may be based on a mistaken belief. If a tax receipt in law were neither necessary nor sufficient to establish rights in a holding, taxing small landholders because they believe otherwise is nothing but the exploitation of ignorance. That this case is not quite as fanciful as it sounds is conceded, by implication, by the other reason advanced in the Report for levying AHT on RVs below 5000 Rs. That is, that 'it will make it necessary to maintain up-to-date records of rights in land'.[23] If the smallholder's belief were well founded, there could be no additional advantage—for example, to rural financial institutions who need security for loans—to be had from an up-to-date record of rights in land. Logically, then, these two 'reasons' are alternatives, and the first at least is irrelevant.

But should AHT be imposed on smallholders simply to force into being a better method of registering land rights? It could be said that this is is a rather backhanded way of doing things. Should not a new method of registering land rights be designed in the light of the primary purposes it is intended to serve, rather than as a by-product of a tax which, but for this consideration, would not have to be imposed at all? It could also be said that, given some of the inequitable features of AHT that are justified by the need for administrative ease, it is odd that it should be required to act as a catalyst for the hugely complex administrative task of re-registering all land rights. But maybe this kind of backhandedness is essential; for the sake of the argument, let us concede that it is. All that follows is that every landholder must pay some AHT. What does not necessarily follow is that this should involve a substantial, rather than a merely formal, violation of equity. For what objection can there be to levying AHT at the peppercorn rate of a single rupee on all holdings with RV below the exemption limit of non-agricultural income tax? That is exactly what the Report proposes for all RVs below 600 Rs. If a peppercorn one-rupee payment will serve the catalytic purpose for these landholdings, why will it not do the same for holdings between 600 Rs and the non-agricultural income tax threshold?

If that is so, then there are no good reasons in the Report why landholders with RVs below the non-agricultural income tax threshold should pay any more than the most nominal sum in AHT. To charge them at a peppercorn rate would substantially improve the equity of the tax vertically. It would also permit the specification of a maximum average tax rate, without adding to the administrative complexity of the assessment formulae, which, in turn would further improve the vertical equity of the tax—particularly a decade ahead when productivity and prices are likely to have risen substantially. These two improvements to equity could be made at no cost to the administrative ease objective. There would, however, be a loss of revenue. But, as has been indicated in sub-section (b), it is likely that the revenue loss from exempting landholders with RVs below 5000 Rs could be more than compensated by shortening the average period for output and prices in the estimation of rateable values. Shortening the averaging period would have the added advantage that it would improve the equivalence of rateable values and taxable income as tax bases, and render less urgent the task of determining the multiplication factor that would bring them to equivalence (as discussed in sub-section (a)).

(e) *Horizontal Inequity and the Alleged Incentive Effect*

It has been suggested that further improvements in vertical equity could be had at relatively little cost in administrative ease by substituting the sum of percentages of slabs method of assessment for the existing simple formulae. The former method would give the flexibility required to bring the degree of progression of AHT between the exemption limit and the maximum average rate more closely into line with the progression of the non-agricultural income tax. The best justification, in terms of equity, itself, for *not* proceeding in this way arises from the interdependence of vertical and horizontal equity. The point here is that, if equals are not being treated equally, the inequity involved is magnified the more progressive the tax is made. The Committee themselves were certainly aware of this point, since it is made in the course of their objections to imposing a progressive surcharge on the existing Indian land revenue system.[24]

In outline, the procedure for deriving AHT rateable values consists of (i) allowing for differences in the quality of land, (ii) allowing for differences in the pattern of crops grown, (iii) estimating a 'normal' output for each crop, and valuing it at a 'normal' price and (iv) deducting a uniform percentage of the figure derived from steps (i)–(iii) in respect of all cultivation costs (except irrigation costs to be deducted in the light of individual circumstances). Doubtless determining the tax base in this way will give greater horizontal equity than that in the existing land revenue system, but, equally obviously, it leaves something to be desired as well. It is a *faute de mieux* procedure. An attempt to treat equals equally is made with steps (i) and (ii), but not with steps (iii) and (iv), with the exception of irrigation costs. What this procedure does is to secure as much horizontal equity as is possible without undertaking the individual assessment of gross agricultural revenues and costs—which, if it were feasible, would dictate the replacement of an 'ideal land tax' by a normal agricultural income tax. As long as we continue to accept that an agricultural income tax is not administratively feasible, little more can be done to improve the horizontal equity of the AHT, and this may be a defensible basis for reluctance to increase the progressivity of the AHT via adoption of the sum of percentages of slabs assessment method.

Having said that, however, it must also be noted that the Report itself wrongly attempts to show that the horizontal inequity of the AHT has a beneficial effect in providing an incentive to raise 'standards of cultivation'. In a curious passage, the Report says that 'as a matter of policy, we should expect the standards of cultivation in larger agricultural holdings to be above the average; if they are not, it would be right and proper to introduce into the fiscal measures of this kind the bias necessary to improve the standards of cultivation in larger holdings and to bring them at least on par with the average'.[25] This is specifically in the context of using output norms in deriving rateable values.

This 'incentive' defence of horizontal inequity is riddled with ambiguities and confusions, as is frequent in discussions of incentives in ideal land tax proposals. The major ones may be briefly listed as follows:

A. 'Standards of cultivation' is a term that is never defined. If what is meant is physical standards of cultivation—the thoroughness of weeding, the precision of planting, spraying and harvesting etc., or the care of conservation of water and soil resources—one would expect the standards to be higher on small landholdings, for reasons long ago explained by Sen.[26] If, on the other hand, cultivation standards are measured by private profitability per acre, it is debatable whether this is something which ought to be encouraged as a matter of public policy in a land-scarce country which cannot meet its basic food needs from domestic production, and where opportunities to earn off-farm incomes are strictly limited.

B. The assumptions being made about farmer motivation are never spelled out. Under assumptions of standard microeconomic rationality, the imposition of AHT should have no effect on production decisions. *Ex hypothesi,* an individual's AHT payment will not change in any one year regardless of how much is produced or of the costs (except irrigation) of producing it. It is thus a fixed cost, and it is an elementary proposition that the profit-maximising output does not vary with changes in fixed costs. So much the worse for standard microeconomic assumptions, might be the riposte, one for which good arguments have been marshalled.[27] But some alternative set of behavioural assumptions is needed before the logic behind the supposed working of fiscal incentives can be discovered.

C. Presumably the underlying idea is that farmers producing less than normal output will try and reduce the proportionate burden of their AHT payment by producing more. There is no reason why, if this is the case, the incentive will only work for large landholders, as the Report suggests. Nor is there any reason why, if this psychology is accepted, it should apply only to farmers producing below the output norm. If they will react to reduce their tax penalty, why will not farmers producing above normal output react by producing more, to increase their tax advantage? If everyone produces more in this way, the result will be to raise rateable values in the following year. The question then becomes, how long will farmers continue to seek the AHT tax advantage, when it becomes clear that they must redouble their efforts in each successive year to stay ahead of the game? What kind of illusions must be attributed to them to ensure that private and public interest remain, so conveniently, the same?[28]

D. One result which the incentive effect (assuming it works as under C) will not have is to make the dispersion of farmers' net outputs converge on the norm. But it is only in the case of nil dispersion that the horizontal inequity implicit in the AHT tax base will be eliminated.

E. By producing the alleged incentive effect as a desirable feature of the AHT, there is a clear suggestion that tax penalties on those farmers who fail to achieve normal net output is in the public interest and does not constitute a serious injustice. But there may be a host of perfectly acceptable reasons for such failure in individual cases, and it cannot be assumed that the only reason is laziness or awkwardness. Can the Committee have forgotten that they were prescribing for a social system in which a certin rural class dominates access to credit, fertiliser, irrigation and advice at the expense of the mass of farmers?[29] If a tax based on presumptive norms were thought to be intrinsically just, why not advocate the same base for corporation and income tax? Why not tax a person on the average income of his tax bracket, regardless of whether he earned more or less? Or a company as if it had realised the industry average rate of return on assets, regardless of whether it actually made losses? Would not such methods create an incentive for the unsuccessful to achieve the (ever-receding) average? Why is it that essentially the same proposal, which seems comical when applied to the non-agricultural sector, can be seriously advocated by intelligent men for the agricultural sector?

To posit confidently a specific incentive effect of a given tax is almost always a mistake, because it is virtually certain that, on closer analysis, the question will turn out to be much more complicated than it seems.[30] In the case of the alleged AHT incentive effect, it is so poorly defined that it is difficult to know where to begin and end in unravelling the complexities. But, in the light of comments A–E above, it seems fair to conclude that if there are any incentive effects at all, they will not be such as to remove over time the horizontal inequities which must result from the recommended method of establishing rateable values. If the Committee were right about 'standards of cultivation' moving towards the average, then one need have no scruples about steepening the degree of progression in the rate structure. But since in all likelihood they are wrong, one must argue at least for caution in moving towards greater progressivity, out of respect for the equity objective itself.

III CONCLUSIONS

(i) There are a variety of possible resolutions of the conflict between tax equity and administrative ease. Simply to abandon the equity objective is morally unacceptable. A crude land tax, as proposed by Bird, comes perilously close to this, and, in Indian conditions of land fragmentation, cannot even offer compensation in the form of large, additional government revenues.

(ii) The proposed Indian Agricultural Holdings Tax is in the tradition of Wald's 'ideal land tax', but in the absence of sound criteria by which to set a revenue target, it takes equity as its primary objective. Logically, the objective of equity can only be met by an agricultural income tax, which is often said to be administratively impossible. If that were true, then equity could be approached only by some variant of the ideal land tax. It still needs, however, to be convincingly demonstrated that the impossibility is one of administrative technique *per se*, rather than one arising from certain broader characteristics of the polity. More research on this area of tax administration seems to be called for.

(iii) The AHT proposal in its detail is noticeably inconsistent with the equity objective its proposers define for themselves. These inconsistencies cannot be justified either in terms of the need to meet an unacknowledged minimum revenue constraint, or as an unacknowledged political tactic.

(iv) Although the rate structure formula was designed to be administratively simple, it is only slightly more so than the ascending percentages of slabs method, which gives much greater flexibility to raise the degree of progression. In any case, with no addition to administrative burdens the equity of the AHT can be improved by setting a maximum average rate of tax and exacting only a peppercorn payment for those with rateable values below the lowest income assessable to non-agricultural income tax. The revenue loss from the latter can be made up by shortening the averaging period used in assessing rateable values. The peppercorn rate will serve well enough side objectives concerned with establishing land rights.

(v) The only valid reason in equity why the rate progression should not be steepened is the horizontal inequity which necessarily arises from the presumptive element in the determination of rateable values. A defence of these inequities by an appeal to their production incentive effect rests on very shaky logical foundations: the conflict between revenue buoyancy and production incentives is never recognised.

(vi) Short-run improvement in Indian land taxation must involve the 'ideal land tax' in some form. The only sense in which Professor Bird's crude land tax would represent an improvement on the existing land revenue system in India, is that it would bring all-India uniformity, if even that were possible under existing political arrangements. But the AHT proposals can only be used to rally support for an ideal land tax if it is amended along the lines already suggested above. Such changes will not guarantee its political success. But if, in current Indian political conditions, tax reformers are condemned to frustration, as little of it as possible should be of their own devising. Taking a longer view, the design of the ideal land tax can be further simplified administratively if an effective egalitarian land reform makes a proportional rate of tax equitable. Further, a thorough-going socialist revolution would open up the possibility of assessing individual agricultural incomes by a Chinese-type method of democratic tax appraisal, in situations where the best bureaucratic efforts cannot do the job alone.[31]

REFERENCES

1 R. M. Bird, *Taxing Agricultural Land in Developing Countries*, Harvard University Press, Cambridge, Mass. 1974, pp. 221, 282–86.

2. *Report of the Committee on Taxation of Agricultural Wealth and Income* (Chairman: Professor K. N. Raj), Government of India, Ministry of Finance, New Delhi, 1972.

3 Bird, *op. cit.*, p. 294.

4 T. M. Joshi, N. Anjanaiah, and S. V. Bhende, *Studies in the Taxation of Agricultural Land and Income in India*, Asia Publishing House, London, 1968, pp. 197–212. *Cf.* A. C. Angrish, *Direct Taxation of Agriculture in India*, Somaiya Publications, Bombay, 1972, pp. 224–29.

5 I. M. D. Little, 'Tax Policy and the Third Plan', in P. Rosenstein—Rodan (editor), *Pricing and Fiscal Policies*, Allen and Unwin, London, 1964, pp. 66–68. *Cf. National Accounts Statistics 1960–61—1973–74*, Government of India, Central Statistical Organisation, New Delhi, February 1976, p. 12 (Table 4) and p. 67 (Table 26).

6 *Report*, pp. 1–2.

7 *Report*, p. 9.

8 *Report*, p. 8. *Cf.* Raj Krishna, 'Intersectoral Equity and Agricultural Taxation in India', *Economic and Political Weekly*, Special Number, August, 1972.

9 K. N. Raj. 'Direct Taxation of Agriculture', *Indian Economic Review*, Vol. VIII (New Series), No.1, April, 1973, p. 5.

10 Bird, *op. cit.*, p. 221.

11 Bird, *op. cit.*, pp. 63–64; *Report*, p. 19, p. 39.

12 Bird, *op. cit.*, pp. 209–10.

13 *Cf.* M. H. Best, 'Political Power and Tax Revenues in Central America', *Journal of Development Economics* Vol. 3, No.1, March, 1976, p. 61, note 22.

14 E.g., J. S. Garg, 'Resource Mobilization in the Agricultural Sector: Tax on Agricultural Income—An Appraisal', *Indian Journal of Agricultural Economics*, Vol XXX, No. 3, July–September, 1975, p. 62.

15 M. J. K. Thavaraj, 'Raj Committee Report', *Social Scientist*, Vol. 1, No. 10, May 1973, p. 62.

16 Raj, *op. cit.*, p. 9. *Cf.* C. H. Hanumantha Rao, 'Agricultural Taxation:

Raj Committee's Report'. *Economic and Political Weekly*, Vol. VII, No. 48, 25th Nov. 1972, p. 2346.

17 V. Sivaramakrishnan and G. S. Oka, 'Feasibility of a Switch-over to Agricultural Holdings Tax: A Case Study of Andhra Pradesh and Punjab', Discussion Paper (IES Training Programme, Batch VIII, Seminar 3) Institute of Economic Growth, Delhi, 18 Feb. 1976, p. 5.

18 *Report*, p. 9.

19 *Report*, p. 40.

20 *Report*, p. 11. *Cf.* P. S. Appu, *Ceiling on Agricultural Holdings*, Government of India, Ministry of Agriculture, New Delhi, 1972, pp. 62–65.

21 *National Accounts Statistics, op. cit.*, p. 16 (Table 5).

22 *Report*, p. 43.

23 *Ibidem*.

24 *Report*, pp. 19–20.

25 *Report*, p. 40.

26 A. K. Sen, 'An Aspect of Indian Agriculture', *Economic Weekly*, Annual Number, 1962.

27 M. Lipton, 'The Theory of the Optimising Peasant', *Journal of Development Studies* Vol. 4 No. 3, April 1968, pp. 327–48.

28 *Cf.* Bird, *op. cit.*, p. 219 and G. N. Ecklund, *Financing the Chinese Government Budget*, Edinburgh University Press, 1966, pp. 45–46.

29 *Cf.* Bird, *op.cit.*, p. 221.

30 *Cf.* M. Peston, 'Incentives, Distortion and the System of Taxation', in B. Crick and W. A. Robson (editors), *Taxation Policy*, Penguin Books, London, 1973, p. 59.

31 Ecklund, *op.cit.*, pp. 36–39.

PART FOUR

ECONOMIC EFFECTS OF TAXATION

Chapter 11 was presented to the Sixth Conference of Economists of the Economic Society of Australia and New Zeland at Hobart in May 1977. The author of it would like to thank the Australian National University for generous financial assistance towards the cost of field work in Thailand; the Bank of Thailand for its ever-ready co-operation in providing research facilities and valuable data; and Dr. P. Drysdale for very helpful comments. For any remaining errors and deficiencies, the usual disclaimer applies.

Chapter 11

Domestic Price Stabilisation of a Staple Export Crop: an Evaluation of the Rice Premium Tax in Thailand

N. V. LAM*

I. INTRODUCTION

The rice export premium tax[1] has been the subject of an on-going debate in Thailand for the last two decades.[2] It has also attracted attention from several economists, particularly as far as its incidence on the agricultural sector is concerned.[3] The influence of the premium as a stabilising device for domestic rice prices has not been as thoroughly or systematically investigated. This paper attempts to analyse in detail rice price stabilisation policies in Thailand, with special reference to the export premium, during the period 1956–74.

Since its introduction in 1955, the rice premium has been a specific tax, except during 1967–68 when it was experimentally converted to an *ad valorem* basis (Table 1). Originally, the export premium was intended to provide the government with a major revenue source, and also as a policy measure to 'ensure an adequate supply of rice for the domestic market at reasonable prices' [*Ayal, 1965: 335*]. However, premium share in fiscal receipts was steadily declining from 15 per cent between 1955–58 to less than 1·5 per cent during 1970–73. The increasing frequent adjustments in premium rates, especially since the late 1960s, can thus be regarded as primarily designed for stabilisation purposes. In this task, the rice is supplemented, especially during periods of severe rice shortage, by

*Institute of Applied Social and Economic Research, Papua, New Guinea.

TABLE 1
PREMIUM RATES FOR MAJOR
GRADES OF RICE EXPORTS, 1956–74
(Baht/Ton)

Adjustment Date	*100% 5%*	*10%, 15%, 20%*	*25% and over*	*A1 Super*
1–1–1956	935	935	730	470
23–4–1958	"	"	"	590
18–6–1959	"	"	650	470
14–11–1959	"	840	600/650	"
30–12–1959	890	"	500/650	450
2–8–1960	"	"	"	540
30–11–1960	"	"	500/650	500
17–4–1961	"	"	600	540
6–6–1961	"	890	650	"
3–4–1962	950	950	700	600
16–1–1967[1]	30%	25%	25%	25%
1–3–1968[1]	40%	35%	35%	35%
1–11–1968	1450	1300	1300	800
15–9–1969	1100	1100	1100	500
3–12–1969	1000	900	900	"
1–11–1970	750	675	675	375
21–4–1971	"	nil	nil	nil
19–5–1971	"	"	"	"
1–9–1972	"	500	"	"
27–10–1972	"	"	"	"
9–8–1973	"	"	"	650
18–9–1973	5000[2]	1300	"	"
6–12–1973	3000	2700	2300	1300
31–1–1974	4500	4000	3000	2000
22–3–1974	5100	4600	4100	2350
26–6–1974	4500	4000	3500	2000
30–10–1974	3750	3250	2750	1250
25–12–1974	2100	1700	1300	600

Notes: 1 *Ad valorem* rates
2 Premium rate for 5% rice was 1400 baht/ton
Source: Data supplied by the Bank of Thailand.

administrative regulations, in terms of export licences or permits, quantitative export restrictions, including a total export ban, and the imposition of an invisible tax, in the form of a percentage of rice export quantity to be surrendered to the government at officially lower prices.

Rice exports from Thailand consist of four main types: cargo rice, white rice, parboiled rice and glutinous rice. Each type is divided into two groups, whole rice and half-broken rice, and within each group, there exist various grades based on the proportion of whole or half-broken grains in the rice.[4] The most important types of rice exports are white rice and parboiled rice, and the most important grades—100 per cent white rice, and A1 Super (half-broken) rice—accounted for almost 42 per cent of total rice export value during 1955–74.

In this paper, the stabilisation impact of the rice export premium, and of other non-premium measures as well, will be analysed with special reference to their influence on the behaviour of domestic and export prices[5] of 5 per cent rice. The selection of this particular rice is necessary for two reasons. Firstly, 5 per cent and 100 per cent rice are quality rice grades, normally not subject to concessional government-to-government export contracts. Their prices are therefore more sensitive to the interacting forces of internal and overseas demand and supply.[6] Secondly, there is the question of data availability. My field work in Thailand resulted in, among other things, the collection of monthly data, from both published and unpublished sources, on 5 per cent rice exports extending back to 1956.

The extent of price fluctuation or instability is measured by means of the usual standard error of estimate, which yields *trend-corrected* variations, and the standard deviation coefficient, which indicates *variance* from mean. Both coefficients are then divided by the mean of the relevant variable being measured for comparison purposes.[7] The 'normalised' standard error is denoted as the I index and the coefficient of variations, C index. These instability indices will also be supplemented by *range deviation* coefficients, showing the absolute difference between the highest and lowest values exhibited by a variable in any specific period of time.

Where relevant, arguments will also be illustrated with elasticity coefficient, e, measured at mean.[8] And when test of significance is necessary, the t test is used and the level of significance, following normal practice, is set at 5 per cent, unless where otherwise indicated.

II. STABILISATION POTENTIAL OF THE RICE PREMIUM

Being a specific tax, except between 1967–68, the export

premium must be frequently adjusted, and these rate adjustments must be appropriate in magnitude and timely in implementation so as to exert an effective stabilisation impact. For example, serious inflationary pressures on domestic rice prices can be generated by rising rice export prices, due to a strong external demand or a local rice shortage. In this case, internal rice prices or the reduced flow of rice supplies can be insulated from exogenous factors by an upward movement in premium levies. Such a change must be sufficiently large not only to *restore* the real premium levels, which are being eroded by rising export prices, but also to *discourage* both overseas demand and local export incentives. On the other hand, deflationary influences on both domestic or external rice prices, attributable to a local rice surplus or reduced export demand, can be checked by a downward adjustment in premium rates. Such an alteration must, of course, be of adequate magnitude not only to eliminate the rise in the real premium burden, due to falling overseas prices, but also to induce more export demand by increasing the competitiveness of Thai rice and export margins.

In addition, the rice premium can also be designed to restrain intra-year price fluctuations due to seasonal factors. Premium reductions between December and April, when both local and external prices are normally depressed by the arrival of the new rice crop, will strengthen paddy and rice price levels. Thai farmers, who sell two-thirds of their paddy output during this period, would greatly benefit from such a policy. Later in the year, premium rates can be gradually raised to relieve inflationary pressures on prices now that rice stocks are being exhausted.

It is clear, therefore, that the rice premium can effectively *narrow down* the range of variations in local rice prices and hence, factor incomes associated with rice production and marketing. Such a stabilisation potential, as thus *defined,* can, however, be fully realised only when changes in premium rates are proportionately greater than the rate of externally or seasonally-induced fluctuations in rice export prices. Whether or not premium revenue will be increased or reduced in any particular period, because of these anti-cyclical adjustments, depends on the percentage variations in export quantities relative to those of premium rates. Given the lack of a definitive estimate of the price elasticity of overseas demand for Thai rice, such changes are presently impossible to predict. What is apparent, however, is that a successful insulating premium policy will, other things being equal, cause premium revenue to be proportionately more responsive to changes in rice export earnings over time. In other words, premium tax collections tend to be elastic with respect to fluctuations in rice export proceeds. The larger the elasticity value, the more unstable will be the premium revenue, but the greater stabilisation impact the premium policy will exert. Consequently, private rice export returns, defined as total rice export earnings minus premium levies, can be expected to be comparatively more stable than gross rice export proceeds.

III. AN EVALUATION

Generally, it can be said that the rice premium and other non-premium measures have failed to achieve much insulating or stabilisation effect. On an aggregate basis, this failure is indicated by the very high correlation between the average export and domestic prices of the most important rice export grades, namely 100 per cent, 5 per cent, 10 per cent, 15 per cent and A1 Super rice, for the period 1956–74. The 45 coefficient values were within the range of 0·84 to 0·99 with a standard deviation of 0·04. Besides, premium tax collections appear to be highly unresponsive to changes in rice export earnings. The elasticity coefficient of premium revenue amounted to only 0·53 between 1956–73. Moreover, rice export proceeds, net of premium levies, are considerably more unstable than total rice export value. The I index for the latter was only 0·225 compared to 0·281 for the former during the same period.[9]

As far as the behaviour of 5 per cent rice prices is concerned, domestic prices have fluctuated more severely than export prices for most of the years since 1956. Variations in local prices averaged over 12 per cent, according to the I index, and 8 per cent, as evidenced by the C index, higher than the instability in export price levels during 1956–74 (Table 2). Besides, the extent of intra-year variability in internal rice prices was quite substantial in absolute terms, averaging 30 per cent and 20 per cent on a monthly and quarterly basis respectively.

TABLE 2
FLUCTUATIONS IN DOMESTIC (PD) AND
EXPORT PRICES (PX) OF 5% RICE, 1956–74

	I Index		*C Index*		*Range Deviation (%)*			
					Monthly		*Quarterly*	
	Px	*Pd*	*Px*	*Pd*	*Px*	*Pd*	*Px*	*Pd*
1956	·022	·068	·044	·065	13	25	10	15
1957	·034	·041	·053	·043	16	17	11	12
1958	·025	·019	·028	·092	8	35	5	27
1959	·027	·047	·028	·044	10	16	6	10
1960	·041	·048	·047	·075	15	24	11	15
1961	·038	·045	·041	·101	16	42	8	28
1962	·077	·034	·073	·067	26	23	15	18
1963	·028	·043	·025	·042	8	11	5	9
1964	·049	·030	·063	·035	26	22	3	9
1965	·038	·070	·050	·119	18	40	12	30
1966	·022	·086	·071	·131	22	54	20	37
1967	·066	·093	·137	·101	49	46	42	23
1968	·045	·023	·098	·050	36	20	29	14
1969	·038	·063	·035	·080	12	25	6	20
1970	·049	·927	·063	·026	26	10	15	5
1971	·051	·077	·069	·095	24	33	14	21
1972	·068	·076	·095	·194	36	67	27	55
1973	·114	·061	·302	·087	137	35	99	17
1974	·079	·079	·078	·072	31	36	22	7

Source: Computed from data supplied by the Bank of Thailand.

A review of Thailand's experience with the rice premium, particularly during years of highly volatile movements in rice prices, clearly indicates two major problem areas which have reduced its potential as a stabilisation device. Firstly, the export premium was, up to 1967, not sufficiently flexible to cope with sometimes very rapidly changing market conditions. Secondly, there exists a serious lag in policy recognition and implementation. As a result there were several premium as well as non-premium measures which proved to be inappropriate in magnitude and untimely in implementation during 1956–74. The following evaluation of the premium policy will therefore be conducted in two stages, with 1967 as the dividing year.

(a) The Rice Premium During 1956–66

From Table 1, where premium rates for 1956–74 are detailed,

the rice premium appears to be a highly inflexible tax. Premium levies for all grades of rice exports remained *constant* between 1962–66. And over the period 1956–66 as a whole, rates were adjusted only twice for 100 per cent and 5 per cent rice, and three times for 10 per cent through 25 per cent rice. It is true that premium rates for lower quality rice of 25 per cent broken grains and over and A1 Super (half-broken) rice were more frequently changed. However, these alterations were either partial or too small relative to the total of unadjusted rates. Besides, several of these modifications were necessitated by government-to-government export contracts, which involved both special export prices and concessional premium rates.

The failure of the government to rely more actively on premium rate adjustments for domestic rice price stabilisation during 1955–66 resulted in a number of notable developments. Firstly, the premium rate structure for *all* rice exports bore little relation to the prevailing market conditions. For example, 1958, 1961 and 1966 were years of relatively serious price inflation due to poor rice harvests and/or very strong export demand. Yet, the ratios of the average rice premium[10] over the average weighted prices[11] of rice exports during these periods were significantly *lower* than those ruling in the rice-surplus years of 1956–57, 1959–60 and 1963–64 (Table 3). Partly as a result, premium tax revenue tended to be relatively unresponsive to changes in rice export earnings, the elasticity coefficient being 0·84 during 1956–66. Besides, private export returns, that is gross rice export values minus premium levies, were also more unstable than total rice export proceeds. The respective I index was 0·149 and 0·140.

Secondly, the rice premium also caused domestic rice prices to be more unstable than export prices. Such a *destabilising* impact was exerted in two ways. Directly, the generally inflexible premium rate structure completely failed to insulate local rice prices from export price fluctuations. These external variations, if transmitted unchanged or only slightly reduced to wholesale price levels, would cause *proportionately* greater variability in domestic prices. The lower the latter, the greater would be the percentage change. Since local prices of major rice export grades averaged about 60 per cent of their export prices during 1956–66 (Table 3), a 10 per cent change in

TABLE 3
AVERAGE WEIGHTED PREMIUM RATE AND EXPORT PRICE, AND PERCENTAGE OF DOMESTIC TO EXPORT PRICES OF MAJOR RICE GRADES, 1956–74

Year	*Average Weighted* Rice Premium *(1)*	Export Price *(2)*	*% of (1)/(2)*	*Percentage of Domestic/Export Prices of Rice* 100%	5%	10%	15%	A1 Super
1956	685	2431	28	61	59	58	58	71
1957	648	2315	28	61	58	53	53	64
1958	716	2558	28	61	60	59	56	65
1959	680	2269	30	60	58	58	53	57
1960	643	1892	34	58	57	56	52	59
1961	644	2299	28	59	58	59	61	61
1962	719	2479	29	63	62	73	60	62
1963	737	2543	29	59	58	58	54	64
1964	727	2304	31	58	55	54	52	53
1965	711	2318	31	58	55	63	52	59
1966	706	2646	27	68	67	72	65	68
1967	967	3224	30	63	65	72	59	62
1968	1537	3809	40	49	50	51	50	50
1969	1032	3067	34	60	59	56	50	43
1970	795	2677	30	67	63	58	54	66
1971	371	2110	18	64	61	73	76	74
1972	309	2382	13	66	56	79	67	82
1973	607	4975	12	54	70	73	71	37
1974	3643	1781	37	39	38	38	37	35

Sources: Average weighted premium rates and export prices for 1956–63: [*Chuchart and Tongpan, 1965: 8*].
Other figures computed from data supplied by the Bank of Thailand.

export price levels would, given relatively constant premium rates, inflate internal prices by over 15 per cent. This direct transmission of external influences is probably one of the major reasons for the generally greater instability of domestic prices.

Indirectly, the failure of premium rates to move upwards or downwards with changing export prices meant, in effect, a rate reduction during periods of rising external prices, and an additional levy in times of depressed rice market conditions. Thus, export margins and incentives were, in fact, increased in years of rice shortage and *vice versa.*

The above observations are wll illustrated in the two most

serious rice price crises during 1955–66 (Table 2). Rapidly increasing export prices, due to a poor rice harvest in most rice producing countries in South East Asia in 1961, resulted in a steady *de facto* reduction in premium rates. For example, the ratio of average weighted premium rate over that of rice exports fell from 34 per cent in the rice surplus year of 1960 to just 28 per cent in 1961. Yet, stabilisation measures consisted wholly of minor premium changes, which were too partial and marginal to be effective. The subsequent heavy export volume constituted a needless drain on limited rice stocks, which totalled less than 60 per cent of the normal level in October and November. It was also responsible for the 42 per cent increase in 5 per cent rice price.

The other emergency, caused by a poor season and aggravated by strong external demand, started late in 1965 and lasted, with varying degrees of seriousness, till late in 1967. The rice premium, as a stabilisation option, was completely ignored between 1965–66. The government relied wholly on administrative regulations, the imposition of heavy invisible taxes in July and August, and an export ban in November 1966 to restrain the local rate of rice price inflation. These non-premium measures proved, however, to be of limited success. This could be primarily attributable to considerable lags in policy responses, as a result of official inability to fully appreciate the intensity of export demand. Indeed, invisible taxes should have been higher so as to overcome the *cushioning* effect of falling real premium rates. For example, the ratio of the average weighted premium to that of export prices was declining from 31 to 27 per cent between 1965–66 (Table 3). The premium/external price ratio for 5 per cent rice stood at 32 per cent in January and only 26 per cent in October 1966. In addition, the November export ban should have been imposed earlier, preferably in July or August. This is because in a period of severe rice price inflation, few stabilisation measures, short of a total export ban, would be greatly effective for two reasons. Firstly, only an export ban would completely isolate domestic prices from external influences which, if sufficiently strong, would render *some* rice exports profitable despite complex administrative regulations and/or higher visible or invisible taxes. Such exports constitute, of course, a further drain on already limited local stocks. Secondly, a ban would completely eliminate opportunities for rice speculation. There would be no need for private exporters or overseas buyers to order unnecessarily large quantities of rice to avoid higher taxes. Besides, rice wholesalers and retailers would not be reluctant to release accumulated stocks for sale at existing prices. Moreover, greater confidence would be instilled in the public and thus panic buying be reduced.

The 1965–66 rice crisis produced intense public pressures in favour of greater government intervention against high rice prices. This finally led to official realisation that the rice premium should have played a more active, instead of negating, stabilisation role, even at the expense of revenue considerations. The subsequent *radical* shift in premium policy emphasis and its impact on domestic rice prices since 1967 are reviewed below.

(b) The Rice Premium during 1967–74

There were three notable developments in this period. Firstly, the rice premium was changed from a specific levy to a fixed *ad valorem* tax in 1967–68. Secondly, in response to very slack export demand, premium rates were abolished or greatly reduced for all grades of rice exports, except 100 per cent and 5 per cent rice, between April 1971 and August 1973. Lastly, the export premium was raised to the highest levels, since its introduction in 1955, during the rice price crisis of 1973–74.

As a whole, however, the rice premium and other stabilisation measures appear to be only *marginally* more successful in this period. Firstly, it is true that export prices tended to fluctuate more seriously than domestic rice prices in the inflationary year of 1967 and particularly 1973. However, the *degree* of annual instability in local prices remained generally very severe. The monthly range deviation in domestic prices of 5 per cent averaged over 33 per cent between 1967–74 (Table 2). Secondly, private returns to the rice sector were still more unstable than the total earnings of rice exports. The respective I index of 0·397 and 0·503 for 1967–73 was very substantial, even in absolute terms. Thirdly, premium tax collections remained unresponsive to changes in rice export proceeds. The elasticity coefficient was only 0·31 during 1967–73, although this value was certainly distorted because of the abolition of premium rates for most grades of rice exports between 1971 and 1973.

The rather limited effectiveness of domestic rice price stabilisation during 1967 was due to two reasons. Firstly, there still existed official failure to predict and implement appropriate non-premium measures in response to changing market conditions. For example, to check the developing rice crisis, a fixed export target, geographical export restrictions and varying invisible taxes were imposed early in 1967. These vigorous measures succeeded in stopping further price rises, which had amounted to between 15 to 19 per cent between January and March. Consequently, non-premium restrictions were relaxed. This mistake caused a strong export surge, forcing local and external rice prices up by 25 and 15 per cent respectively during April to September. In particular, the monthly prices for 5 per cent rice varied by as much as 46 per cent between the peak and trough level (Table 2).

The second factor for such domestic instability was the *unsuitability* of the rice premium tax, in its existing structure, as a stabilisation measure. Although the conversion of premium rate to a fixed *ad valorem* basis in January 1967 constituted a step in the right direction, it was clearly not enough to insulate financially domestic prices from external forces. It is true that a fixed *ad valorem* structure enabled the government to maintain the real premium levy during a period of rapidly rising export prices. Such a *constant* real tax rate, however, produced little export disincentive effect because the government would fail to absorb a proportionately increasing share of the windfall profits being reaped by the rice industry. On the other hand, during years of slack external demand and falling export prices, the fixed *ad valorem* rate structure would be too burdensome as it contributed nothing to increase the competitiveness of Thai rice.

A steeply progressive *ad valorem* rate structure, with a cut-off point at some floor price levels below which no premium would be paid, would have been a more effective change in 1967. Its automaticity would conveniently eliminate the need for frequent adjustments and highly accurate market forecasts, and the possibility of administrative abuses. Its graduated schedule would be more effective as a stabilisation device in boom as well as lean years. This point will be taken up again when a policy proposal for rice export tax is made in the next section.

Between 1968–70, domestic and overseas rice surpluses considerably weakened external demand. However, the government was not able to significantly increase rice export volume as various premium reductions were not sufficiently large to produce additional demand. It was not until 1971 that a radical strategy was experimented with. Domestic rice price support measures were instituted and more importantly, the export premium for all white rice grades, except 100 per cent and 5 per cent rice, was abolished in May. This latter policy represented an *ad valorem* premium reduction of between 33 to 40 per cent for all rice exports of 10 per cent broken grains or over. Consequently, rice export volume was increased by 48 per cent in 1971, and this effectively helped stop the downward movement in local rice prices.

The relatively successful experience in 1971 contrasted sharply to government failure in rice price stabilisation during 1972 (Tables 2 and 3). Heavy export demand continued, and this started to push up prices early in this year. Yet, premium levy for 100 per cent and 5 per cent rice remained unchanged, and this represented an average drop in real premium rates of about 15 per cent. Besides, the premium was not re-introduced for inferior grades of rice exports. Moreover, premium tax for 10 per cent to 20 per cent rice was not re-imposed until September, and the rates, relative to existing prices, were comparatively much lower than those applicable even during years of relatively 'normal' rice marketing conditions (Tables 1 and 3).

Only during 1973–74 could domestic rice price stabilisation be comparatively regarded as most successful throughout the entire period under examination. This was partly due to more flexible, frequent and timely rate adjustments. In fact, the premium was very substantially raised, for example from 750 to 5000 baht per ton of quality rice exports in September, to choke off the emerging local rice shortage and price inflation. Besides, there was also the absence of extreme demand and supply (shortage) conditions. However, the rice premium, in its present form, requires frequent discretionary changes which, to be effective, necessitate highly accurate marketing forecasts. Such a requirement is unlikely to be easily met, as indicated by the historical experience with premium rate adjustments reviewed above. Besides, frequent premium changes are not only administratively very inconvenient but also wide open for political abuses and speculation. These represent an undesirable feature of the existing premium levy, which would be eliminated in the policy proposal for an anti-cyclical rice export taxation to be discussed below.

IV. A PROPOSAL FOR RICE EXPORT TAX

Although the rice premium has historically proved to be of very limited success in stabilising domestic rice prices, it has exerted a *profound* economic impact on the Thai economy. Indeed, it is generally agreed that the premium has seriously blunted incentives, reduced output and distorted the allocation of resources, particularly in the agricultural sector [*Ingram, 1971: 259*].

Premium incidence has been analysed in detail elsewhere [*Lam, 1977*]. It is sufficient to note here that, over the period 1961–72, the rice premium deflated the prices of paddy and rice by about 30 per cent, and those of other rural commodities by about 20 per cent. These represented an (implicit) income transfer from the rice surplus to the rice consuming sector amounting to over 11 per cent of agricultural income. In addition, the total tax burden borne by Thai farmers, adjusted for the distribution of neutral taxes and income transfer generated by the premium, averaged over 50 per cent of fiscal receipts and over 25 per cent of rural income. This was, indeed, a very substantial and inequitable tax incidence as total income per man employed in the agricultural sector, adjusted for various imputed rents, amounted to only a quarter of income per man employed elsewhere in the economy [*Usher, 1965: 12*].

It can be argued that heavy rural taxation under the present system may be justified for development purposes. After all, recent theories of economic development have stressed the need to channel agricultural surplus into capital formation, especially through the public sector. However, criticism can still, at least, be levelled at the *form,* if not at the level, of rural taxation in Thailand. Firstly, the rice premium is an extremely inefficient means for disguised public capital formation. Almost two-thirds of its burden represents a subsidy to rice consumers rather than funds available for government investment. The most immediate effect of the premium is, therefore, a reduction in the urban cost of living.[12] In this context, it is questionable whether those investment decisions encouraged or discouraged by the premium are economically and/or socially optimal. This is because the lowered domestic prices and costs do not reflect their true value in the external market, and hence may not provide the right signal to guide domestic capital formation [*Leff, 1969: 353; Silcock, 1967: 245–47; Usher, 1965: 16*].

Secondly, the premium-generated deflationary impact on paddy and rice prices has tended to obstruct the modernisation of a substantial part of Thai agriculture by chaining rice farming to a low productivity technology [*Bertrand, 1969: 184*]. It is true that Thai farmers can compensate for lower revenue by increasing output via marginal cultivation. There is, however, a limit beyond which intensive and/or extensive farming of available land will no longer be profitable under the prevailing methods. Improved technical inputs, such as fertilisers, pesticides, higher yielding varieties and mechanical force may have to be relied on to raise rice output. The benefits/costs factors are, however, often against the application of improved inputs [*Behrman 1968: 89–90; Bertrand, 1969: 184*]. For example, the cost of nitrogen relative to farm prices of corn is four times as high in Thailand as in the United States. The cost of the same fertiliser relative to the farm price of paddy is higher in Thailand than in all other Asian and Far Eastern countries except Burma. Consequently, usage of major chemical fertilisers such as nitrogen, phosphates and potash per unit area in Thailand remains lowest, except again in the case of Burma. In addition, most of the chemical inputs being applied in Thailand are not for the rice crop but mainly for vegetable and tobacco crops, and mulberry bushes [*Behrman 1968: 88–89*]. Partly because of this, rice yield in Thailand is relatively low. A comparison with Malaysia reveals yields up to two-thirds and one half above those obtainable in Thailand [*Corden and Richter, 1967: 132*].

These developments, of course, represent a marked contrast to the often-cited Japanese experience. The disincentive effects of heavy rural taxation in Japan were more than offset by means of far reaching changes in land tenure, and the creation of an elaborate agricultural network for the extensive propagation of better or newer farming techniques. Tax receipts captured from the resulting rural surpluses were then spent on public capital projects [*Bertrand, 1969: 184; Food and Agricultural Organisation, 1967: 481–88*].

And the consensus amongst most economists, who are concerned with the question of reforms of rural taxation in general and the economic effects of the premium in particular, is that the rice premium should be abolished.[13] This would, at once, remove the most highly regressive and substantial fiscal burden borne by the farmers. The premium's removal would cause some loss in fiscal receipts but this, in itself, is not a serious problem. In fact, premium levy averaged less than three per cent of government income during 1969–74. Besides, it is not certain that the loss of premium collections would lead to an absolute fall in public revenue. Higher paddy prices and output, and greater farm income may considerably stimulate external trade and domestic activities. Total tax yields may even be increased. The public financing problem arises because about two-thirds of premium incidence represents a subsidy to the rice consuming population. Without it, the urban cost of living would average about ten per cent higher [*Lam, 1977: Table 1*]. Compensation to certain politically influential groups, such as public servants and the armed forces, may be necessary. And this would constitute some burden to public finances.

A more serious problem is that the complete removal of the rice premium would also eliminate the potentially very effective stabilising impact that this tax may exert. The need for an anti-cyclical export levy is undeniable, especially when it is remembered that the range of externally generated fluctuations in monthly and quarterly rice export prices amounted to as high as 49 and 42 per cent respectively as in 1967, the premium being constant (Table 2). Besides, an anti-cyclical rice tax would also provide a convenient means to enable the government to absorb substantial windfall profits, which would generate additional inflationary pressures in an export boom. This need is well illustrated by re-introduction of the rice premium, and the subsequent drastic increases in premium rates, to supplement other stabilisation efforts during the rice crisis of 1973.

The tax proposal set out in this paper involves, firstly, the *retention* of the rice export premium at the 'higher' range of rice export prices. However, its application would be automatic once external rice prices reach a certain level. This is to eliminate the administrative inconvenience of frequent rate adjustments, which may be subject to abuses and speculation on the one hand, and policy lags in recognition and implementation on the other. Its rates would be structured on an *ad valorem* and steeply sliding-scale basis so that an increasingly greater share of export proceeds is collected during periods of rising export prices.

Secondly, the rice premium would be completely *abolished* for any other (lower) export price levels. This would effectively remove the substantial income transfer from the price-producing sector to other rice-consuming units. The subsequent better allocation of resources according to their true market values, in general, and increases in rice farming income and incentives, in particular, are admittedly achieved at the expense of some increase in the urban cost of living.

Thirdly, the re-structured export premium would have to be supplemented by discretionary measures in the form of export controls, quantitative as well as geographical, and the imposition of invisible export taxes during years of severe shortages.

The above proposal involves the determination of firstly, the export price levels above which a premium is payable and secondly, a tax schedule to be adopted. The first problem is very difficult because it is impossible to determine the new equilibrium price levels, following the premium removal, due to the absence of definitive estimates of external and domestic price elasticities of rice demand and supply. It is reasonable, however, to suggest that an anti-cyclical export levy should be paid when external prices for 100 per cent rice exceed 3800 baht/ton (b/t); 5 per cent and 10 per cent rice, 3650 b/t; 15 per cent and 20 per cent rice, 3450 b/t; all other inferior grades of white rice and half-broken rice, 3100 b/t; and parboiled rice, 3300 b/t. These arbitrary levels are supported by three considerations. Firstly, only during periods of serious domestic rice shortage and/or very strong rice export demand, as in 1967–69 and 1973–74, did export prices exceed these levels. In these cases, a stabilising tax is essential not only to reduce export demand and incentives but also to set up absolute ceilings for local rice prices.

Secondly, these proposed price levels would, in effect, permit internal rice prices to moderately increase by 20 to 40 per cent above the average levels during 1970–75. The subsequent rise in the urban cost of living would, therefore, not be as serious as if the premium was completely removed. More important is the fact that the price elasticity at mean of rice output has been estimated, in Behrman's exhaustive study on agricultural responses in Thailand, to be about 0·25 [*1968: 182–220*]. Rice farming activities and the amount of rice surplus for export can thus be expected to be considerably increased. This would, among other things, eventually reduce the urban cost of living to some extent, given the relatively inelastic internal demand for staple foodstuffs.

Thirdly, the proposed price ceilings in general or for a particular grade of rice export can be easily adjusted to allow for temporary or long-run changes in local or overseas agricultural costs and prices.

As far as the tax rate is concerned, the objective is to try to contain strong export demand and discourage export incentives as *quickly* as possible, so as to reduce the range of domestic rice price fluctuations. This requires a very steeply progressive rate structure, which can be achieved by means of a non-linear polynomial tax function. The schedule suggested here takes the form of $Tp=(10)(d/100)^3$, where Tp represents the export tax payable and d, the positive difference between the actual external prices and the 'posted' or ceiling prices for relevant grades of rice. It can, therefore, be seen that as d varies between 100 to 400 baht, Tp will increase from 10 to 640. Thus, there would be no incentive for private exporters to contract, for example, 100 per cent rice exports at prices in excess of 4115 b/t. The proposed tax schedule would, other things being equal, effectively limit the maximum fluctuation in export, and hence local, rice prices to about ten per cent of the posted or ceiling levels.

V. CONCLUSION

In sum, it can be said that the rice export premium tax has generally failed as a policy measure to stabilise domestic rice prices in Thailand. Due to the trade-off between revenue and stabilisation considerations, it became a rather inflexible anti-cyclical device until 1967. And as such, the premium levy regrettably exerted a destabilising impact on local rice prices, and also frustrated other non-premium measures. The rice premium has, since the late 1960s, been comparatively more frequently and timely adjusted, and hence marginally more successful in narrowing down the range of domestic rice price instability.

In its existing form, however, the premium requires not only accurate marketing forecasts but also frequent and appropriate rate adjustments to be fully effective. These conditions cannot be expected to be easily met, as evidenced by Thailand's experience with the rice premium during 1956–74. The anti-cyclical rice export tax proposed in this paper would eliminate these difficult and administratively inconvenient requirements. It would also substantially reduce the very heavy and inequitable premium tax burden borne by the agricultural sector, and the range of local rice price fluctuations generated by external demand or local supply factors.

NOTES

1. Henceforth, referred to as rice premium, export premium, premium tax or just the premium.
2. Indeed it has been noted that the rice premium controversy is comparable, in importance and scope, to the Corn Law debate in nineteenth-century England [*Ingram, 1971: 244*].
3. A partial list of more significant references can be found in the bibliographical section of this paper. See also [*Ingram, 1971: 243–44*].
4. There are nine grades in the white rice group, varying from 100 per cent (whole) rice to 5 per cent through 45 per cent broken rice. Half-broken rice is divided into four grades and eight sub-grades. For a detailed description of different types and grades of rice exports, see [*Renaud and Suphaphiphat, 1971: 103–05*].

5. Except where otherwise stated, domestic and export prices of rice refer to the Bangkok wholesale prices and the f.o.b. export prices respectively. Also, the various statistical data used in this study can be found in the *Monthly Bulletin* and *Annual Report* published by the Bank of Thailand, unless otherwise indicated.
6. Although parboiled rice is an important export item, averaging 17 per cent of rice export value for 1955–74, it is not consumed domestically. Low quality whole rice, that is rice with 25 per cent or more broken grains, is mostly exported under government-to-government contracts, involving special prices and concessional premium rates.
7. The 'normalised' standard error of estimate is comparatively a more commonly used index to measure the extent of short-term trade instability. For further methodological details, see Massell [*1964: 49*] and Neuberger [*1964: 287*].
8. This elasticity estimate is defined as $e = b(\bar{X})/(\bar{Y})$, where b is the linear regression coefficient of Y_t on X_t, and $\bar{Y}$ and $\bar{X}$ are the mean value of the dependent and independent variable respectively.
9. The respective C index is 0·191 and 0·250.
10. Derived by multiplying premium rates for all grades of rice exports by the relevant export quantities, on a monthly basis if necessary. The sum of these products is then divided by the total export volume. Since the export premium can be changed at any time during the month, the 15th day is chosen as the dividing line. If the rates are changed before this date, rice exports are assumed to be subject to the old rates of the whole month, and *vice versa.*
11. Derived by multiplying the average export prices for different grades or types of rice exports by their relative weights, on a monthly basis when necessary. The sum of these products is then divided by the total weight.
12. The rice premium is estimated to have reduced the urban cost of living in Thailand by about ten per cent during 1962–72 [*Lam, 1977:* Table 1].
13. See, for example, Behrman [*1968: 185–87*]; Ingram [*1971: 244*] and Usher [*1967: 25*].

REFERENCES

Ayal, E., 1965, 'The Impact of Export Taxes on the Domestic Economy of Underdeveloped Countries', *Journal of Development Studies, vol. 1,* July, pp. 330–62.

Behrman, J. H., 1968, *Supply Responses in Underdeveloped Agriculture,* Amsterdam: North Holland Publishing Co.

Bertrand, T., 1969 'Rural Taxation in Thailand', *Pacific Affairs,* vol. 43, Summer, pp. 178–87.

Churchart, C. and S. Tongpan, 1965, *The Determination and Analysis of Policies to Support and Stabilise Agricultural Prices and Incomes of Thai farmers,* Bangkok: Department of Lands.

Corden, W. M. and H. V. Richter, 1967, 'Trade and the Balance of Payments', in T. H. Silcock (ed.), *Thailand—Social and Economic Studies in Development,* Canberra: ANU Press.

Food and Agriculture Organisation of the United Nations, 1967, 'The Role of Agricultural Land Taxes in Japanese Development' in R. Bird and O. Oldman (eds), *Readings on Taxation in Developing Countries*, Baltimore: John Hopkins University Press, 2nd ed.

Ingram, J. C., 1971, *Economic Change in Thailand 1850–1970*, Stanford: University Press.

Krisanamis, P., 1967, *Paddy Price Movements and Their Effects on Central Plain Farmers*, Bangkok: NIDA.

Lam, N. V., 1977, 'Incidence of the Rice Export Premium in Thailand', *Journal of Development Studies*, vol. 14, no. 1.

Leff, N. H., 1969, 'The "Exportable Surplus" Approach to Foreign Trade in Underdeveloped Countries', *Economic Development and Cultural Change*, vol. 17, no. 3, April, pp. 346–55.

Long, M. and C. Aranjakananda, 1963, 'Rice Marketing in Thailand', *Bangkok Bank Monthly Review*, July, pp. 19–24.

Massell, B. F., 1964, 'Export Concentration and Fluctuations in Export Earnings', *American Economic Review*, vol. 54, no. 2, March, pp. 47–63.

Muscat, R. J., 1966, *Development Strategy in Thailand*, New York: Praeger Publishers.

Neuberger, E., 1964, 'Is the U.S.S.R. Superior to the West as a Market for Primary Production?', *Review of Economics and Statistics*, vol. 46, no. 3, August, pp. 287–93.

Renaud, B. M. and P. Suphaphiphat, 1971, 'The Effect of Rice Export Tax on the Domestic Rice Price Level in Thailand', *Malayan Economic Review*, vol. 16, April, pp. 84–107.

Sanittanont, S., 1967, *Thailand's Rice Export Tax: Its Effects on the Rice Economy*, Bangkok: NIDA.

Silcock, T. H. 1967, 'The Rice Premium and Agricultural Diversification' in T. H. Silcock (ed), *Thailand—Social and Economic Studies in Development*, Canberra: ANU Press.

Silcock, T. H., 1970, *Economic Development of Thai Agriculture*, Canberra: ANU Press.

Usher, D., 1965, 'The Economics of the Rice Premium', Bangkok, mimeographed.

Usher, D., 1967, 'The Thai Rice Trade', in T. H. Silcock (ed), *Thailand—Social and Economic Studies in development*, Canberra: ANU Press.

Van Roy, E., 1968, 'The Pursuit of Growth and Stability through Taxation of Agricultural Exports: Thailand's Experience', *Public Finance*, vol. 23, no. 3, pp. 294–313.

Chapter 12

Fiscal Incentives for Firms in Some Developing Countries: Survey and Critique

S. M. S. SHAH and J. F. J. TOYE*

Among governments of developing countries, it is a widespread practice to operate schemes which give tax concessions (or, more rarely, subsidies from public expenditure) to newly established firms or old firms starting new activities. The rationale for such schemes seems straightforward enough, and is conveyed by the description as 'fiscal incentives'. It is that governments which want to promote economic growth in a mixed economy should use appropriate fiscal means to induce private sector firms to make their contribution to the desired expansion of national output.

This paper begins with a summary analysis of relevant aspects of tax legislation in 28 developing countries which are known currently to offer fiscal incentives to the private sector. It then discusses briefly attempts so far made to measure the impact and effectiveness of fiscal incentives in promoting the growth of private sector investment. Finally, it argues that the conventional rationale of fiscal incentives is a dubious one, and that any explanation of their popularity with governments of developing countries must rest on an analysis which fuses social and political with purely economic considerations.

*S. M. S. Shah is a member of the Pakistan Revenue Service.

I. FISCAL INCENTIVES IN 28 DEVELOPING COUNTRIES

The first task in presenting the summary of legislation on fiscal incentives in 28 developing countries is to choose the categories by which to order the available information. There are a number of economic distinctions that can be used to categorise fiscal incentives.

The first distinction which can be noted is between two different senses of the notion of the 'capital' of the firm. They are capital in the sense of money paid for the durable inputs to production (K^o), and capital in the sense of the present value of the entire stream of earnings (pre-tax profits) of the firm (J^o). These two different concepts relate to each other as follows:

$$J^o = \int_0^{\infty} r^o K^o e^{-t} = \frac{r^o K^o}{i}$$

where r^o is the firm's rate of return, i is the ruling interest rate, and where it is assumed that (a) risk and (b) corporation tax are absent, and (c) that the firm earns $r^o K^o$ in perpetuity. As Usher has pointed out, certain fiscal incentives are proportional to J (e.g. 'tax holidays') while certain other fiscal incentives are proportional to K (e.g. 'investment allowances' or 'investment tax credits') [*Usher, 1977: 122, 134*].

This dichotomy takes us part of the way, but it is a little too simple. In the first place, one should not be misled into thinking that, because the benefits of a fiscal incentive are not proportional to investment, they must necessarily be proportional to earnings or profits. To do so would be to lose sight of fiscal incentives such as the waiver or rebate of import duty on capital goods, and sometimes also on raw materials, granted to new or expanding firms. The benefit of import duty exemption schemes is, obviously, proportional only to the value of imports absorbed by the firm. Thus an exhaustive categorisation can be only (1) schemes where benefits are proportional to investment and (2) schemes where benefits are not proportional to investment. One should also not be misled into thinking that because the benefits of certain fiscal incentives are proportional to investment, they necessarily take no account of whether a potential beneficiary firm is earning small profits or large. Some schemes, such as investment grants, are not conditional on the firm's reaching a minimum profit level. But others, such as investment allowances or tax credits, grant benefits only to firms which succeed in earning sufficient profits to cross the threshold of corporation tax liability.

Therefore, it seems to make better sense to adopt a two-way classification capable of distinguishing four different types of scheme from each other, as in Table 1.

TABLE 1
A CLASSIFICATION OF TYPES OF FISCAL INCENTIVE SCHEME

	(A) $J^{o} > J^{*}$	*(B)* $J^{o} \leqq J^{*}$
(1) $S \neq f(K^{o})$	Tax holiday Tax deductible loan interest	Import duty exemption
(2) $S = f(K^{o})$	Tax Credit Investment allowance Accelerated depreciation	Investment grant

Notes: (i) S is the amount of public subsidy
(ii) J* is the level of corporate profits at which tax becomes payable.

This classification distinguishes four types of fiscal incentive scheme, as follows:

(A1) Subsidy is independent of scale of investment, but conditional on a maximum level of profits. The main scheme of this type is the tax holiday defined as total (or partial) exemption of new or expanding firms from direct taxation for a specified period.

(A2) Subsidy is dependent on the scale of investment and conditional on a minimum level of profits. There are a variety of schemes of this type, including 'special first year' and subsequent annual percentages of an asset's cost that are deductible from taxable income. The allowances are also known as accelerated depreciation, because they allow the asset to be written down for tax purposes faster than would be possible under normal accountancy depreciation rules. Also in this category fall tax credits, investment allowances and development rebates, which allow a further percentage of the asset's costs to be deducted from taxable income, over and above the depreciation provisions for writing down the asset's historic cost.

(B1) Subsidy is independent of the scale of investment and not conditional on a minimum level of profit. The main scheme of this type is the waiver or rebate of duty paid on imported capital goods (and sometimes also raw materials) by new or expanding firms.

(B2) Subsidy is dependent on the scale of investment but not conditional on a minimum level of profit. The example here is the investment grant whereby a given share of a firm's investment cost is paid for by the government.

Other distinctions can be made than those used in this classification of types of incentive scheme. One is the different phasing of benefits in different types of scheme. Investment grants confer all their benefits right at the start of any new economic activity. Import duty exemption confers initial benefits in respect of capital good imports and continuing benefits in respect of raw materials imports. Tax holidays and tax credits spread their benefits over quite a number of years while a project is establishing itself. The exact pattern of benefits depends on the timing of profit accrual and the detailed provisions of the scheme.

But, although the exact timing of benefits (in conjunction with the appropriate discount rate) is crucial to firms, and governments, who wish to know the present value of alternative forms of subsidy, it does not provide a clear-cut criterion for categorising incentive schemes.

Another distinction that is sometimes made is that between schemes which subsidise new firms and schemes which subsidise new investment. The main objection to this is that it seems to add very little to the distinction which has already been adopted between schemes whose benefits are not proportional to investment, and those whose benefits are proportional to investment. Further, although this distinction is perfectly clear, it may be doubted whether it would effectively discriminate between different schemes, as each

TABLE 2
SUMMARY OF FISCAL INCENTIVE SCHEMES IN 28 DEVELOPING COUNTRIES
TYPE (A1) SCHEMES ONLY

Country	Source*	Tax Holiday (years)	Loss Carry-over (years)	Dividends	Annual Profit Limit	Other Conditions	Interest Deductible from Profits
1. Afghanistan	62(b)	4	—	Exempt	—	—	Yes
2. Bangladesh	53	5	—	Ex.	—	—	—
3. Barbados	21(a)	7/9	5/7	Ex. until year 9/11	—	—	Yes
4. Ecuador	37, 61, 62(d)	5	6	Ex.	—	—	Foreign loans only
5. Fiji	21(f), 58, 66	5	6	Ex.	15% K	—	—
6. Guyana	14, 15, 32	5	—	Ex.	—	—	—
7. Ghana	37	4/10	—	Ex.	—	—	—
8. India	18, 21(d)	5	3	Ex.	7% K	—	Long term foreign loans
9. Indonesia	55	2/3	indefinite	Ex.	—	see notes	—
10. Ivory Coast	37	5	—	Ex.	—	—	—
11. Jamaica	21(a)	5	6	Ex.	—	—	Yes
12. Malaysia	21(e), 34 41, 62(f)	2/5	—	Ex.	—	see notes	—
13. Mauritius	21(d), 58	5/8	indefinite	Ex.	—	see notes	—
14. Niger	37	10	—	—	—	—	—
15. Nigeria	44, 49, 50, 62(d)	2/5	4	Ex.	—	see notes	—
16. Paraguay	62(c)	5	—	—	30% to 50% K	—	—
17. Pakistan	3, 6, 19, 20 21(d), 29, 53	4 (to '65) 2 (to '71)	—	Ex.	5% to 10% K	—	Foreign loans only

18. Peru	65	3	—	Ex.	—	—	—
19. Senegal	37	8	—	—	—	—	—
20. Sri Lanka	4, 5, 53	5	—	Ex.	10% K	see notes	—
21. Sierra Leone	37, 58	5	indefinite	Not Ex.	—	—	—
22. Singapore	21(e), 28	5/10	—	Ex.	—	see notes	Yes
23. Sudan	21(b), 60	3/10	5	Ex.	10% K	see notes	—
24. Surinam	11	5/10	—	Ex.	—	see notes	—
25. Tanzania	21(b)	—	—	—	—	—	—
26. Trinidad and Tobago	21(a)	5/10	5	Ex.	—	see notes	Yes
27. Uraquay	68	10	—	—	—	—	—
28. Zambia	21(c)	—	—	—	—	—	—

*The figures in this column refer to the numbered sources in the Reference list at the end.

Notes

9. *Indonesia*. If capital investment is \$2·5 million or less period of tax holiday is 2 years. If more than \$2·5 million, 3 years.
12. *Malaysia*. If capital investment is M\$250,000, tax holiday period is 2 years; if up to M\$500,000, 3 years; if up to M\$1 million, 4 years; if over M\$1 million, 5 years.
13. *Mauritius*. If 100 employed, 2 extra years tax holiday; if 200 employed 3 extra years; if up to 350 employed, 4 extra years; if over 350 employed, 4 extra years.
15. *Nigeria*. If capital investment less than N. 10,000, no holiday.
21. *Sri Lanka*. 20 per cent additional tax relief, if over 50 employed.
22. *Singapore*. If capital expenditure exceeds \$10 million, tax holiday extended to 10 years.
23. *Sudan*. If capital expenditure is up to £50,000, period of tax holiday is 3 years; if capital expenditure is up to £150,000, period is 5 years. Holiday is extendable by a further 5 years.
24. *Surinam*. Period of tax holiday is up to 10 years, depending on the size of the capital investment.
26. *Trinidad and Tobago*. Period of tax holiday on a sliding scale between 5 and 9 years. 10 years tax holiday for capital intensive and enclave enterprises.

ideal polar type is unlikely to be found in practice. A scheme which was to benefit only new firms would presumably have to prevent old firms from setting up new subsidiary companies in order to benefit from it. A scheme which was to benefit only new investment, in the economist's sense, would presumably have to prevent new firms from doing 'old' investment, that is starting off operations with a purchase of second-hand assets. It therefore seems that one would not be able to sort out real world schemes into two groups using this criterion.

From the existing literature on fiscal incentive schemes in developing countries, a summary analysis can be prepared of the form which such schemes take in 28 developing countries. This analysis is shown in Tables 2 (for types (A1) schemes) and 3 (for type (A2), (B1) and (B2) schemes. It will be noted that, of the 28 developing countries for which information is readily available, no less than 18 are former British colonial territories. Because of this obvious bias in the sample, it may be that the conclusions to be drawn from this sample cannot be extended to cover developing countries as a whole.

Inspection of Tables 2 and 3 immediately suggests a number of points. The first concerns the relative popularity with developing country governments of the different types of fiscal incentive scheme. The most popular type of scheme with developing country governments is type (A1)—the tax holiday. Out of our 28 countries, 26 offer some form of tax holiday.[1] Only Tanzania and Zambia did not do so. The second most popular type of scheme is (A2), provision for the accelerated depreciation of investment in determining tax liability, and associated investment tax credits. Sixteen of our 28 countries offer one or more of the following concessions: an especially high depreciation allowance in the first year of operation; an especially high annual depreciation allowance; an investment allowance, investment tax credit or development rebate over and above the normal or the concessionally high depreciation allowances; a special allowance for the regular working of more than one shift. The third most frequently observed type of scheme is the exemption of imported plant and machinery (and sometimes also parts and raw materials) from customs duty or other import taxation. This exemption operates in ten of the 28 countries. Type (B2), the investment grant, is the least

TABLE 3

SUMMARY OF FISCAL INCENTIVE SCHEMES IN 28 DEVELOPING COUNTRIES = TYPE (A2), (B1) AND (B2) SCHEMES

Country	*Source**	*(A2) First Year Allowance*	*Annual Allowance*	*I.A., I.T.C. or D.R.*	*Extra Shift Allowance*	*(B1) Import Duty Exemption*	*(B2) Investment Grant*
Afghanistan	62(b)	—	—	—	—	—	—
Bangladesh	53	10/30%	—	—	—	P+M Ex.	—
Barbados	21(a)	20% on P+M	—	I.A. 40% on P+M	—	—	—
Ecuador	37, 61, 62(d)	—	29% (5 yrs.)	—	—	P+M Ex.	—
Fiji	21(f), 58, 66	20% on P+M	At taxpayer's discretion	I.A. 55%	—	—	Up to 50% K (hotels only)
Guyana	14, 15, 32	40% on P+M 10% on B	—	—	—	P+M Ex. (10 yrs.)	—
Ghana	37	—	—	—	—	—	—
India	18, 21(d)	25% of K†	—	D.R. 15/25	D.S.=50% D	—	—
	31, 53, 57			40%††	T.S.=100% D	—	—
Indonesia	55	—	—	—	—	P+M+R Ex.	—
Ivory Coast	37	—	—	—	—	—	—
Jamaica	21(a)	20% of K	—	I.A. 20%	D.S.= +20% of I.A.	—	—
Malaysia	21(e), 34 41, 62(f)	80% of K	20% (1 yr.)	I.T.C. 25%	—	—	—
Mauritius	21(d), 58	—	—	—	—	—	—
Niger	37	—	—	—	—	—	—
Nigeria	44, 49, 50 62(d)	—	—	—	—	P+M+R Ex.	—

Paraguay	62(c)	—	—	—	—	—	—
Pakistan	3, 6, 19, 20 21(d), 29, 53	10/30% on P+M	15% p.a.	I.T.C. 10%	D.S.=50% D T.S.= +100% D	P+M+R Ex.	—
Peru	65	—	—	—	—	P+M+parts Ex.	—
Senegal	37	—	—	—	—	—	—
Sri Lanka	4, 5, 53, 62(a)	33⅓/80%	—	I.T.C. 10% D.R. 20/40%	—	P+M Ex.	—
Sierra Leone	37, 58	—	—	—	—	—	—
Singapore	21(c), 28	20/100% (discretionary)	33½%	—	—	—	—
Sudan	21(b), 60	—	—	—	D.S.= +3×D	P+M+parts Ex.	—
Surinam	11	—	(optional)	—	—	P+M+R Ex. (First 3 yrs.)	—
Tanzania	21(b)	—	12½% p.a.	I.A. 20%	—	—	—
Trinidad and Tobago	21(a)	0/40% on P+M after holiday	—	—	—	—	—
Uruguay	68	—	—	—	—	—	—
Zambia	21(c)	—	—	I.A. 20%	—	—	—

*The figures in this column refer to the numbered sources in the Reference list at the end.

Key to table: I.A. is investment allowance, I.T.C. is investment tax credit and D.R. is development rebate.
P is plant, M is machinery, B is buildings, R is raw materials, K is capital expenditure, D is depreciation, D.S. is double shift and T.S. is triple shift.
† with effect from June 1974. †† up to and including May, 1974.

popular of all the incentives. Among the 28 countries in Tables 2 and 3, only Fiji offered investment grants, and then only in the hotel construction sector. It would be interesting to speculate on the reasons for this particular popularity ranking.

But before we do so, there is a second point that emerges from Tables 2 and 3. It is that, in practice as opposed to theory, tax holidays and tax credits, subsidies to earnings and subsidies to investment are not alternatives. Almost half of the countries in the sample were operating both tax holidays *and* accelerated depreciation or other tax credit schemes. It is not clear merely from reading the tax legislation how these two different types of scheme are operated in a complementary fashion. There seem to be three possibilities. It could be that tax holidays are enjoyed by new firms, while tax credits are given to all new investment that is not undertaken by new firms. Firms could be allowed to opt, to benefit under one scheme or the other, according to which provides the greater subsidy. More likely, however, is that firms first of all enjoy their tax holidays, and, when these are exhausted, they then enjoy the different kinds of depreciation allowance and tax credit that are also available to them [*cf. Heller and Kauffman, 1963: 108–9*].[2] Again, while in theory there is a clear distinction between subsidies proportional to investment and subsidies not proportional to investment, in practice this distinction is often blurred. This happens when tax holidays, normally considered a form of subsidy not proportional to investment, are offered on a sliding scale, with the length of the holiday linked to the amount of capital expenditure involved. This kind of link has been made in Indonesia, Malaysia, Nigeria, Singapore, Sudan, Surinam, as indicated in the notes to Table 2.

The third point that arises out of Tables 2 and 3 is that the most popular type of scheme, the tax holiday, usually has a number of additional features which makes it more attractive than an initial period of x years during which no business taxes are payable. As well as the tax-free period, which in the sample typically lasts between five and ten years, about half of the countries allowed a further period, after the tax holiday, during which losses made in the tax holiday period could be used to offset later, otherwise taxable, profits. The period during which losses can be carried forward in determining tax liability is normally between four and six years. Almost all the countries which offer tax holidays also exempt dividends paid out to shareholders from the levy of personal income taxes,[3] so that there is no special reward for firms that retain profits in order to re-invest. Only six countries set an upper limit to profits that can go untaxed, and the maximum varies from between seven and 50 per cent of initial capital expenditure allowable as tax-free profits in any one year.

The final proposition that can be drawn from Tables 2 and 3 is that the use of fiscal incentive schemes has a certain geographical pattern. As already noted, some countries offer both tax holidays and accelerated depreciation and other tax credits. These thirteen 'hyper-generous' countries can be divided into two geographical categories. Nine are islands, or have such small island-like economies that they could be called quasi-islands. They are Barbados, Fiji, Jamaica, Singapore, Trinidad and Tobago, Ecuador, Guyana, Malaysia, and Surinam. The remaining four are the South Asian neighbours India, Pakistan, Bangladesh and Sri Lanka, which falls also into the category of islands, of course.

II. THE ECONOMIC IMPACT OF FISCAL INCENTIVE SCHEMES

It has been shown in Section I that fiscal incentive schemes are a much used tool of fiscal policy in developing countries. One is bound to go on to ask whether they are an effective tool of fiscal policy. By the effectiveness or impact of a scheme is understood its power to change behaviour from what it would otherwise have been, in a direction which the relevant policy-makers prefer.

The first and crudest method which has been used to measure the impact of fiscal incentive schemes is to investigate whether, in the period after they are introduced, the share of investment in gross national product rises. This test has been applied in studies of these schemes in Mexico [*Katz, 1972*], Ecuador [*Tanzi, 1969*], Malaysia [*Karunaratne and Abdullah, 1977*] and Pakistan [*Hamid and Hussain, 1974*]. The obvious objection to it is that investment's share in G.N.P. may change for many different reasons. Thus any recorded change that is observed after introducing a fiscal incentive scheme cannot be assumed to be a consequence of its introduction. The results from this method would be valid only if it could be shown independently that non-scheme influences on the investment/G.N.P. share were constant over the period of measurement. Since no attempt was made to control for non-scheme variables in the four studies mentioned above, their results do not require further discussion.

A second method applied to measure the impact of these schemes is to interview a representative sample of businessmen who have benefited from the schemes. The aim is to ascertain by direct questioning how many of them were influenced in making their investment decisions by the availability of the scheme's benefits. This approach was used in case studies of schemes in Mexico [*Stanford and Christensen, 1959*], Jamaica [*Chen-Young, 1967*], Pakistan [*Azhar and Sharif, 1974*], Brazil [*Goodman, 1972*] and Nigeria [*Olaloku, 1976*]. There are many ways in which questionnaire/survey results can be invalidated. Sample size can be too small, the sample can be inadequately stratified, the response rate can be inadequate or non-random, questions can be ambiguous or otherwise inadequate, the respondent may not have the requisite information and so on. In addition, the researcher may classify and/or interpret the responses subjectively, as has been discussed frequently before [e.g. *White, 1956; Eisner, 1957; Lund, 1976*].

It is not possible to scrutinise fully the exact methods used in the five case studies cited. One merely has to keep the sources of potential bias in mind when considering their results. In the Mexican study of 24 firms enjoying tax exemptions, 14 reported that they would have 'definitely' invested exactly as they had done, even without the tax exemptions. A further nine firms said that they 'probably' would have invested as they had without the tax exemptions. Only one firm said that it would not have invested as it did, but for the fiscal inducement. Of 55 Jamaican firms asked to state the influences on their investment decision, only two volunteered a mention of tax exemptions. Of forty Pakistani firms studied, only eight were reported to have had their investment decision swayed by tax exemptions. On the other hand, in Goodman's study of North East Brazil, the regionally differentiated tax incentives under Article 34/18 were reported as a decisive influence on the choice of plant location.[4]

In common with the first method, the survey/questionnaire approach assumes that the impact of incentive schemes is to be looked for solely in the area of investment behaviour, focusing either on the decision whether to invest at all, or on where to locate an investment. But the effect on investment does not emerge from these studies very clearly. Results are reported for numbers of firms, not for the net value of investment that has been induced or re-located. There is no systematic attempt to distinguish large investors from small investors, or capital-intensive enterprises from labour-intensive enterprises.

Nevertheless, the evidence of these studies does seem to point towards the ineffectiveness of these schemes in inducing new investment. It could be argued that the method is biased in favour of this conclusion, because businessmen will understate the impact of tax incentives in the hope of encouraging the government to make them even more generous. But one could just as well suppose an opposite bias in favour of overstating the impact of tax incentives: if the government became convinced that these incentives were having very little impact, it might decide to withdraw them to boost tax revenue. One might reasonably suppose that these two sources of bias offset each other, and, if so, the original conclusion of apparent ineffectiveness still stands.

When interpreting the results of these survey/questionnaire studies a further limitation of the method needs to be borne in mind. They draw their evidence only from those businessmen who did decide to invest in the country concerned. Therefore they do not necessarily capture the full net impact on investment of fiscal incentive schemes. This is because the investments which are actually subsidised by the scheme may crowd out the investments which other firms might otherwise have been willing to make without the subsidy. The subsidised firms might even compete existing firms out of the market. The possible losses of investment caused by the fiscal incentive scheme have to be accounted for to assess its full net impact, and these are excluded by assumption when the survey/questionnaire method is used. One is led to conclude that the impact of incentive schemes on investment is small even on the optimistic assumption that they are causing no loss of investment.

The third method of assessing the effectiveness of tax incentives relies on inferences made from the published profit levels of tax exempt firms. The net present value of a firm's profits is calculated first with ruling tax exemptions (NPV_e) and then assuming no tax exemptions were enjoyed (NPV_n). Both figures are then compared with Q, the critical minimum rate of profit which firms require, and without which they will not invest. Inferences are then drawn about the impact of the tax incentive as follows.

(a) If $NPV_n < Q$, and $NPV_e < Q$, the incentive was not sufficient to make the venture attractive as an investment, and thus was ineffective.
(b) If $NPV_n > Q$ and $NPV_e > Q$, the venture was profitable and would have been undertaken regardless of the incentive, which, hence, was ineffective.
(c) If $NPV_n < Q$ and $NPV_e > Q$, the incentive has been effective because it alone has made the investment sufficiently attractive to the firm to ensure that it was in fact undertaken.

This procedure is valid only on certain assumptions which need to be spelled out carefully. They are, in part,
(i) that the firm's objective is the maximisation of profits;
(ii) that the firm does not face any capital constraint;
(iii) that the firm enjoys perfect foresight, so that realised profits are a correct reflection of the *ex ante* profit possibilities which faced the firm when it took its economic decisions;
(iv) that the value of Q can be quantified. (If Q is set equal to $r/1-e^{-rb}$ (where r is the private discount rate and b is the life of the project), each firm is assumed to have only one project);
(v) that the tax burden of the firm is not shifted.

In addition, it must be noted that this method, in common with the survey/questionnaire approach excludes by assumption any loss of investment arising from the competition of subsidised firms or investments with other existing or potential unsubsidised firms or investments [*Usher, 1977: 140*].

This method has been employed to analyse the impact of tax incentives in Pakistan [*Azhar and Sharif, 1974; Kemal, 1975*] and Colombia [*Billsborrow and Porter, 1972*]. The first Pakistan study uses the formula $Q = r/1 - e^{-rb}$, and concludes that 20 per cent of tax exempt firms had been stimulated to invest by the tax holiday. The second Pakistan study uses the same formula for Q, but increases the value of b to lengthen the time horizon. It concludes that the proportion of tax exempt firms stimulated by the tax holiday to invest was 30 per cent. The Colombia study does not attempt to calculate the value of Q for each firm. Instead, the NPV_n and the NPV_e are compared with the average profit rate for the industry (two or three digit S.I.T.C.) in which the firm operates. On this basis only four out of forty Colombian firms were found to have been stimulated to invest by the tax exemptions.

In order to meet the objection that to assume profit-maximising firms is unrealistic, the third method can be varied to fit the assumption that investment results from the firm's liquidity, rather than its expectations of profit. There is considerable support in the literature for a liquidity motive for investment in relation to developed economies [e.g., *Thomas, 1972; Agarwala and Goodson, 1969; Lund, 1976*]. One could argue that the scarcity of capital and the weakness of capital markets in developing countries indicate an even greater reliance there on internal sources for investment funds. However, a study of Colombia using a similar method to that outlined above found that it showed only a small number of firms that satisfied the effectiveness criterion that had been set [*Billsborrow and Porter, 1972*].

A fourth method of measuring the impact of fiscal incentive schemes has been tried using data for developed economies [*Helliwell, 1976; 157–255*]. Its foundation is the neo-classical theory of capital investment, on which is built a variety of closely related computable investment-models. From such models, the effect on aggregate investment of changes in tax variables can be estimated. To our knowledge, this method has not yet been applied to data for tax incentives in developing countries. No doubt it will be before long; but the effort will be wasted because of the often discussed flaws in the production function approach to capital theory [*cf. Usher, 1977: 141–44*].

Thus, at the moment, empirical evidence on the impact of fiscal incentive schemes derives from only two methods, the survey/questionnaire approach and *ex post* analysis of profit levels. The results from both seem to show that those schemes have very little impact on the level of aggregate investment, but might be somewhat more influential in steering investment, once it has been decided on the principle, to the location which policy-makers prefer. At the same time we have seen that both the methods used to arrive at these conclusions have important defects which make their results unreliable, but unreliable to an unknown degree.

Logically, then, it is not possible to arrive at a single definite conclusion about the economic effect of these schemes. It would be reasonable to come to either of two conclusions. The first is that, if two independent procedures discover the same result, i.e. that fiscal incentive schemes have little impact on investments, that result becomes probable, even though each method taken separately is rather crude. The second is that the agreement of the results of the two procedures is no more than a coincidence of errors, and that one is obliged to remain entirely agnostic on the issue of whether these schemes affect investment or not. The most that can be said is that their impact is either slight or unknown.[5]

III A PUZZLE AND SOME EXPLANATIONS

The puzzle which now has to be posed to the reader is a simple one. In Section I it was shown that fiscal incentive schemes were widespread and popular in developing countries. In Section II it was shown that their impact on their major policy target, the level of investment, is either slight or unknown. Why should schemes whose impact is either slight or unknown be so widespread and popular in developing countries? What is the explanation of this apparent paradox?

Let us begin by indicating, in a rough and ready way, four possible types of explanation. One could argue that because in developing countries normal tax rates are so low, the importance of fiscal incentives has been greatly exaggerated, and that the size of the subsidy which they create is very small. The absence of any firm evidence of impact can then be explained in terms of the weakness of the incentive effect which the schemes generate [*cf. Heller and Kauffman, 1963; 67*]. A second, closely related argument is that, even where tax rates are high, the evasion of taxes is endemic, particularly in the unorganised sector. Fiscal incentive schemes are not really intended as incentives, but are either a formal recognition that the government would not be able to collect substantial revenues from the favoured firms if it tried, or an admission that, although the revenues could be collected, it would be unfair to do so given the general poorness of tax compliance. This explanation says that the slight or unknown impact of these schemes is irrelevant, because they are really a means of legitimising non-collection of revenues or of getting large firms domestic and foreign to register their activities for government monitoring.

Another quite different line of explanation relies on the notion of fierce competition between countries with poor resource endowments and little in the way of technology and labour skills for footloose foreign manufacturing investment. In the vain attempt to out-bid each other for the available scarce foreign manufacturing investment, these countries compete away their potential revenues from corporate taxation. As this happens, the foreign firms decide where and how much to invest in accordance with non-tax criteria, knowing that they will pay precious little to the exchequer wherever they go. Thus the competition hypothesis simultaneously explains the ubiquity of the schemes and their slight or unknown effects.

The final explanation is a variant of the competitive hypothesis. It suggests that governments are indeed forced to forego corporate revenue which they might otherwise collect, but not because their neighbouring country is offering a more attractive package of tax exemptions. The compulsion arises, in this explanation, directly from the power of large domestic and foreign firms to pressure the government of the country they have invested in, or want to invest in, to take measures favourable to their economic well-being.

The first of these explanations, that the weakness of the incentive results from the lowness of the normal corporation tax rates, is not very satisfactory as it stands. The reason is that most developing countries prefer to have high nominal rates of corporation tax (to impress the ignorant with the seriousness of the government's attempts to mobilise resources) and then to grant exemptions selectively. This is certainly so for the South Asian countries which operate incentive schemes. This explanation might be still relevant for the large international firms, however. As long as only one or two developing countries impose low rates of corporation tax, large international firms can, by manipulating intra-firm transfer prices, ensure that profits are brought to taxation in countries where corporation tax rates are lowest. Then all the other developing countries will find it very difficult to influence the size and/or the location of the investment of such firms by selective dispensation from their high nominal tax rates. But where a firm does not have the size and sophistication to decide the tax jurisdiction in which its profits are declared, and when nevertheless it is making a substantial profit in relation to its investment, the offer of tax exemption or tax allowances cannot be described as insignificant or inconsequential.[6] It is usually a very important windfall gain, even if there are other powerful influences on its decisions, of when, where and how much to invest. One is still left with the task of explaining why such an important windfall gain is handed by governments to private firms.

The claim that the nominal tax liabilities of these firms could not be collected by the governments of developing countries if they wished to collect them is not very persuasive. Much is always made of the technical obstacles to tax collection from farmers and petty traders in developing countries. But to try and extend the argument to the large, organised industrial firms, operating in urban areas with extensive direct or indirect involvement in foreign trade is to stretch an already thin argument to the point of destruction. This is particularly so for countries which have set up fiscal incentive schemes of which the benefits are discretionary and not automatic. It is absurd to claim that a developing country possesses the administrative skills to operate a selective incentive scheme efficiently but does not have the administrative skills to collect a corporation tax. The alternative claim, that in equity foreign investors should be granted parity with tax-evading domestic investors also loses its force. If there are no immovable technical obstacles to collecting corporation tax from domestic firms, equity is served just as well by refusing tax exemption to foreign and domestic firms alike.

To explain the ubiquity and inefficacy of incentive schemes as the results of a competition in tax liberality has the unpleasant ring of truth. This explanation is most convincing with respect to developing countries which are very small and/or very poor. Among the ultra-generous of the 28 developing countries surveyed in Section I was a group of island or quasi-island economies. This group, consisting of five Caribbean economies plus Malaysia, Singapore, Fiji and Ecuador is, with possible addition of Senegal and Sierra Leone, Bangledesh and Sri Lanka, that to which the competitive hypothesis is more likely to apply.

But the competitive hypothesis is not *prima facie* appropriate to economies like those of Indonesia and Nigeria or, in South Asia, India and Pakistan which have substantial natural resource endowment and a large internal market. Here the potential for industrialisation based on home resources, skills and market is substantial, and indeed already partly realised. If such countries compete for foreign investment by forgoing tax revenues to no purpose, they do not do so as a result of external pressures. For them, such policies must result either from gullibility or from internal political pressure. It is rather hard to maintain that developing countries have been insufficiently warned of the disadvantages of fiscal incentive schemes. Even supporters of private sector development have come forward to warn of the doubtfulness of most alleged advantages of these schemes and of the likelihood of most of the drawbacks.

Furthermore, if one looks at the strategy of economic development adopted for these large and relatively well-endowed economies, it is clearly inconsistent with fiscal incentive schemes. In most, the main instrument used by the government to promote indigenous industrialisation has been administrative control of foreign trade and payments in a manner that stimulates domestic production of import substitutes. Often this stimulus is so powerful that the government in addition has to start licensing the installation of extra industrial capacity in order to try to prevent scarce investment resources being diverted to non-priority uses. The combination of foreign trade control and industrial licensing actually creates spare industrial capacity in approved industries, partly by allowing bottlenecks in the supply of imported spare parts and raw materials, and partly by making it profitable to keep factories idle and sell import entitlements on the black market. It cannot be economically desirable for the government to operate both an industrial licensing system (which implies that certain investments have to be prevented) and an automatic fiscal incentive scheme (which implies that investment in general has to be encouraged). The latter makes even less sense when the economy has already developed a sizeable margin of spare industrial capacity. To introduce an additional tax incentive for firms which work their capital equipment in double or triple shifts (as has been done in India, Pakistan, Sudan and Jamaica) is a backhanded admission that investment stimulants are redundant.

If a developing country adopts and persists with a policy about which even private enterprise pundits are lukewarm; which is inconsistent with the economic strategy being pursued; and without the compulsions of distress which make the policy unavoidable for small islands; it does not seem unreasonable to suggest that its government is doing the bidding of those who make windfall gains from these schemes, that is, of large-scale monopoly capitalists. This supposition is buttressed by the pattern of incentive schemes as shown in Tables 2 and 3. The most popular type of scheme is the tax holiday, which of all types, provides the largest element of subsidy to firms which earn high profits [*Heller and Kauffman, 1963: 85; Usher, 1977: 131-132*]. The basic tax holiday is in most countries added to, extended and elaborated by other types of tax concession. The almost complete avoidance by developing country governments of investment grants, which is the only type of scheme that would ensure that the cost of the subsidy would appear in the government's budget and accounts, seems to be an attempt to exploit the public's 'expenditure blindness', just as revenue-raising often exploits the public's 'tax blindness' [*cf. Prest, 1978: 28–29*].

It is no surprise, therefore, that when fiscal incentive schemes are thought up by the developing country's government and its capitalist paymasters, 'little or no opposition to their enactment is likely in most countries'. As the same point is rather delightfully put elsewhere, 'while arguments that the country would be better off in the balance with tax incentives than without . . . may be oversimplifications, they appeal to important segments of the politically articulate public' [*Heller and Kauffman, 1963: 7*]. The power of capitalism is the power to weep at academic criticism all the way to the bank.

NOTES

1. In some countries, like Costa Rica, Ecuador and Sierra Leone, only part of corporate earnings is exempt from tax; while in Israel corporate earnings are exempt from one type of tax, income tax, but not exempt from another type, profits tax *(Lent, 1975; Smith, 1975; Tanzi, 1969*]. Normally the period of exemption begins on the 'production day', i.e. the day when normal quantities of output start to be produced. There are some departures from this norm: for example, in Antigua exemption for hotels begins when construction work is complete; in Dominica, Grenada and St. Vincent exemption begins from the date of granting of import licences [*Smith, 1975*].
2. Some countries including Guyana [*Gaugadin 1973, 1975; Jetha, 1976*], Ghana [*Lent, 1975*] Nigeria [*Phillips 1967, 1968*] and Malayasia, Sabah and Singapore [*Smith, 1975*] explicitly provide for the postponement of all depreciation allowances so that they can be claimed once the tax holiday is over.
3. Dividend exemption applies during the tax holiday itself and, quite commonly, for a further period up to two years after the end of the holiday (e.g. in Guyana [*Gangadin, 1973, 1975*]. Most developing countries exempt distributed dividends up to the total amount of tax-free profits, but India, Pakistan, Sri Lanka and Suden limit dividend distribution to between 5 and 10 per cent per year of capital expenditure [*Qureshi, 1971; Singhal, 1973; Siliman, 1973*]. Some developing countries have special provisions designed to prevent individuals liable to pay income tax at the highest rates using the income to buy assets for 'close companies' which they control and which do not pay dividends. 'Close company' provisions exist in India, Barbados and Trinidad and Tobago [*Govt. of U.K. (a)(d)*].
4. Regionally differentiated tax incentives are fiscal incentive schemes which give greater benefits to firms or investments which locate themselves in regions or areas designated by the government as less developed than the remainder of the country. Regionally-differentiated schemes can be classified in the categories already adopted in the text.

   Type (A1).

   In Pakistan, industrial undertakings starting production between 1.7.1975 and 30.6.1981 gain exemption from taxation of profits up to 10 per cent of capital expenditure for 10 years if located in underdeveloped areas, compared with only up to 5 per cent of capital for five years if located in a developing area [*Govt. of Pakistan, 1976; Qureshi, 1977*]. In Peru, 'pioneer industries' are given 15 years tax holiday if located in Selva, ten years if in Sierra, five years if in coastal zone (except Lima and Collao) and three years if in Lima and Collao; and a similar differentiation exists in respect of 'basic industries' [*Vargas, 1970*]. Similar schemes in which length of tax holiday is related to location of investment apply in Afghanistan, Bangladesh, Jamaica, Malaysia, Puerto Rico and Venezuela [*Govt. of U.K.; Tax News Service; Mathai, 1976; Woodward, 1974*].

Type (A2)

In Brazil since 1961 firms have been allowed to reduce their tax liability by 50 per cent if they invest their tax savings in projects approved by Sudene, the agency responsible for developing the North-East (Nordeste) region. This 'investment tax credit scheme of Article 34/18' was extended to the Amazon region in 1966, and is said to have 'transformed a market of 20 m. people with a very little purchasing power into an important producer and consumer market' [*Mendive, 1964; De Sousa, 1968; Goodman, 1972, 1976; Hirschman, 1968*]. An additional percentage of investment tax credit for firms in underdeveloped regions is given in Argentina, Pakistan and Malaysia [*Risueno, 1968; Govt. of Pakistan, 1976; Govt. of U.K.*]. In India, if a company sells its existing business in an urban area and moves to an underdeveloped region, it is given a tax credit certificate for the capital gains tax due on the sale.

Type (B1)

Pakistan allows total exemption from import duty on machinery installed in underdeveloped areas compared with a rebate of only 25 per cent with respect to developing areas [*Govt. of Pakistan, 1976*]. Brazil, Peru and India give exemptions from sales taxes, local excises and other state, local or municipal duties and fees for enterprises operating in backward areas.

Type (B2)

India gives a 10 per cent investment grant for all investments in backward or underdeveloped areas, up to a maximum of five million rupees. Morocco offers a 20 per cent investment grant for investment in underdeveloped regions.

Information on regionally-differentiated fiscal incentive schemes is summarised in Table 4.

5. If one had been led to the conclusion that fiscal incentive schemes have no effect on investment, one would have no interest in examining the different kinds of economic effects produced by the different types of fiscal incentive scheme. Since our conclusion leaves some room for agnosticism on the impact of these schemes on investment, it is necessary to look at this point. It is often said that tax incentives for investment are one of the government measures which encourage the use of excessively capital-intensive technology which is inappropriate to

	Country	Upper limit to profits	Length of holiday in UDA's	IA,DR,ITC†	Special, Initial Allowance	High Annual Allowance	Grants	Other Tax Concessions
1.	Afghanistan	—	6 yrs	—	—	—	—	Duty free Import of P+M & spare parts, exemptiom of Registration fee and 'Sukuk'.
2.	Argentina	—	—	50% ITC	—	—	—	—
3.	Bangladesh	—	7 yrs	—	—	—	—	Duty free import of P+M
4.	Brazil	—	—	50% ITC	—	—	—	Duty free import of P+M; & state & municipal tax exemptions.
5.	India	20% of capital	10 yrs	ITC equal to capital gains tax liability	—	—	10% of capital	Municipal and state tax relief
6.	Jamaica	—	11–15 yrs	—	—	—	—	—
7.	Malaysia	—	5–8 yrs	30% ITC	—	—	—	—
8.	Morocco	—	—	—	—	—	20% of capital	—
9.	Pakistan	a) 5% of capital	5 yrs	15% ITC	—	—	—	Duty free import of P+M
		b) 10% of capital	10 yrs	30% ITC	—	—	—	exemptions of sales tax
10.	Peru	30%–50% of capital	5,10,15 yrs* 'P' 20 and 55 yrs 'B'	—	—	—	—	Duty free import of P+M & raw materials; exemption of sales tax, licence fees and stamp duty
11.	Sudan	Finance Minister's discretion to grant special relief for enterprises located in 'rural areas'						
12.	Puerto Rico	—	10–17 yrs	—	—	—	—	—
13.	Venezuela	15%–100% of profit	5 yrs	—	—	—	—	—

†Investment allowance, development rebate and investment tax credit.
*Different rates of relief depending on different locations.
(a) Developing areas (b) Underdeveloped areas
'B' = Basic Industries 'P' = Pioneer Industries.

labour-surplus developing economies [e.g. *Morawetz, 1974; 142, 158*]. There are several ways in which this could happen. Most obviously, schemes of types (A2) and (B2) confer benefits in accordance with capital expenditure and thereby encourage the producer to choose a more capital-intensive method of production than he would otherwise have done. Secondly, a selective tax incentive scheme which is more accessible to large-scale operators will have the effect of making industry more capital-intensive than it would otherwise be if the large-scale operators already tend to use the more capital-intensive techniques. Thirdly, one could argue that tax incentives whatever their form are a subsidy raising the real rate of return in the industrial sector. If they succeed in inducing capital to move from other sectors where the marginal capital/labour ratio is lower, one could say that the economy as a whole becomes more capital-intensive. A debate has taken place on the policy measures needed to eliminate these types of pro-capital bias arising from fiscal incentive schemes. One suggestion is to graduate the benefits from these schemes in accordance with the volume or intensity of labour employment of the project [*Lent, 1971; Gupta, 1976; Olaloku, 1975*]. Another suggestion is to subsidise the use of labour directly [*Prest, 1971; Ahluwalia, 1972*]. A third is to tax capital rather than subsidise labour [*Peacock and Shaw, 1971*]. Using a Cobb-Douglas production function and assuming that for either policy a balanced budget must be maintained, Peacock and Shaw argue that a capital tax will be more effective in increasing employment and easier to administer. After various criticisms, their model in a modified version shows that, when the level of output is constrained, the government incurs the same level of budget deficit whether it uses a labour subsidy or a capital tax, a result confirmed by a CES production function analysis [*Banks, 1971; Gulati and Krishnan, 1971; Peacock and Shaw, 1972, 1973; Oyejide, 1972*]. Thus as it is administratively easier, the capital tax would be the superior policy. The importance of these results in practice depends, of course, on the existence of significant scope for factor substitution in the real world. Apart from that, if the government's trade and monetary policies are the major pressures towards excessive capital intensity of production, one may be pardoned for wondering whether the government will have the slightest interest in finding fiscal means to nullify them.

6. There is an exception to this statement which is worth noting. If a foreign company is making large profits in a developing country which operates a tax exemption scheme, the beneficial effect of this to the company will be removed if it is taxed in its home jurisdiction on its world-wide earnings, with foreign tax paid deductible from its domestic tax liability. It is ironical that double taxation agreements, which were intended to make foreign investors' lives happier, do do this, but at the same time make it impossible for them to benefit from tax exemptions granted by the host government. What is foregone by the developing country's government is reaped by the home government. Thus international firms which cannot succeed in bringing their profits to tax

in a low-tax third country will contribute part of their surplus to their home government and not to the government of the developing country in which they operate [*cf. Hymer, 1972: 54*].

REFERENCES

1. Agarwala, R. and G. C. Goodson, 1969, 'An analysis of the Effects of Investment Incentives Behaviour in the British Economy', *Economica*, pp. 377–88.
2. Ahluwalia, M. S., 1972, 'Taxes, Subsidies and Employment', *Quarterly Journal of Economics*, pp. 393–409.
3. Ahmad, K., 1973, 'Incentive Taxation for Economic and Social Development', *Pakistan Economic and Social Review*, pp. 154–66.
4. Ambalavaner, S., 1972, 'Ceylon: Summary of Import Taxes and Levies', *Bulletin for International Fiscal Documentation*, pp. 2–16.
5. Ambalavaner, S. and Saravanamuttu, M., 1976, 'Sri Lanka Budget for 1976', *Bulletin for International Fiscal Documentation*, pp. 76–79.
6. Azhar, B. A. and S. M. Sharif, 1974, 'The Effects of Tax Holiday on Investment Decisions: An Empirical Analysis', *Pakistan Development Review*, pp. 409–32.
7. Banks, F. E., 1971, 'Fiscal Measures to Improve Employment in Developing Countries: a Comment', *Public Finance/Finances Publiques*, pp. 473–76.
8. Billsborrow, R. E. and R. C. Porter, 1972, 'The Effects of Tax Exemptions on Investment by Industrial Firms in Colombia', *Weltwirtschaftliches Archiv*, pp. 396–425.
9. Chen-Young, P. A., 1967, 'A Study of Tax Incentives in Jamaica', *National Tax Journal*, pp. 292–308.
10. De Sousa, R. G., 1968, 'Taxation in Brazil', *Bulletin for International Fiscal Documentation*, pp. 415–55.
11. Dudler, H. J., E. Furst, M. Hardon and H. Lambert, 1971, 'The Economy of Surinam', *IMF Staff Papers*, pp. 668–750.
12. Eisner, R., 1957, 'Interview and other Survey Techniques and the Study of Investment', in N.B.E.R. Studies of Income and Wealth, Vol. 19, *Problems of Capital Formation*, Princeton U.P., Princeton, pp. 513–84.
13. Fromm, G. (editor), 1971, *Taxation Incentives and Capital Spending*, Brookings Institution, Washington D.C.
14. Gangadin, V. J., 1973, 'Guyana: a Brief Outline of Income Tax, Corporate Tax, Capital Gains Tax, Withholding Tax and Property Tax, with special reference to Foreign Corporations operating in Guyana', *Bulletin for International Fiscal Documentation*, pp. 455–63.
15. Gangadin, V. J., 1975, 'Fiscal Incentives in Guyana', *Bulletin for International Fiscal Documentation*, pp. 223–30.
16. Goodman, D. E., 1972, 'Industrial Development in the Brazilian North-East: an Interim Assessment of the Tax Credit Scheme of Article 34/18' in Roett, R., (editor), *Brazil in the Sixties*, Vanderbilt U.P., Missouri.
17. Goodman, D. E., 1976, 'The Brazilian Economic "Miracle" and Regional Policy: Some Evidence from Urban North-east', *Journal of Latin American Studies*, pp. 1–27.

18. Government of India (Ministry of Finance), 1976, *Finance Act 1976*, New Delhi.
19. Government of Pakistan (Finance Division), 1972, *Fiscal Policy in Pakistan: and Historical Perspective*, Vol. I and II, 1948–70, Islamabad.
20. Government of Pakistan, 1976, *Tax Structure of Pakistan*, Islamabad.
21. Government of U.K. (Board of Inland Revenue), series, *Income Tax Outside the U.K.*, Vols. II to V, H.M.S.O., London.
    (a) Vol. II, Group 6, Caribbean Countries: Barbados, Jamaica, Trinidad and Tobago.
    (b) Vol. III, Group 8, Sudan, Tanzania.
    (c) Vol. III, Group 8, Zambia.
    (d) Vol. IV, Group 2, India, Pakistan and Mauritius.
    (e) Vol. V, Group 12, Malaysia and Singapore.
    (f) Vol. V, Group 13, Fiji.
22. Gulati, I. S. and T. N. Krishnan, 1971, 'Fiscal Measures to Improve Employment in Developing Countries – a Comment', *Public Finance/Finances Publiques*, pp. 477–82.
23. Gupta, A. P., 1976, 'How Fiscal Policy Can Help Employment Generation', *Economic and Political Weekly*, pp. 631–36.
24. Hamid, N. and K. Hussein, 1974, 'Regional Inequality and Capitalist Development', *Pakistan Economic and Social Review*, pp. 255–88.
25. Heller, J. and K. Kauffman, 1973, *Tax Incentives for Industry in Less Developed Countries*, Harvard Law School International Tax Program, Cambridge, Mass.
26. Helliwell, J. F., (editor), 1976, *Aggregate Investment: Selected Readings*, Penguin, London.
27. Hirshman, A. O., 1968, 'Industrial Development, the Brazilian North-East and the Tax Credit Scheme of Article 34/18', *Journal of Development Studies*, pp. 5–28.
28. Hong, L. F., 1976, 'Taxation in Singapore', *Bulletin for International Fiscal Documentation*, pp. 411–20.
29. Hussain, S. M., 1969, *Incentive Policies for Industrial Development: Pakistan Experience*, Lahore.
30. Hymer, S., 1972, 'The Multinational Corporation and the Law of Uneven Development', in Radice, H. (editor), 1975, *International Firms and Modern Imperialism*, Penguin, London, pp. 37–62.
31. Jain, U., 1976, 'Tax Incentives in India', *Bulletin for International Fiscal Documentation*, pp. 514–22.
32. Jethna, N., 1976, 'The Structure of Major Taxes in Guyana', *Bulletin for International Fiscal Documentation*, pp. 47–59.
33. Jhaveri, N. J., 1970, 'Bhootalingam Committee on Depreciation: an Evaluation of its Recommendations', *Economic and Political Weekly*, pp. 451–57.
34. Karunaratne, N. D. and Abdullah, M. P., 1977, 'Incentive Schemes and Foreign Investment in the Industrialisation of Post-Independent Malaysia', mimeo.
35. Katz, B. S., 1972, 'Mexican Fiscal and Subsidy Incentives for Industrial Development', *American Journal of Economics and Sociology*, pp. 353–60.

36. Kemal, A. R., 1975, 'The Effects of Tax Holiday on Investment Decisions: Some Comments', *Pakistan Development Review*, pp. 245–48.
37. Lent, G. E., 1967, 'Tax Incentives for Investment in Developing Countries', *I.M.F. Staff Papers*, pp. 249–323.
38. Lent, G. E., 1971, 'Tax Incentives for the Promotion of Industrial Employment in Developing Countries', *I.M.F. Staff Papers*, pp. 399–419.
39. Lent, G. E., 1975, 'Tax Incentives in Developing Countries', in R. M. Bird and O. Oldman, (editors), 1975, *Readings on Taxation in Developing Countries*, Third edition, pp. 363–77.
40. Lund, P. J., 1976, 'The Econometric Assessment of the Impact of Investment Incentives', in A. Whiting, (editor), 1976, *The Economics of Investment Subsidies*, H.M.S.O., London, pp. 245–65.
41 Mathai, M. K., 1969, 'Incentives for Investment in Malaysia', *Bulletin for International Fiscal Documentation*, pp. 503–15.
42. Mendive, P., 1964, 'Tax Incentives in Latin America', *U.N. Bulletin for Latin America*, pp. 103–16.
43. Morawetz, D., 1974, 'Employment Implications of Industrialisation in Developing Countries: a Survey', *Economic Journal*, pp. 491–542, and in R.E.S./S.S.R.C., 1977, *Surveys of Applied Economics*, Vol. 2, Macmillan, London, pp. 115–68.
44. Olaloku, F. A., 1976, 'Fiscal Policy Options for Employment Promotion in Nigeria's Modern Manufacturing Sector', *Bulletin for International Fiscal Documentation*, pp. 318–27.
45. Oyejide, T. A., 1972, 'Fiscal Measures to Improve Employment in Developing Countries – a Comment', *Public Finance/Finances Publiques*, pp. 283–88.
46. Peacock, A. T. and G. K. Shaw, 1971, 'Fiscal Measures to Improve Employment in Developing Countries – a Technical Note', *Public Finance/Finances Publiques*, pp. 410–17.
47. Peacock, A. T. and G. K. Shaw, 1972, 'Fiscal Measures to Improve Employment in Developing Countries – a Reply', *Public Finance/Finances Publiques*, pp. 489–90.
48. Peacock, A. T. and G. K. Shaw, 1973, 'Fiscal Measures to Create Employment: the Indonesian Case', *Bulletin for International Fiscal Documentation*, pp. 443–53.
49. Phillips, A. O., 1967, 'Nigerian Industrial Incentives, Import Duty and Approved User Scheme', *Nigerian Journal of Economic and Social Studies*, pp. 315–27.
50. Phillips, A. O., 1968, 'Nigeria's Experience with Income Tax – A Preliminary Assessment', *Nigerian Journal of Economic and Social Studies*, pp. 33–62.
51. Prest, A. R., 1971, 'The Role of Labour Taxes and Subsidies in Promoting Employment in Developing Countries', *International Labour Review*, pp. 315–32.
52. Prest, A. R, 1978, 'The Taxable Capacity of a Country', Chapter 1 of this volume, pp. 13–32.

53. Qureshi, N. M., 1977, 'New Orientations in Tax Policies: Pakistan, India, Sri Lanka and Bangladesh', *Bulletin for International Fiscal Documentation*, pp. 7–16.
54. Risueno, M. M., 1968, 'Taxation in Argentina', *Bulletin for International Fiscal Documentation*, pp. 304–18.
55. Rochmat Soemitro, S. H., 1968, 'Investment of Foreign Capital in Indonesia', *Bulletin for International Fiscal Documentation*, pp. 496–510.
56. Sastry, D. U., 1975, 'Investment Behaviour in the Indian Capital Goods Industry', *Indian Economic Journal*, pp. 56–77.
57. Singhal, H. K., 1973, 'Taxing for Development: Incentives affecting Foreign Investment in India', *Harvard International Law Journal*, pp. 51–88.
58. Smith, A. H., 1975, 'Income Tax Incentives for New Industries in Developing Countries', *Bulletin for International Fiscal Documentation*, pp. 64–77.
59. Stanford, G. R. and J. B. Christensen, 1959, *Tax Incentives for Industry in Mexico*, Harvard Law School, Cambridge, Mass.
60. Suliman, A. A., 1973, 'Fiscal Incentives for Industrial Investment in the Sudan', *Bulletin for International Fiscal Documentation*, pp. 315–23.
61. Tanzi, V., 1969, 'Tax Incentives and Economic Development: the Ecuadorian Experience', *Finanzarchiv*, pp. 226–35.
62. B.I.F.D., series, *Tax News Service (Non-Europe)*. Part II.
    (a) B.I.F.D., 1972, Sri Lanka, p. 28.
    (b) B.I.F.D., 1975 Afghanistan, p. 3.
    (c) B.I.F.D., 1976, Paraguay, p. 13.
    (d) B.I.F.D., 1976, Ecuador and Nigeria, p. 38.
    (e) B.I.F.D., 1976, Venezuela, p. 50.
    (f) B.I.F.D., 1976, Malaysia, p. 56.
63. Thomas, R., 1972, 'The Fiscal Incentives to Invest: Liquidity and Profitability Aspects', *Scottish Journal of Political Economy*, pp. 273–85.
64. Usher, D., 1977, 'The Economics of Tax Incentives to encourage investment in less developed Countries', *Journal of Development Economics*, pp. 119–48.
65. Vargas, H. de L., 1970, 'Taxation and Incentives in Peru', *Bulletin for International Fiscal Documentation*, pp. 91–108.
66. Ward, M., 1971, *The Role of Investment in the Development of Fiji*, D.A.E. Occasional Paper 26, Cambridge U.P., Cambridge.
67. White, W. H., 1956, 'Interest Elasticity of Demand – the Case from Business Attitude Surveys Re-examined', *American Economic Review*, pp. 565–87.
68. Woodward, R. S., 1974, 'The Effects of Intra-Island incentives in Puerto Rico', *National Tax Journal*, pp. 261–73.

Index of Subjects and Persons

Ability-to-pay principle, 174
Accelerated depreciation provisions, 271, 275–277
Agriculture Holding Tax (India), 223–225, and 227–244 passim.
Aid allocation criteria, 38–39
Aid creditworthiness, 39
Aid leverage effects, 38
Allende, S., 152
Allingham M.G., 161, 168
Arrow, K. J., 170

Bahl, R., 20–21, 73–74
Belaunde, 136
Benefits of public expenditure (Indian agriculture), 211
Bird, R. M., 22, 138, 222–223, 225, 227, 242–243

Capitalist industrialisation, 126–127, 146
Capital of the firm, 270
Cardenas, 152
Central American Common Market, 6, 84, 102
Centrally–planned economies, 31
Chelliah, R. J., 20, 52, 73
Chenery, H. B., 48
Churchill, W., 56
Clark, C., 9, 27
Consumption functions, 104–107, 177
Critical minimum rate of profit, 282–283
Cross-subsidies among water consumers, 185–186

Demand for public expenditure, 43
Democratic institutions, 9–10, 152, 244
Detection of tax evasion, 163, 168
Developmental public spending, 127–128
Development planning, 1, 103
De Wulf, L., 53, 138
Diwedi, D. N., 203

Earmarked property taxes, 186–190
Eastern European economies, 29
Echeverria, 136
Econometric model of El Salvador, 103–116
Econometric studies of taxable capacity and tax effort, 19, 62, 69–73
Economic surplus, 8, 23–24, 50–51, 129
Equity, 177, 208–211, 224–227, 228–230, 238–239
Excess profits of public corporations, 16–18
Export functions, 113–114
Export taxes, 2–3, 94, 112, 133–135; *See also* Rice Premium Tax

Family size and water consumption, 177, 180, 183
Fertilizer cost and use, 262–263
Fiscal crisis of the state, 6, 125–126, 153
Fiscal deficit, 141
Foreign capital transfers, 37, 116
Functional taxation, 1
Furtado, C., 140–141

Gandhi, V. P., 53–54, 201–203
Gini coefficient, 54
Government of India, 194, 195, 223

Haig/Simons principle of taxation, 18
Hindu Undivided Family, 224

'Ideal land tax', 222–223, 225, 227, 242–244

Import duty exemption, 270, 272–277
Import functions, 109–111
Import-substituting industrialization, 6, 111, 119, 135
Import tariffs and licenses, 134, 215, 217, 287
Incentives to work, 24–26, 239–242
Incidence of Thai rice premium tax, 261
Income distribution between sectors, 201
Income tax evasion, 7, 10, 161, 285
Income tax withholding, 28
Indirect taxes, 8–9, 90–91, 133, 137, 139
Industrial capacity licensing, 287–288
Inflationary effects of taxation, 27
Inflation tax, 16, 28, 96, 149
Interdependence of utility functions, 179–180
International comparisons of taxable capacity, 17, 19–22, 34–35, 49
International Monetary Fund, 5, 19, 41–42, 45, 47, 52, 55, 96, 143, 148, 149
Intersectoral price manipulation, 215
Investment decision surveys, 280–281
Investment functions, 107–109, 116
Investment/G. N. P. ratio, 279–280
Investment grants, 270, 275–278
Investment incentives, 8, 85, 95, 112–113, 134, 138, 269–296 passim

Joshi, T. M., 223

Kaldor, N., 23, 83
Kalecki, M., 4, 9, 10
Keynes, J. M., 2, 10
Khusro, A. M., 196
Kubisheck, 137
Kuznets, S., 48

Land rights and agricultural taxation, 236–237, 244
Large international firms, 285–286
Lewis, W. A., 19, 34–35
Lorenz curve of income distribution, 164–167, 171–172, 201
Lctz, J. R., 53,75
Lump-sum cash transfers, 179
Lusk consumption units, 203

Macroeconomic fluctuations, 2
Managerial autonomy of public utilities, 177
Marginal cost pricing, 177, 179
Mathew, E. T., 211
Money creation, 149–150
Morgenstern, O., 48, 168
Morse, E., 53, 75
Musgrave, R. H., 44, 51, 53, 63

Numerology, 56

O'Connor, J., 125–126, 129
Optimal resource allocation, 64–69
Optimal taxation theory, 18–19
Overvalued exchange rate (India), 215, 217

Pareto's law of income distribution, 54
Pareto's optimality in consumption, 179
Pinochet, 153
Pitt the Younger, 19
Please, S., 35–36
PL 480 food aid, 215–216
Political constraints on taxation, 23–24, 46, 96, 113, 177, 233–234, 263, 287, 288–289
'Populist' governments, 176
Presumptive tax assessment, 238–239, 241, 243
Price elasticity of demand for water, 178–179
Progressivity of public utility charges, 174, 180–182, 190
Progressivity of taxation, 22, 36, 49, 51, 53–54, 85, 91, 138, 140, 161, 208, 228–230, 265
Public enterprise profits, 143–144, 176

Public sector investment, 112, 128–129, 141
Public utility prices, 7, 143–4, 174

Raj, K. N., 8
Rao, V. K. R. V., 196–197
Representative tax systems approach, 21–22
Revenue target, 230–233
Rice export tax proposal (Thailand), 261–266
Rice premium tax (Thailand), 3, 249, 254–261
Rice price stabilization, 251–253, 255–261
Risk aversion, 161, 168, 170–172
Rural saving/investment ratio, 198–199
Rural taxation in Japan, 263
Rural-urban migration, 195–198
Rural-urban transfers, 3, 193–194, 261

Sacrifice principle of taxation, 18, 51, 53–55
Sahota, G. S., 53–54
Sandmo, A., 161, 168
Shifting of taxes on capital, 180
Shoup C. S., 15, 24, 29, 40
Srinivason, T. N., 161, 162–168
Social security revenues, 14, 16, 140, 143–145
State in Latin America, 125–129, 150–151, 152–153
State borrowing abroad, 147–149
State domestic borrowing, 145–147
Subsistence estimates (Uttar Pradesh), 203–204

Tanzi, V., 47, 49
Tax administration, 222, 226–227, 234–236, 259–260, 286–287
Tax blindness, 9, 28–29, 152
Tax buoyancy, 51, 84, 88–91, 94–95, 243
Tax burden, 57, 140
Taxable capacity, 5, 13–14, 21–22, 44, 48, 64, 134, 200
Tax effort, 20–22, 44–48, 52, 62, 75–77, 112
Tax elasticity, 51–52, 83, 86, 91–94, 132, 251, 253
Tax/G. N. P. ratios, 14–15, 17–18, 20–21, 27, 40–41, 46, 51, 75, 116
Tax handles, 44, 63–64, 131
Tax holidays, 271, 273–275
Tax justice, 18–19, 22
Tax legislation, 269
Tax performance, 4–5, 51
Tax pressure (in Latin America), 131–132
Tax reform and the O.A.S., 136
Tax structure evolution, 40–41, 134–137
Turnover taxes, 29

Undertaxation of agriculture, 7, 199–200, 217, 261–262
Urban cost of living, 261, 263, 264–265

Value added taxation, 28, 48, 135, 137
Vargas, 152
Videla, 153
Von Neumann, 168

Wald, H. P., 222–223, 225
Water consumption survey (Penang), 181–182
Webb, R. C., 138
Wealth taxes (Latin America), 134
Willingness to be taxed, 134
Willingness to tax, 43–46
World Bank (I.B.R.D.), 148–149, 176–177

www.ingramcontent.com/pod-product-compliance
Lightning Source LLC
LaVergne TN
LVHW011115300926
849160LV00008B/393
* 9 7 8 0 4 1 5 8 3 3 9 0 5 *